PROGRAMMING IN
ZORTECH C++
– *with Version 2*

John M. Hughes

SIGMA PRESS – *Wilmslow, United Kingdom*

First published in 1990 by
Sigma Press, 1 South Oak Lane, Wilmslow, Cheshire SK9 6AR, England.

British Library Cataloguing in Publication Data
A CIP catalogue record for this book is available from the British Library.
ISBN: 1-85058-166-5

Typesetting and design by
Sigma Hi-Tech Services Ltd

Distributed by
John Wiley & Sons Ltd., Baffins Lane, Chichester, West Sussex, England.

Printed in Great Britain by
Dotesios Printers Ltd, Trowbridge, Wiltshire

Contents

Thanks   to

JOHN HAGGINS
and
STEVE TEALE
of Zortech Ltd

for their help during
the writing of this book

About this book

This book is about the C++ programming language, and in particular the implementation of Version 2 of that language produced by Zortech Ltd for personal computers running under the MS-DOS and PC-DOS operating systems.

Virtually everything that you will read in this book is also applicable to other implementations of the C++ language. However, C++ is still young, and slight differences exist between versions of the language produced by different software houses; wherever we are aware of such differences, we have drawn attention to them in the text.

This book also contains certain material relating specifically to the Zortech implementation, including the operation of the ZED editor, the C++ compiler and the BLINK linker.

At the time of writing, versions of C++ from other software houses are not compiled directly into executable machine code but are first interpreted into a form which can then be processed using a standard C compiler. The Zortech approach enables much faster production and debugging of your programs than the previous system using an interpreter – compiler combination.

Why program in C++?

Like its predecessor C, C++ is an extremely powerful language: you can do practically anything you want with it *provided that you understand exactly what you are up to*. It is this power which makes C++ such a pleasure to use, and which explains its increasing popularity among both professional programmers and interested amateurs.

There is, however, another side to this power. If you don't understand what you are doing, then your programs won't work; or worse, they will work unreliably. Some programming errors are extremely difficult to track down, let alone correct, and it is the responsibility of the programmer to make sure that he or she has thought of everything that might go wrong and has built all these possibilities into their software. For instance, if you have an array containing 10 elements and mistakenly try to access the (non-existent) eleventh element, most programming languages will prevent you. C++ (and C) will not.

Another feature of C++ which beginners frequently find disconcerting is that professionally-written code often looks completely unintelligible. This is because professional programmers make use of several shortcuts which are quicker to code and which may run faster than the more obvious methods which a newcomer might use. Don't let this put you off; before long you will be writing almost equally complex code yourself.

What you need

The hardware you will need before you can use Zortech C++ Version 2 is briefly described: an IBM-compatible computer running DOS Version 2.11 or later, equipped with a hard disc and at least one floppy drive. A mouse is useful but not essential.

It is less easy to describe the mental equipment and experience that you need to program in C++. We assume that most readers will have some prior experience of programming in a high-level language – Basic or Pascal, perhaps – but this is by no means essential. Writing short programs isn't very difficult, and even if you have no programming experience at all you may well astonish yourself with the speed of your progress. However, novices should be very sure that they completely understand the material in the first three or four chapters of the book before trying to go any further, or they will rapidly find that they are out of their depth.

What is C++?

C++ is a high-level block-structured object-oriented language based on the popular C language. Programs written in C are, with very few exceptions, upwardly compatible with C++.

High-level languages: First, C++ is a **high-level language**. High-level languages such as Pascal and Basic are problem-oriented, whereas low-level languages such as assembly language and machine code are machine-oriented. Programs written in high-level languages are 'portable', at least in theory; that is, a program written in a high-level language to run on one kind of computer should run with the very minimum of alteration on a completely different type of computer.

In practice, some degree of portability is often sacrificed in favour of writing code which makes use of the specific features of individual machines, such as their graphic or musical capabilities. These exceptions aside, you should find that your C++ programs can be recompiled to run on completely different machines from the one on which they were originally written.

A feature of high-level languages is that for the most part you don't need to know what is going on in your computer at the machine level: the detailed manipulation of bits and bytes and CPU registers is handled automatically, and is not the concern of the programmer.

However, there are cases when it becomes necessary to know what is going on, and to control it, at a very low level. For instance, encryption and Comms routines often depend on the programmer's ability to manipulate individual bits.

C++ has a wide range of machine-level commands. Consequently it can be used for such tasks as writing compilers and operating systems – tasks which at one time could only be done in assembly language or machine code.

Block-structured languages: Nowadays, it is commonly accepted that the best way of creating a complex program is to break it down into a number of separate blocks or functions, each of which can be tested and debugged separately, rather than to write a mass of 'spaghetti code' full of JUMP and GOTO instructions.

Block structured languages such as C++ allow the **scope** of variables to be tightly controlled, minimising any possibility of accidental interference between one section of a program and another; provided that a block of code works perfectly in isolation, you can be quite certain that it will continue to work correctly when incorporated into a complete program.

Object-oriented languages: One of the problems with conventional computer languages is that they often have rather a poor 'fit' with the data they are required to handle.

Imagine, for example, a database program which handles the records of a large library system. Such a system would be relatively simple to design using a traditional programming language provided that all the records were basically of the same kind; an individual field would hold the title of a book, the author's name, the name of the publisher, the number of pages, the ISBN number and so on.

However, this record-structure isn't easily capable of being adapted to handle some of the other items which a library might stock such as compact discs, cassette tapes, videos and so on. Compact discs do not have pages, for example, and videos do not have ISBN numbers.

Object oriented languages allow you to create data types which closely reflect the situation existing in the 'real world'. For example, in the case described above it would be possible to define a base type – a **Library Object** – and then to define a number of sub-types which are derived from it, including books, videos, records and so on.

Object-oriented languages often use rather different jargon from that with which you may be familiar. For instance, instead of a program passing a set of arguments to a function, they are likely to talk of sending a message to an object.

Many newcomers to Object Oriented Programming find this new jargon rather distracting. As far as possible, this book uses the conventional language with which most programmers will be familiar.

C and C++

C++ is a superset of C; a great deal of C code is perfectly acceptable in C++, and where problems do occur they can usually be easily resolved. However, C++ is much more than the C language with a few handy bolt-on extras. Some areas – especially function calls – have been completely redesigned, and so even programmers who are already familiar with writing C code will need to spend some time familiarising themselves with the new techniques used in C++.

C++ as a compiled language

With a very few exceptions, of which Basic is the best-known, modern computer languages are **compiled** into machine code. This means that the **source** code – the C++ code which you have written – is converted by a piece of software called a **compiler** into an intermediate stage called the Object Code. This is stored on disc with the file-extension .OBJ.

(If you are using a version of C++ which requires both an interpreter and a compiler, the order of events is that the C++ code is first interpreted into C code and this is then compiled into an .OBJ file.)

The .OBJ file is then processed by a second program called a **linker**. As its name implies, several different .OBJ files can be joined together at this stage to produce a single program; indeed, this is the way in which virtually all 'real' C++ programs are constructed.

The linked code is given the file-extension .EXE. It is now a 'stand-alone' program which can be run in the same way as any other program by simply typing in its name at the DOS prompt; alternatively, if the program is relatively short (normally under 64K for program and data together) it can be further converted by a utility called EXE2BIN into a .COM file. The advantage of doing this is that .COM files load faster and occupy less space than .EXE files.

Because it is impossible to backtrack from the final .EXE or .COM file to the original C++ source code, your software is safe from tampering by other people. Compiled programs are also much faster-running than almost all interpreted programs. Of course, the compilation and linking processes themselves do take some time, but once they have been successfully completed they will not have to be repeated unless you subsequently wish to alter the program in some way.

A note about type-styles and programs

In running text, all references to C and C++ keywords, operators and function-names are printed in **bold type**; terms which are introduced for the first time are also printed in bold.

To guard against errors in typesetting the code, all listings have been taken directly from working programs; as far as we are aware, all the code in this book is bug free, and should work perfectly provided that it is entered *exactly* as it appears here.

1

Starting out

This chapter describes the installation of the Zortech C++ programming package from the distribution discs onto a hard disc, and the process of configuring the installed package to work with your equipment.

Next, the process of writing, editing, compiling, linking and running a simple C++ program is described. The chapter ends with a brief description of elementary C++ syntax including a list of keywords.

Installing C++

The minimum hardware configuration for running Zortech C++ Version 2 is an IBM PC, XT, PS/2 or compatible computer, running DOS Version 2.11 or above. Most common monitor standards are supported. At least 512K of RAM is needed, and a hard disc with at least 1 megabyte of free space is required. If you are installing the complete Developer's Edition, up to 3 megabytes will be needed. (Although it was just possible to install Version 1 of Zortech C++ on a floppy-disc system, Version 2 cannot be used in this way; it is possible to install the Zortech C compiler – provided with C++ – onto a floppy disc system, but this will not be described here.) A mouse is not essential, but you may find it useful for editing your code.

The Developer's Edition consists of four distinct elements: the compiler; the debugger; the tools; and the library source code. An upgrade for OS/2 is available as an optional extra.

The standard installation procedure is as follows. Put Compiler Disc 1 into Drive A; make Drive A the default drive by entering **A:** and pressing [RETURN]; and then enter

```
ZTCSETUP
```

and then follow the instructions on the screen.

Configuring C++

When the program has been installed, use a text editor (such as EDLIN) or your favourite word processor to make the following changes to your AUTOEXEC.BAT file; this should be in the root directory of Drive C.

First, if the AUTOEXEC.BAT file already includes a PATH command, make sure that it includes the entry

```
C:\ZORTECH\BIN
```

If no PATH command currently exists in the AUTOEXEC.BAT file, then create one by inserting the following line:

```
PATH C:\ZORTECH\BIN
```

Next, you may add the following two commands after the PATH command:

```
SET INCLUDE=C:\ZORTECH\INCLUDE
SET LIB=C:\ZORTECH\LIB
```

These are only required if you intend to carry out compilation directly from the DOS command line; if all your work will be done from the ZED editor, these lines are not necessary.

If you want the help system to be installed automatically whenever the computer is started, then you can include the line

```
ZTCHELP
```

below the PATH command in the AUTOEXEC.BAT file. This may be worth doing if you use your computer primarily for programming in C++. However, because the ZTCHELP program is memory-resident, it does take up a certain amount of memory which is then not available to you for other purposes, and if C++ programming is not your main occupation, you may prefer to invoke ZTCHELP only when it is needed. Provided that no other programs have subsequently been loaded 'above' it in memory, you can in any case uninstall ZTCHELP by entering the command

```
ZTCHELP /r
```

at the DOS command line.

When you have made all the necessary changes to the AUTOEXEC.BAT file, save it and then load the CONFIG.SYS file from the root directory of the hard disc into your text editor and check that it includes the lines

```
BUFFERS=20
FILES=20
```

If not, make the appropriate changes and then save the altered file. You can now exit from your editor.

The C++ programming language environment is now ready to use. However, the new PATH commands and the alterations to the CONFIG.SYS file won't become effective until the next time the computer is started up, so you should reboot the machine with [Ctrl]/[Alt]/[Del] before continuing.

Configuring the C++ environment

You can now if you wish configure the C++ environment. This enables you to set up the system to suit your printer, your screen-type and other items.

Make sure that you are in the root directory of the hard disc on which C++ has been installed, and then enter the command

```
ZCONFIG
```

and press [RETURN]. If the computer responds with the line **Bad command or file name**, then there is either something wrong with the PATH command which you should have inserted in the AUTOEXEC.BAT file; or you have not rebooted the computer since adding the correct PATH command to that file; or the ZCON-FIG.EXE program is missing from the \ZORTECH\BIN\ directory. Check which of these faults exists and correct it.

Assuming that all is in order, you will be shown a screen which is blank except for a menu bar at the top:

```
Hotkeys Files Screen Colors More clrs Lines Windows Box chars Print saVe eXit
Set instant command keys
```

Virtually all aspects of the configuration of the C++ environment can be changed from here. These include the colours of the various menus and screens which you will meet from time to time; the 'hotkeys' which call up Help or which enable you to manipulate text in the ZED editor; and the directories in which files of various kinds will be stored and from which they will be loaded.

It is a good idea at this point to check that the Files option is correctly set. Select this either by pressing [F] or by moving the highlight on the menu bar until it is resting on the Files option and then pressing [RETURN]. A new menu bar will appear listing several options. You can make changes to the areas of the environment controlled by these options by selecting them, entering the changes, and then pressing [RETURN] to confirm them. To back out of any menu, press [Esc].

No changes that you may make will become effective until you have saved them to disc at the end of the session, so if you find that you have made a mess of anything, you can safely abandon your work and start again.

We will now consider the various options which are currently offered on the screen.

Ramdisk: If part of your computer's RAM has been set aside as a ramdisc, then select this option and enter the appropriate drive letter. Some computers which are equipped with a hard disc do not also have a ramdisc; on those which do, it is usually Drive D or E. If you wish to enter the name of a ramdisc here, make sure that it ends in a colon (such as D: for the root directory of the ramdisc) or in a backslash for any other directory (such as D:\TMP\).

Help: Assuming that you have installed C++ on hard disc C as described above, the entry for the Help file should read as follows:

```
C:\ZORTECH\BIN\ZED.HLP
```

This file is a simple text file which can be edited with any ordinary text editor, or even with the ZED editor itself. However, it isn't a good idea to try to edit the file while you are using it!

Backup: By default, the former version of any file which you have amended is retained on the same drive and directory as before, but with the original extension replaced by the extension .BAK to identify it as a backup file.

This is generally helpful, but under certain circumstances it may not guarantee that you always have a backup version of a current file. This is because if you have several files with the same name but different extensions – such as TEST.CPP and TEST.H – then editing either of these files will cause a .BAK file previously created from the other file to be overwritten.

You can overcome this problem by storing all your backup files in their own directory. When this is done, previous versions of the files are no longer given the .BAK extension; instead, they are stored in the special backup directory and retain their own name and extension. Consequently there is no possibility of files with the same name but different extensions overwriting each others' backups. It is also much easier to locate and erase unwanted backup files if they have all been put in the same directory.

To use this facility, you must first create a new directory in which the backup files will be stored. This must be done at the DOS prompt using the MKDIR command. The new directory must be on the same disc as the one you intend to use for the original files.

Assuming that you have decided to create such a directory, you can enter the name of it after selecting the Backup option from the Files menu of ZCONFIG. Enter only the name and path of the directory, ending it with a backslash; do not prefix it with the name of the disc on which it is located as it must be on the same disc as the original file – this restriction is imposed by DOS. Then press [RETURN] to confirm it.

Libs: This option lets you specify the directory in which the C++ libraries have been stored. These comprise files which have both .LIB and .OBJ extensions.

Assuming that the normal installation process has been used as described earlier, the entry should read thus:

```
C:\ZORTECH\LIB\
```

The entry must end with a colon – for a root directory – or with a backslash for any other directory.

Includes: Files which have the .H and .HPP extensions belong in this directory. The correct entry will normally be

```
C:\ZORTECH\INCLUDE\
```

Once again, the entry must end with either a colon or a backslash, depending on whether it refers to a root directory or a directory above the root.

Printer: If your printer is connected to the first parallel port, the entry here should read either LPT1 or PRN. If it is connected to the second parallel port – if you have one – the entry should read LPT2.

If the printer is connected to the first serial port, the entry should read COM1; COM2 would be correct if the printer were connected to the second serial port.

EOF: Edlin, WordStar and some other editors and word processing programs expect to mark the end of a file with a ^Z (Ctrl/Z) symbol; however, many other programs do not use or recognise this symbol.

If you expect to use your own editor to work on files as well as ZED, you should check the editor manual to discover whether it uses ^Z as an End Of File (EOF) marker. If not, set the EOF option to OFF; otherwise, leave it set to ON.

Saving the changed configuration: When all necessary changes to the configuration details have been made, select the Save option from the main menu bar. The changed configuration will be written to disc, overwriting the former version, and control will return to the DOS prompt. Alternatively you can abandon any changes you have made by selecting the Exit option.

Writing your first C++ program

With C++ correctly installed and configured, you are ready to write, compile and run your first C++ program.

Begin by putting yourself in the directory in which you wish the text of the program to be stored. If you don't already have a special directory in which to store your C++ programs, this may be a good time to create it with the MKDIR command. Then put yourself in the new directory and type in the command

```
ZED PROG1.CPP
```

and press [RETURN]. You will be taken straight to the ZED program editor, ready to begin work on the new file PROG1.CPP.

It isn't actually necessary to include the name of the file you will be working on as part of the command line. If you prefer, you can simply type **ZED** and then give a suitable name to the file before saving or compiling it.

It is important that the file is given the extension .CPP; all Zortech C++ program files must be given this extension. If you use the extension .C instead, your work will normally be compiled as an ordinary C program, though you can force the program to be compiled as a C++ program by use of the **–cpp** compiler flag.

Entering the program: Type in the following program very carefully. Be particularly careful to remember the semi-colon after every line in the section between the two braces { and }.

Program 1.1

```
#include <stream.hpp>
main()
{
   char name [20];
   cout << "Please type in your first name\n ";
   cin >> name;
   cout << "Welcome to C++ programming, " << name << "\n ";
}
```

What does the program do?

We shall now take a very brief look at what each line between the braces { } does. Don't worry if some of the terms which you meet in this section don't mean very much at the moment; we shall explain all of them in more detail in due course.

The first line declares an array of characters (often called a **string**) and calls it **name**; there is room in this array to store up to 19 characters plus the 'end of string' marker that C++ adds, making 20 in all.

The second line displays the message which is enclosed in double quotation marks; the final **\n** then makes the cursor jump to the beginning of the next line.

The third line makes the computer wait until you type something and press [RETURN]; the characters you have typed in will be stored in the computer's memory in the array **name**.

The last line displays the message enclosed between quotes, then prints out whatever has been stored in the array **name**, and finally goes to the beginning of the next line. Then the program ends.

Laying out your program

You should lay the program out exactly as it is shown here. In particular, make sure that the first line begins hard against the left margin; the reasons for this are discussed later.

Indenting lines of code: To indent the lines between the braces, press the Tab key when the cursor is against the left margin. ZED also has an auto-indent facility which will automatically indent each line by the same distance as the previous line, provided that the previous line was terminated by pressing [RETURN]. To toggle autoindent on or off, either press the [SHIFT]/[TAB] combination or choose the **Auto** option from the Edit Menu.

If you are using autoindent, press the backspace key before entering the closing brace } at the end of the program to move the cursor back to the left margin.

If you are used to certain other programming languages, including Pascal and most versions of Basic, you may be surprised to notice that everything should be entered in lower-case letters. In C++ (and C) all commands are always entered in lower-case, and the convention is that all variable names are written in the same way. However, constants such as **PI** are conventionally entered in capitals. C and C++ are both case-dependant, so that **name** and **NAME** represent two different variables.

Compiling and running the program

If you did not name your program when you invoked ZED, you must do so now. Press [Esc] [F] [S] to call down the File Menu and invoke the Save option, then type in the name PROG1.CPP and press [RETURN]. Your work will then be saved to disc.

You are now ready to compile, link and run the program. As we pointed out in the Introduction, because C++ is a compiled language – unlike Basic – it can't be run directly from the text you have typed in, which is referred to as the **source code**. Instead, it must be converted into an intermediate format, which is itself saved in a file with the same name but with the extension .OBJ. Finally, this is **linked** and a program file with the extension .EXE is produced. The entire process of compilation and linking is often loosely referred to as compilation.

To begin this process, press [Esc] [C] [C]. Pressing [Esc] takes you out of editing mode into menu mode, and a highlight appears on the menu bar at the top of the screen. Pressing [C] for the first time takes you into the Compile Menu, and pressing it again starts the Compile option running.

A simpler way of starting the compilation process is to press Function Key [F9].

A prompt will appear at the top of the screen asking you to enter the Compiler flags you want. If any characters appear after the prompt, delete them and then press [RETURN].

Compiling the program with no flags forces the compiler to create a Small Memory Model program – that is, one which requires a maximum of 64K of RAM for the program code and another 64K for data. All of the programs we shall be creating in this book fall into this category.

The first stage of compilation: During the first stage of the compilation, the program is scanned by the Preprocessor, which performs any **directives** such as **#include** and **#define**; the effect of an **#include** directive is to treat an additional file as though it were an integral part of the file currently being compiled. If any file mentioned in an **#include** directive cannot be found, then the compilation will fail.

Also during the first stage of compilation, any **syntax errors** are detected; these are discussed in a little more detail later.

The second stage of compilation will then take place, followed by the linking. Then the message *Blink complete* will appear, followed by an indication of the time taken for linking; at the same time, the prompt **Program parameters (or Esc)** will appear at the top of the screen.

Running the program: You can now either return to ZED by pressing [Esc] or you can try out your program by pressing [RETURN]. If you choose the latter, the screen will clear and you will be prompted *Please type in your first name*.

Type in your name and press [RETURN]; the message *Welcome to C++ programming* and your name will then appear. Press any key to return to ZED. You have now created your first C++ program! If you wish to end the session, leave ZED by pressing [Esc] [F] [X]; this selects the eXit option from the Files Menu. You can now run the new program from the DOS command line by just typing in PROG1.

Curing problems

Whichever way you have chosen to compile your first program, you may find that something has gone wrong and that you therefore end up with an error message instead of an .EXE file.

If this happens to you, don't worry! As time goes on, you will become more familiar both with C++ errors and the messages that they generate, but to begin with you must expect that many errors will occur, often because of simple typing slips. In any case, with both C and C++ by far the most difficult problems to track down are those which appear while the program is actually running – **run-time** errors – rather than **compile-time** errors.

Syntax errors: Syntax errors are those caused by some error in the way you have used some feature of the C++ language; the most common cause is simply that you have mistyped something, or perhaps omitted a semi-colon.

When any such error is found, you will be returned to ZED with the cursor located at the point at which the error was detected. However, the error may well have occurred somewhere else, so you will have to look carefully above the cursor position to locate the precise location of the error. A diagnostic message will appear on the screen; such messages can be very helpful once you have acquired some skill at reading between the lines of what they mean.

Some common errors: For instance, if you forget the semi-colon at the end of a line, the omission may not be detected until the compiler has read several characters of next line. The diagnostic message *Syntax error: ';' expected* will appear on the screen; although this indicates the nature of the error, it doesn't show you where the semi-colon is missing from, for the simple reason that the compiler is unable to work out precisely where it ought to be. (After all, if the compiler could always reliably predict where the missing semi-colon ought to go, it could correct the error itself and then carry on with the compilation.)

Some error messages are less helpful. For instance, if you mistype the << symbol as <, you will be warned *Syntax error: illegal operand types*. In your current state of knowledge about C++ this is a much less useful message.

Another type of error may occur if for some reason the special file STREAM.HPP can't be found. (This file is provided as part of the C++ package.) STREAM.HPP should be in your Include directory, and if you are warned that it **can't be opened** you should check that you have typed in its name correctly in the first line of the program; that the # symbol is in the first column; that the file really is present in the Include directory; that the filename has been enclosed between chevrons < and >; and that your setup has been properly configured (with ZCONFIG as described earlier in this chapter) so that the compiler knows where to look for that file.

Once any fatal error has been found, the compilation process is abandoned. This means that any further errors in your program won't be discovered until you recompile it. Compiling a long program can therefore be a fairly time-consuming business, especially if many errors are found. For this reason – and for many others – it is not generally a good idea to try to compose a C++ program when you are sitting at the keyboard. Instead, write the program out carefully on paper, and only type it in when you are sure that it is as bug-free as you can make it.

Command line compilation

You can if you wish use your own word processor or line editor instead of ZED. If you do so, you must save the completed program as an Ascii file, giving it a name which ends in the extension .CPP.

You can then compile the program from the DOS command line by using the program ZTC.EXE. Assuming that your program has been stored in the root directory of a disc in Drive A under the name PROG1.CPP, the command to compile and link the program would look like this:

```
ZTC A:PROG1.CPP -IC:\ZORTECH\INCLUDE
```

The purpose of the flag **-I** which occurs immediately (no space) in front of the drive specifier C: is to specify the path which must be searched for any 'include' files – that is, files which are specified by an **#include** directive, such as STREAM.HPP.

If you compile the program from the command line in this way, you won't be offered the opportunity of running it once the linking process is complete. The completed .EXE file will be placed in the default directory – which should normally be the \ZORTECH\BIN\ directory – and you can run it directly from there.

The elements of a C++ program

We shall now look at the elements of a simple C++ program as they are shown in the program which you have already typed in.

Program layout

Both C and C++ are **free form** languages; that is, with very few exceptions, the compiler doesn't care where individual statements are placed in a line. This is quite different from Fortran, for example.

Consequently, it is not an absolute requirement of either C or C++ that a program should be laid out with the various levels of indentation which you will see in this book. Indeed, different programmers use several different styles and manners of indentation. What *is* important is that you should adopt some consistent format by which you can identify at a glance the 'level' of any statement or group of statements; that is, whether they form a part of any loop or other similar structure, which function they belong to, and so on.

The system of indentation used in this book has been chosen because it is simple to understand, and we recommend that you adopt it; but if not, use some other system which you find logical. Whatever happens, don't be enticed into writing code which has no logical layout at all, or you will quickly lose your way when you try to debug it. Since debugging programs is a far more important (and difficult) activity than writing them in the first place, it follows that anything you can do to simplify the debugging process for yourself or someone else must be worthwhile.

Using comments

One of the best ways of simplifying the debugging process is to include plenty of comments in your programs. Comments have no 'overhead'; no matter how many you use, they will have no effect on the speed with which your program will execute. There is thus no reason not to use them liberally.

Comment formats: C++ supports two different formats for placing comments in your source code. The first, and simplest, is to precede each comment by a double slash, //; everything which follows this symbol *on the same line* is treated as a comment and is thus ignored by the compiler. Comments of this sort cannot be extended beyond the end of the line on which they start. This usage is identical to the use of the REM statement in Basic. Comments of this type are peculiar to C++; code including them will not compile with a C compiler.

The second way of inserting comments is to enclose each comment between /* and */ markers. Comments of this sort can be as long as you wish; for instance, when testing a program you can 'comment out' sections of code which you don't wish to compile by putting /* at the beginning of each section and */ at the end. Comments of this type can be used in both C and C++ code.

Program 1.2 shows what our first program would look like if it were liberally commented in the usual C++ style.

Program 1.2

```
#include <stream.hpp>
main()
{
    char name [20]; // defines variable name and prompts for it
    cout << "Please type in your first name\n'';
    cin >> name; // inputs name
    // prints message
    cout << "Welcome to C++ programming, " << name << "\n";
}
```

About main(): Every C++ program must contain at least one **function**, or self-contained block of statements, called **main()**. The use of other functions is described in later chapters, especially Chapters Five and Six; for the moment you only need to know that a typical C++ program may – and usually will – contain several other functions as well as **main()**.

A program can only have one **main()** function. The code which it contains is enclosed between two braces, { and }. Execution of the program begins immediately after the opening brace, and terminates when the closing brace is reached. If you are familiar with Pascal, you will realise that the braces are a close equivalent to the Pascal **BEGIN** and **END** keywords.

Reserved words in C++

The Zortech Version 2 implementation of the C++ programming language has a set of 54 keywords, and these are **reserved**; that is, they cannot be used as variable or function names, etc. Some other implementations use a slightly different list.

The full list of keywords is as follows:

asm	far	public
auto	float	register
break	for	return
case	fortran	short
catch	friend	signed
cdecl	goto	sizeof
char	huge	static
class	if	struct
const	inline	switch
continue	int	this
default	long	template
delete	near	typedef
do	new	union
double	overload	unsigned
else	operator	virtual
entry	pascal	void
enum	private	volatile
extern	protected	while

Program statements

Every program statement in C and C++ must end with a semi-colon, which functions as a statement terminator. Even the last statement of a program must end with a semi-colon. This is different from Pascal, where semi-colons are used as statement separators, and where they are therefore not needed before the Pascal keyword **END**.

Semi-colons are not used after the closing brace of a function, including **main()**; a function is a block of statements, and not a single statement, and thus it does not need a semi-colon to terminate it.

Line endings are not significant in C++ (except for comments which begin with //, which are end-of-line terminated). It is thus perfectly proper for several statements to follow each other on the same line, provided that each statement ends with a semi-colon. For instance, the following would be quite acceptable from the syntax point of view in our first program:

```
cout << "Please type in your first name\n "; cin >> name;
```

Lay your code out like this whenever it makes it easier to read and understand.

Variable and function names

Variables and functions can have **identifiers** or names of up to 127 characters, all of which are significant. Underline characters and numbers are allowed as well as letters, though it is not good practice to use underlines at the beginning or end of names, or to use double underlines at all.

The names of identifiers are case-significant, so that NUMBER, Number and number all refer to different variables. The convention is to use only lower case letters.

Include files

The first line of your first C++ program may have puzzled you; it read

```
#include <stream.hpp>
```

The purpose of the **#include** directive is to force the compiler to read another source file – in this case, one called STREAM.HPP – into your program. This is necessary because many C++ programs make use of functions and other elements which were written by other people. As far as the compiler is concerned, using the **#include** directive has the effect of inserting the specified file into the rest of the code at the point where the directive occurs.

Most **#include** files are of the kind called **header files**; we shall be meeting these in a little more detail in Chapters Five and Six. Header files generally have the extension .H if they contain ordinary C code – which is for the most part capable of being compiled by the C++ compiler – and .HPP if they contain C++ code.

About variables

C++ requires you to declare the **type** of every variable before you use it. This is done in the first line after the opening brace of **main**(). In our first program there was one variable declaration, which took the form:

```
char name [20];
```

This states that **name** is a variable of type **char**; that is, it contains alphanumeric characters rather than any of the other types which are permissible in C++, such as integers or floating point numbers.

name is actually an array variable which can contain up to 20 characters; this is the meaning of the '[20]' which follows the variable name. We shall look at arrays in detail in Chapter Four.

Variable types

C++ provides several types of variable, and also allows you to define your own types. The following are the most important predefined types:

```
char      Integers -128 to 127
int       Integers -32,768 to +32,767
long      Integers -2,147,483,648 to +2,147,483,647
float     Real 1.e -36 to 1.e +36 (precision 7 digits)
double    Real 1.e -303 to 1.e +303 (precision 13 digits)
```

The first three types are used for holding integers (for most purposes characters are treated as if they were integers), and the last two for holding real numbers; that is, those which have a fractional part, such as 3.14159 or -0.123.

You will sometimes come across variables of type **short int**, or just **short**. In some implementations variables of this type are accommodated in a single byte, and thus have the same range as variables of type char; in Zortech C++, short ints are the same as ints.

Signed and unsigned types: All the above variable types can be further distinguished by the reserved words **signed** and **unsigned**; **signed** is the default.

For instance, in Zortech C++ type char is treated by default as **signed**. Since a single byte is allotted for storing one character, reserving the high-order bit for use as a sign-bit means that a variable of type char can have any numeric value between -128 and 127. If a variable is declared as **unsigned char** then all values will be treated as positive and the range will extend from 0 to 255, allowing the extended character set above Ascii 127 to be used.

Declaring variables

Variables are declared by specifying the type first and following it by the name(s) of the variables of that type which you wish to declare. For instance, to define integer variables **num1** and **num2** and a float variable **fraction**, you would use the following code:

```
int num1, num2; float fraction;
```

Input and output

In our first C++ program, input and output were handled by means of **cin** and **cout**. It is tempting to regard these as straightforward commands, analogous to the INPUT and PRINT commands in Basic. In reality, however, **cin** and **cout** are members of the predefined C++ **streams** classes; this is why the header file mentioned in the first line of the program is called STREAM.HPP. We shall be looking at streams in much more detail in Chapter Eleven.

Escape characters: Referring back to our first program, you will have noticed that both the output lines included the character sequence **\n**. This is an **escape sequence** of control characters which instructs C++ to move to a new line.

C++ and C have several such sequences, as follows:

```
\\          Backslash
\?          Question mark
\a          Sound bell
\b          Backspace
\f          Formfeed (new page)
\n          Newline
\r          Carriage return
\t          Horizontal tab
\v          Vertical tab
\'          Single quote character
\"          Double quote character
\0          Null
```

For reasons of code portability, it is a good idea to use these sequences – duly enclosed in their own double quotation marks or included within the double quotation marks of a complete character string – rather than relying on using the Ascii code of a character. To sound the console 'bell', for instance, you could write

```
cout << "\a ";
```

To move onto a new line, display a warning on the screen, sound the bell and then move onto another new line, the statement might look like this:

```
cout << "\nError - press a key to continue\a\n ";
```

Formatted output

So far we have used **cout** to produce what might be called 'unformatted output'; that is, the items to be shown on the screen have all been displayed according to a set of defaults which C++ uses unless it is told to do something else.

The reason why C++ works in this way is because it lets you write simple code that will meet most of your needs. However, there may be occasions when you would find it useful to take greater control of the way in which your output is handled, and C++ provides a variety of tools for this purpose. This process is referred to as **formatting**; in general this simply means that the program's output is converted from one format to another – for instance, the representation of numbers may be altered from base 10 to base 8.

Simple functions for formatted output

C++ offers several functions which you can use to modify the format in which your data is displayed. They are all very easy to use, and you do not need to know anything about the way in which functions work in C++ before you can include these in your programs.

There are five simple formatted output functions. They are **chr()**, **dec()**, **hex()**, **oct()** and **str()**.

chr(): C++ regards integers and single characters – or, to be formal, variables of types int and char – as being largely interchangeable. This is a very useful characteristic, but in implementations of C++ before Version 2 it gave rise to some strange consequences.

Look at the following code fragment:

```
char letter;     // declare a variable of type char
letter='a';      // it is given the value 'a'
cout << letter   // and then output
```

In some versions of C++, the last line of this code would have output not **a** but **97**, which is the Ascii equivalent of 'a'. To get around this, it was necessary to write the last line like this:

```
cout << chr(letter);
```

which forced the character rather than the Ascii code to be displayed. Alternatively, the following could be used, with the same effect:

```
cout.put(letter);
```

In Zortech C++ Version 2 this anomaly has been corrected, and the line **cout << letter** in the program fragment printed above will simply display **a**.

dec(): The **dec()** function displays the contents of a numerical variable in decimal (denary, or base 10) format; if the value is not an integer, it is truncated to an integer first. (Numeric variables are described in detail in Chapter Two.) For instance, consider the fragment on the next page:

```
float number;       // number is variable of type float
number=12.345;      // and is given the value 12.345
cout << dec(number);   // and then output as an integer
```

The output from the last line of this code will be **12**.

hex(): The **hex()** function displays the contents of a numerical variable in hexadecimal (base 16) format; if the value is not an integer, it is truncated to an integer first. Consider the following:

```
int number;          // number is variable of type int
number=16;           // and is given the value 16
cout << hex(number);   // and then output in hex
```

This will output **10** which is the hexadecimal equivalent of the number 16.

oct(): The **oct()** function displays the contents of a numerical variable in octal (base 8) format; if the value is not an integer, it is truncated to an integer first. The output from the following code will therefore be **20**, which is the octal equivalent of the denary number 16:

```
int number;          // number is a variable of type int
number=16;           // it is given the value 16
cout << oct(number);   // and then output in octal
```

str(): The function **str()** has the effect of displaying a character string as a string. For instance, if the character string **string** contains "This is a string ", then the output from the following line will be **This is a string**.

```
cout << str(string);
```

The value of this apparently pointless operation will now be explained. All the functions we have just described have an additional facility which is to specify the width of the field within which the values which are being output will be displayed.

For instance, where **number** is a variable of type int containing the value 12345, the following line will cause that value to be output in denary form, with the value appearing right-justified within a field which is 20 characters wide:

```
cout << dec(number,20);
```

Similarly, the following line will allocate a field 30 characters wide for the string variable **string**, displaying the words "This is a string " at the extreme right of the field:

```
cout << str(string,30);
```

Where the field-width specifier is omitted, or where it is equal to zero, the correct amount of space required to display the contents of the variable will be allocated automatically.

Where the field-width specified is insufficient to display the contents of the variable, the value output will be truncated to fit the space allocated, and no warning will be given. You must accordingly be very careful to ensure that for normal programming purposes you never specify a field-width which is inadequate to display a value accurately, as there will be no indication that the answer shown is wrong.

Where the field-width specified is a negative number, the value displayed will be left-justified within the space rather than right-justified, which is the default.

Advanced formatted output

More complex formatted output is also available. This is accomplished by means of the **form**() function, which allows the use of several formatting sequences – sometimes called **conversion commands** – as follows:

```
%c        single character
%d        denary (base 10) integer
%e        scientific (exponential) notation
%f        floating point value
%g        general numeric format
%o        octal (base 8) value
%p        pointer value
%s        string
%u        unsigned integer value
%x        hexadecimal (base 16) value
```

The appropriate formatting sequence or sequences must be placed between double quotation marks before the values to which they refer; an exception is when the only item in the print list is a string which is enclosed between double quotation marks. To print the '%' character, use the sequence %%.

The following short program illustrates the principle of the formatting characters:

```
#include <stream.hpp>
main()
{
    int number; // a variable of type int
    number=123; // with the value 123
    cout << form( "%x%s ",number, "\n "); // output in hex
    cout << form( "%o%s ",number, "\n "); // then in octal
    cout << form( "%d%s ",number, "\n "); // and in denary
}
```

In the first line after the opening brace {, the variable **number** is defined as an integer. Then it is given the value 123.

The calls to the function **form**() in the next three lines result in the value of **number** being printed three times: first as a hexadecimal number; then as a number in base 8; and finally as an ordinary denary number.

In each **print list** the formatting sequence ends with **%s**; this is because each print list ends with the control string **"\n "**.

Specifying the number of decimal places: One particular advantage of using **form**() is that it allows you to specify the number of decimal places to be used in displaying a number of type float or double.

Consider the following fragment of code:

```
float fraction;
fraction=123.456;
cout << form( "%3.2f%s ",fraction, "\n ");
```

The output from this will be **123.46**. This is because the formatting sequence **%3.2f** specifies that the floating point number to which it applies is to be output with up to three digits before the decimal point and two after the decimal point. Note that the value displayed is rounded up where this is appropriate.

form() and printf()

If you are already familiar with the original C programming language, you will realise that the C++ **form**() function works in almost exactly the same way as the **printf**() function does in C. Indeed, there is nothing to prevent you from using the old **printf**() function if you prefer, though it is certainly less easy to use than **cout**, as the latter allows the use of a series of defaults which make most C++ output much easier to understand than the C equivalent.

A little about streams: Input and output streams are dealt with in some detail in Chapter Eleven, but this section will introduce the concepts briefly.

The original C language treats all input and output as sequences – or 'streams' – of characters. This remains the case even where non-printing characters are involved – so-called **binary** output.

It was consequently necessary in C to allow for some system of converting all input and output into the appropriate format; hence the use of the formatting sequences, which specify what this format is to be.

C++, on the other hand, is capable of handling most sorts of numeric and string output directly, without the use of formatting sequences.

fprintf() and **sprintf()**: In addition to **printf**, which was used in C for screen output, you can also use the functions **fprintf()** and **sprintf()**. These work in a very similar way to **printf()**; **fprintf()** is used to pass values to a file and **sprintf()** to pass values to a memory buffer. We shall meet **printf()** again from time to time, but **sprintf()** will not be described further. **printf()** and its fellows, including **puts()** and **gets()** which are described below, are found in the STDIO.H file, so you must place the directive **#include <stdio.h>** at the top of a program which uses any of these.

About puts()

As well as **printf()** and the other functions described above, you can also use the function **puts()**. This is a much simpler and faster function to use than **printf()**: its only purpose is to output character strings, and it can't be used to convert data from one format to another. Indeed, it can't be used to output numeric data at all.

A typical use of **puts()** is shown in this short program:

```
#include <stdio.h>
main()
{
    puts ( "This shows how to use puts()\n ");
}
```

puts() recognises the same control characters as **cout**, including the sequence **\n** for a newline.

Input techniques in C++ and C

In C++, most keyboard input is accomplished by means of **cin** and the >> operator. Like its counterpart **cout**, this has the great advantage that any variables of any type can be input without additional work on the part of the programmer.

For instance, the following fragment will input values for three variables: one of type float, one of type int, and one of type char:

```
float fraction;char letter;int number;
cin >> fraction >> number >> letter;
```

To enter values for these three variables, they should either all be entered on a single line, terminated by [RETURN] and separated from each other by spaces (not by commas), or the [RETURN] key should be pressed after each one has been entered. Either technique will work equally well.

Unfortunately, **cin** does have one important disadvantage. Consider the following code:

```
char string[80];
cin >> string;
```

The variable **string** will hold up to 80 characters, and you might consequently imagine that the second line of code would ensure that any group of characters which might be typed in, as far as the next press of the [RETURN] key, would be assigned to **string**.

However, this is not the case; if the user were to type in the expression "This is a string ", only the word "This" would be assigned to variable **string**. This is because **cin** regards the space character as marking the end of a variable. (It is because of this peculiarity that in Program 1.1, only the user's first name was asked for; if two names had been typed in, the second one would have been ignored.)

At times this can be useful. For instance, the lines

```
// declare some variables
float number_1, number_2; char symbol;
// and input values
cin >> number_1 >> symbol >> number_2;
```

would allow you to type in an expression like **30 + 62** and then automatically assign the first value to variable **number_1**, the + to **symbol**, and the second value to **number_2**.

However, where a complete string including spaces must be input and stored as a single variable, a different technique must be found. The simplest solution is to use the C function **gets()**. This is part of the **stdio.h** library, so you must place the line **#include <stdio.h>** at the beginning of your program.

gets() can be used to input a string of characters terminated by pressing [RETURN]; any errors you may make in entering it can be corrected with the backspace key in the usual way. For instance, the following program is the equivalent in C of Program 1.1, though it will also work perfectly well if compiled as a C++ program:

Program 1.3

```
#include <stdio.h>
main()
{
   char name [20];
   puts( "Please type in your name ");
   gets(name);
   puts( "Welcome to C++ programming ");
   puts(name)
}
```

A further alternative is provided by the C function **scanf()**. This is rather more complicated than **gets()**; you can think of it as more or less the counterpart of **printf()**. **scanf()** is not described here because using it relies on an understanding of **pointers** which are introduced in Chapter Six; in any case, **scanf()** can always be replaced by **gets()**, which is both simpler to use and more flexible.

Postscript to Chapter One

By the time that you have completed this chapter, you should have your C++ compiler properly installed and configured on your hard disc, and have learned how to enter, compile, link and run a simple C++ program.

You should also understand one of the conventional ways in which a C++ program may be laid out, and understand the use of the statement terminator ; and the braces { and }.

Finally, you should be able to use **cin** and **cout** and the operators >> and <<, and understand something of the use of the C input/output functions **puts()**, **printf()** and **gets()**.

Exercises to Chapter One

1. Write a program to output the following on the screen using **cout** and the << operator:

```
This is a character string.
This is another one.
```

2. Rewrite the above program using the **printf()** function.

3. If you haven't yet entered and run Program 1.1, do so now.

2

Simple Work with Numbers

The ability to carry out calculations is at the heart of every computer language. C++ has a particularly wide variety of techniques for carrying out numerical work of all kinds, and in this chapter we shall examine these.

Simple arithmetic

Program 2.1 is intended as a gentle introduction to arithmetic in C++. Its purpose is to input a value in degrees Celsius and then to output a corresponding value in degrees Fahrenheit. The conversion is carried out using the formula **Fahrenheit = (Celsius x 1.9) + 32**.

Program 2.1

```
#include <stream.hpp>
main()
{
   float fahrenheit, celsius;
   cout << "Enter a value in degrees Celsius\n";
   cin >> celsius;
   fahrenheit=celsius*1.9+32;
   cout << "This is equivalent to " << fahrenheit
      << " in Fahrenheit\n";
}
```

If you are used to programming in Pascal, Program 2.1 won't look too surprising; if the only programming language you have ever used is Basic – or if you have never programmed before – then you will find that there are some concepts here which may be entirely new to you.

Declaring variables

We mentioned in Chapter One that it is necessary in C++ to declare variables before you can use them. The first line of **main()** is just such a declaration:

```
float fahrenheit, celsius;
```

This code alerts the compiler to the fact that the program will need space to store two variables – to be named **fahrenheit** and **celsius** – and that both of these will be of type **float**; that is, they are real numbers which may include a decimal point and a fractional part.

Both these variables have been declared inside **main()**. They come into existence at the moment when they are declared, and they cease to exist as soon as the closing brace of **main()** is reached. It is a fundamental error – but a very common one among inexperienced programmers - to attempt to use a variable which has not yet been declared.

Another error which you must guard against is that of attempting to declare a variable twice, even if the two declarations are consistent with each other.

Declaration and initialisation

Declaring an ordinary variable like **fahrenheit** or **celsius** doesn't of itself give that variable any value – not even zero; consequently, the value of **celsius** remains indeterminate until you have typed in a figure when prompted to do so. Giving a value to a variable which as yet has no determinate value is called **initialisation**. Even experienced programmers occasionally fall into the trap of forgetting that variables contain no value until they have been explicitly initialised.

Variables are subject to strict rules of **scope** which define those areas of the program within which they exist and can be used; these will be described later. For the moment, you only need to know that a variable declared within **main()** can then be accessed anywhere in **main()** below the point at which it has been declared.

When to declare a variable: In C, it was obligatory for variables to be declared at the very beginning of their scope; for instance, a variable to be used in **main()** would be declared before any of the 'action code' in **main()**. This method is also permissible in C++, and you will find it widely used.

It is also permissible in C++ (though not in C) to declare a variable at the point of its first use, even if this is in the middle of a statement which is doing something completely different; for instance, you will see later that it is quite common to both declare and initialise loop counters within the loop statement itself.

To declare the variable **celsius** of type float and simultaneously initialise it to the value 123.45, you would use this idiom:

```
float celsius=123.45
```

Some programmers feel that it is better style to declare and initialise variables close to the point of their first use; others disagree. In this book we have used both systems, choosing whichever seems clearer at any given point, and there is no reason why you should not do the same.

If you are not used to a programming language which requires you to declare variables before using them, you may at first find it a nuisance. However, this feeling will pass, and you will soon appreciate the fact that certain types of programming error which may arise in many versions of Basic when you mistype a variable name are prevented in C and C++ because of the need to declare variables.

Declaring character variables: Simple variables of type char can also be initialised when they are declared. The form for this is as follows:

```
char letter='A'; // declare a char variable and initialise it
```

Here **letter** has been declared to be a variable of type char and has been initialised to hold the value **A**. The letter has been enclosed between apostrophes, *not* double quotation marks; double quotation marks are only used for string constants – as in the line

```
cout << "Press a key to continue...";
```

It is also possible to initialise a variable of type char by specifying its Ascii value preceded by a backslash, thus:

```
char letter='\65'; // this is the Ascii value for 'A'
```

or by making it equal to an integer (or a variable of type int) like this:

```
char letter=65; // this is the Ascii value for 'A'
```

Prompts and inputs

Returning to our program, the declaration of the variables is followed by the following two lines of code:

```
cout << "Enter a value in degrees Celsius\n";
cin >> celsius;
```

The first of these lines causes the prompt *Enter a value in degrees Celsius* to appear on the screen; the cursor then moves to the beginning of the next line and waits for you to type in a number and press [RETURN].

The next line then takes the value which you have typed in and stores it in the variable **celsius**. Remember that this variable has not been initialised, and consequently contains no determinate value until the figure you have typed in is placed there; had there in fact been some other value stored there, it would in any case have been **overwritten** by the new value and consequently lost, as a variable can only store one value at a time. (For the sake of completeness it should be mentioned that array variables can store a number of values under a single variable name; arrays are introduced in Chapter Four.)

Assignment statements

The next line of code is the one which actually does the arithmetic. It reads:

```
fahrenheit=celsius*1.9+32;
```

This is an **assignment statement**; it is so called because it takes the value on the right hand side of the equals sign = and **assigns** it to the variable whose name appears on the left of the equals sign. In this case, the value stored in variable **celsius** is multiplied by 1.9, and then 32 is added to the result; the final figure is then stored in the variable **fahrenheit**.

In C++, as in many other programming languages, * is used to mean 'multiply', and / is used to mean 'divide'; + and – have their everyday meanings. C++ has many other arithmetic operators as well as these, of course, and we shall be meeting most of them later in this chapter.

The material which occurs on the right of the equals sign in an arithmetical calculation can either be a value or an expression which can be evaluated to yield a value. For instance,

```
fahrenheit=123.456
```

would store the value 123.456 in the variable **fahrenheit**, while

```
fahrenheit=123+456
```

would add the numbers 123 and 456, and then store the result of the addition in the variable **fahrenheit**.

Remember that the = sign does not imply that the variable on its left is equal to the value on its right; rather, it instructs the computer to carry out the appropriate steps to *make* the variable on the left equal to the value on its right. To be quite precise, in C++ the = operator is a **replacement** operator, and its mode of working is from right to left; that is, the value to the left of = is **replaced** by the value to its right.

Multiple assignments: One useful feature of C++ is that it is possible to assign the same value to several different variables in the same line of code. For instance, if you have variables **num_1**, **num_2** and **num_3**, all of type int, and all of which you wish to set equal to some value – zero, for instance – you can do so like this:

```
num_1=num_2=num_3=0;
```

An illegal assignment: Only a single variable can appear on the left hand side in an assignment expression; complete arithmetical expressions are not allowed. The following statement is therefore illegal and will not compile:

```
fahrenheit+2=123+456
```

If you are used to programming in other languages, none of this will seem very strange.

lvalues and rvalues

You will sometimes see references in C++ literature to **lvalues** and **rvalues**. lvalues are expressions which can legally occur on the left of the = operator, while rvalues are expressions which can legally occur on the right of the = operator.

For instance, **celsius*1.9+32** is an rvalue because it can occur in an expression on the right of the = sign. It cannot be used as an lvalue because it is incorrect to write something like **celsius*1.9+32=fahrenheit**.

Outputting the result

The final statement in **main()** is as follows:

```
cout << "This is equivalent to " << fahrenheit
    << "in Fahrenheit\n";
```

These lines print out the value of the variable **fahrenheit** in the middle of a line of explanatory text, and then move the cursor down one line. The occurrence of the closing brace } of **main**() marks the end of the program, and control is returned to DOS (or to ZED if you have compiled and run the program from that editor).

The C++ arithmetic operators

C++ has a very wide range of arithmetic operators. We have already met two of them (* and +) and it is now time to meet several others. They are listed here in descending order of precedence.

Operator	Example	Precedence	Name
++	++a	1	increment
--	--a	1	decrement
*	a*b	2	multiplication
/	a/b	2	division
%	a%b	2	modulo division
+	a+b	3	addition
-	a-b	3	subtraction and unary minus
=	a=b	4	assignment

The increment and decrement operators

The use of several of the operators listed above will probably strike you as fairly self-evident; the major exception will perhaps be the increment and decrement operators which occur at the head of the list. The following section is devoted to the use of these.

The majority of the arithmetic operators in C++ are binary operators – that is, they occur between two **operands**. However, the increment and decrement operators ++ and - - are unary operators, relating to a single operand.

Consider the following code-fragment:

```
int a=5,b=6;
a=a+1;
b=b-1;
```

The purpose of this code is to declare and initialise two variables of type int. The second line increases the value of **a** by 1, and the third line decreases the value of **b** by 1. This code is perfectly correct C++ (and C), and as far as the syntax of the language is concerned there is no reason why you should not write code like this. However, very few programmers would compose such code; instead, they would write:

```
int a=5,b=6;
a++;
b--;
```

which has exactly the same effect in terms of the mathematical result, but from which many compilers can create much faster running machine code.

In fact the Zortech Version 2 compiler does not need the hint provided by the ++ and -- operators. However, most programmers would still expect to use these operators, thus retaining compatibility with older code, as well as creating extremely compact source code.

It would also be possible to achieve the same result with the following:

```
++a;
--b;
```

Here, the ++ and -- come before instead of after the operands to which they are applied. Summing up therefore, all three of the following expressions have the effect of incrementing the value of **a**:

```
a=a+1;a++;++a;
```

A Subtle Distinction

There is, however, a subtle but important difference between the last two expressions in the above line. Consider the following fragment, in which **a** and **b** are integer variables:

```
int a=1,b;
b=a++;
```

The effect of the second line here is to make **b** equal to **a** and *then* to increment **a**, so that **b** is made equal to 1 and **a** is made equal to 2. The result is quite different from that produced by the following very similar code:

```
int a=1,b;
b=++a;
```

Here, **a** is incremented *first* and only afterwards is **b** made equal to it; thus both **a** and **b** are finally made equal to 2.

The rule is that if the increment or decrement operators are prefixed to their operand, then the appropriate incrementing or decrementing operation is performed *before* any other assignment is made; if the increment or decrement operators are suffixed to their operand, then the assignment takes place first, and the incrementing or decrementing takes place afterwards.

Be absolutely sure that you understand this subtlety of the ++ and -- operators. They let you write very compact programs; however, a moment's carelessness can lead you to using the prefixed form instead of the suffixed form and *vice versa*, and since such an error will not be found during compilation, the only warning you will actually have that anything at all is wrong will be when your program produces the wrong results.

Unary minus: Although the minus sign – is generally used as a binary operator (one which is placed between two operands), it can also be used as a unary operator (that is, as one which relates to a single operand). Its effect is to multiply the operand by -1. It can thus be used to change any negative value to its positive equivalent and *vice versa*.

For instance, consider the following code:

```
int a=6;
a=-a;
cout << a;
```

This will output **-6**.

More about multiplication and division

We have already remarked on the use of * to mean 'multiply' and / to mean 'divide'.

Ordinary multiplication and division are generally straightforward, except that when integers (or variables of type int) are divided using the / operator, then any remainder will be truncated.

You can test this for yourself by entering and running the short program on the following page.

Program 2.2

```
#include <stream.hpp>
main()
{
   int num1=13,num2=7;
   cout << "The result of the division is "
      << num1/num2 << "\n";
}
```

If you type this in and then compile and run it, you will see that the result of the integer division of 13 by 7 is given as 1.

The * and / operators can be used on any of the built-in data types available in C++, and – like the other operators – they can also be **overloaded** so that they can be used with data types which you have created yourself. This is a very useful feature; it is described at length in Chapter Nine.

Modulo division

Modulo division with the operator % returns the remainder of an integer division; this operator should not be used with real numbers.

Extending Program 2.2 to show the use of % gives Program 2.3:

Program 2.3

```
#include <stream.hpp>
main()
{
   int num1=13,num2=7;
   cout << "The result of the division is "
      << num1/num2 << "\n";
   cout << "The remainder is " << num1%num2 << "\n";
}
```

This program will show that the result of the division of 13 by 7 is 1, and that the remainder is 6.

Parentheses

Parentheses are used in C++ to change the 'natural' precedence of an operator in the same way as in ordinary arithmetic: an operation which is enclosed between a () pair will take precedence over every other operation. For instance, the expression

```
(3+4)*2
```

will return the result 14 (add 3 and 4 and multiply the result by 2) while the expression

```
3+4*2
```

will return the result 11 (multiply 4 by 2 and add 3 to the result).

As in ordinary arithmetic, parentheses must always be paired; a very common error when entering complex expressions is to omit one or more parentheses.

Type conversions and casts

It is permissible to mix variables of one type with variables of another type. For instance, the following is quite permissible:

```
char num_1;double num_2=123.45;
num_1=num_2;
cout << num_1;
```

If you try it, you will find that it outputs an opening brace {, which is the character which corresponds with Ascii 123.

What has happened here is that the double value has been progressively changed to a float, then to an int, and finally to a char. At each stage there has been a potential loss of accuracy, though in this example this is only evident in the loss of the fractional part of the value of **num_2**.

Type conversion in the other direction is quite legal, but doesn't result in any gain in accuracy.

Pascal generally prohibits this sort of simple type conversion because the resulting loss of accuracy can cause problems; C++ assumes that the programmer knows what he or she is doing and accordingly allows it.

Casts

Another way of changing from one type to another is by the use of **casts**.

For instance, look at the following fragment of code:

```
int number=5; // declare and initialise an integer
cout << number/2; // division produces an integer result
```

As we have already observed, division of an integer or a variable of type int produces an integer result, and so the output from the code will be **2**.

To force the output of the untruncated result, you can 'cast' the integer variable **number** to a float; the code would look like this:

```
int number=5;
cout << float(number)/2; // use a cast for the full result
```

The effect of **float(number)** is to temporarily treat **number** as though it were of type float instead of type int; the output of the second line of code will therefore be **2.5**.

As you can see, the format of a cast is **type(expression)**. This format is only used in C++. The alternative format used in C, and which is also available in C++, is **(type)expression**; the second line of code in the fragment printed above could therefore also have been written as

```
cout << (float)number/2;
```

In C and C++ casts are usually considered to be unary operators, although the C++ versions look very much like functions.

You will probably not find that you need to use casts very often; however, they do provide a useful way of forcing a temporary type conversion.

Bitwise manipulation

As well as the various arithmetic operators described above, C and C++ include a variety of operators with which you can manipulate the individual bits of which binary numbers are comprised; specifically, you can test, change or shift the individual bits of an integer or character variable.

In the discussion which follows, we assume that you understand something of the principles which lie behind binary numbers; if not, you may find it helpful to consult one of the many books which are available dealing with this topic.

Until fairly recently, the creators of high-level languages seem to have assumed that programmers wouldn't need to have access to bit-level programming; indeed, high-level languages were originally intended to make such access unnecessary. Any programmers who *did* need to manipulate individual bits were politely pointed in the direction of writing machine-code routines.

Thankfully, C++ offers a more helpful approach. This is because the language was designed so that it can replace assembly language even in such tasks as writing an operating system. Consequently, virtually everything which it is possible to do in machine code can also be carried out with C++; and this includes bit manipulation.

The shift operators

C++ has two **shift operators**; they are << and >>. The effect of >> is to shift a given pattern of bits one place to the right; << shifts a given pattern one place to the left.

(You will probably have noticed that the shift operators are the same as you have already met when using **cin** and **cout**. In C, these operators were used only for bitwise shifts. In C++ they have been **overloaded** for use with **cin** and **cout**; that is, they have been given a special extended meaning. We shall be looking at the overloading of operators in detail in Chapter Nine.)

To see how these operators work, look at the following fragment of code:

```
int a=2,b; // a couple of variables
b=a<<2; // double bitwise shift to the left
cout << b; // output the result
```

When variable **a** is set to 2 in the first line of the above program, it is stored as the binary number 00000010. The effect of the << operator in the second line is to shift all the bits two places to the left – the number of places to be moved is shown by the '2' after the <<. The two left-most bits 'fall off the end' of the byte as they are shifted, and zeros are shifted in at the right-hand end of the byte; consequently the byte now holds the sequence 00001000.

This is equivalent to 8 in denary arithmetic, and so 8 is output in the last line of the fragment printed above.

You can restore the original value by shifting the contents of the byte to the right two places; the command to do this and assign the resulting value to **b** would be

```
b=a>>2;
```

Once again, bits pushed off the end are lost, and zeros are shifted in at the other end.

In binary arithmetic, shifting a number one place to the left is the equivalent of multiplying it by 2, and shifting it one place to the right is the equivalent of dividing it by 2. One use of the shift operators is therefore to provide very rapid multiplication and division of integers.

ANDs, ORs and NOTs

It is often necessary to change individual bits in a byte without affecting the other bits. For instance, WordStar and some other word processing programs mark the boundaries of words by setting the MSB – the most significant bit – of the last character in each word to 1. (When a bit is **set**, this means that it carries the value 1; when it is **reset** or **cleared**, it carries the value 0.)

One consequence of this feature is that when text composed with these programs is displayed on the screen or printer using the DOS TYPE or PRINT commands, several strange characters are displayed instead of the expected letters; a similar problem arises when the text is exported to other word processing programs which do not recognise the WordStar convention. It therefore becomes necessary to use a conversion program which will reset the MSB of every affected byte back to 0 without affecting the remaining bits in the byte.

It would in fact be possible to do this using nothing more than the two bitwise shift operators we have already met: shifting all the bits one place to the left with << will push the original MSB off the end of the byte, and a subsequent shift to the right will put all the bits back in their original places, with a zero automatically being shifted into the MSB position.

Although this technique would work, it would suffer from the disadvantage that every byte would be operated on twice, with consequent loss of speed when the program is being run. This is clearly inefficient, but there is a better solution as the next section describes.

Bit-level operators: There are four operators which can be used to set or clear individual bits within a byte:

Operator	Name
&	bitwise AND
|	bitwise OR
^	bitwise Exclusive OR
~	one's complement

Bitwise AND: The purpose of a bitwise AND operation is to compare the pattern of bits in two bytes and then to return a 1 for all those bits which are 1 in both bytes and a 0 for all the others. In other words, a 1 is returned if the appropriate bits in byte 1 AND byte 2 are set to 1.

To see how this works, look at the following fragment of code:

```
int a=6,b=7,c;
c=a&b;
cout << c;
```

Here, variable **a** holds the value 6; variable **b** holds the value 7. In binary terms, this is equivalent to the following:

a	00000110
b	00000111

The second line of the fragment sets all the bits of variable **c** to 1 where the equivalent bits of both **a** and **b** are 1, and resets all the others to 0. The result is therefore:

```
c                    00000110
```

Consequently the final line of the fragment will produce the output 6, which is the denary equivalent of the binary value stored in **c**.

The bitwise AND can thus be thought of as a way of clearing selected bits to 0.

Returning to our WordStar example, we want to clear the MSB of those bytes where the MSB is set, while leaving everything else untouched. The easiest way of doing this is to AND each byte with a byte in which the MSB is set to 0 and all the other bits are set to 1; in this way, the MSB of the result will be 0 and all the other bits will be unchanged:

```
original byte              11101101
mask byte                  01111111
result of bitwise AND      01101101
```

In terms of C++ code, this would look something like this:

```
char c;
c=c&127; // This is the denary representation of binary
         // 01111111
cout << c;
```

This operation is called **masking**, and the byte which is ANDed with the original byte is called the **mask**; only those bits which can 'peep through' the mask will be returned by the AND operation. In Chapter Eleven we shall develop a complete program to read a WordStar file and convert it to Ascii.

Bitwise OR: The bitwise OR operator | compares the pattern of bits in two bytes. It then returns a 1 for all those bits which are 1 in either one byte OR the other.

Consider the following fragment of C++ code:

```
int a=6,b=7,c;
c=a|b;
cout << c;
```

Here as before variable **a** holds the value 6, and variable **b** holds the value 7. In binary terms, the situation is thus like this:

```
a               00000110
b               00000111
```

The effect of the assignment statement **c=a|b** is to set a bit in variable **c** where the corresponding bits in either **a** or **b** are set; the other bits are cleared. The result is thus:

```
c               00000111
```

This is the binary equivalent of denary 7, and so this is the value that will be output in the final line of the fragment.

Just as the bitwise AND operator is used to clear selected bits, so the bitwise OR operator is used to set selected bits. Use a 1 in the appropriate position in the mask byte to force a 1 to appear in the result; the other bits will be unaffected.

The bitwise Exclusive OR: The effect of the exclusive OR operator ^ is to compare the bits in two bytes and to return a zero wherever the bits in both bytes are 0 or the bits in both bytes are 1; only when one byte has a 1 in a given position while the other byte has a 0 in the same position does the operator return a 1. In other words, Exclusive OR means 'Either one byte or the other *but not both.*'

The following fragment of code should make this clear:

```
int a=6,b=7,c;
c=a^b;
cout << c;
```

Once again, the pattern of bits in variables **a** and **b** looks like this:

```
a               00000110
b               00000111
```

The effect of the Exclusive OR operation is to return a 1 only in the rightmost position, since in every other position the bit pattern of both bytes is the same:

```
c               00000001
```

The result of the operation is therefore 1.

The bitwise one's complement operator: The last of the bitwise operators is ~. Unlike the other operators, this one is unary; that is, it returns a value based on only one byte rather than one byte and a mask.

The one's complement of a binary number is produced by 'flipping the bits'; that is, by turning every 1 into a 0 and every 0 into a 1.

For instance, consider the following fragment:

```
int a=6,b;
b=~a;
cout << b;
```

The pattern of bits in the byte representing variable **a** has the familiar form:

    a   00000110

The effect of the third line of the fragment is to flip the bits thus:

    b   11111001

You might assume from the pattern of bits that this is the equivalent of denary 249. However, if you incorporate the fragment in a program and run it, you will discover that the answer is given as -7.

The reason for this is that the most significant bit is treated as a 'sign bit'; when it is set, the remainder of the byte is assumed to hold a two's complement (*not* one's complement) negative number; when it is cleared, the remainder of the byte is assumed to hold a positive number.

A two's complement negative number can be arrived at by adding 1 to a one's complement negative number; you can prove this to yourself by changing the last line of the fragment to read **cout << ++b;**. Try this and confirm that it works as you would expect.

Apart from using the one's complement operator in this way to produce a negative number – which is arithmetically the same as using the unary – operator described earlier – another use of the operator is to encrypt text-files so that they cannot easily be read.

This technique involves complementing every byte of the text before saving it to disc. Any attempt to read the text using the DOS TYPE command will then display only garbage.

To restore the plain text, simply complement every byte as it is read back into memory; complementing any value twice merely restores the original value.

Shorthand arithmetic notation

As well as the normal system of arithmetic and bitwise notation described above, all of the binary operators can occur in statements using a special 'shorthand' notation which reduces the amount of typing that you may have to do.

The shorthand notation can be used whenever the same variable occurs on both sides of the = operator, as in the expression **a=a*b**. This can always be replaced by the much shorter expression **a*=b**.

The full list of shorthand expressions is as follows:

Shorthand	*Equivalent expression*
a*=b	a=a*b
a/=b	a=a/b
a%=b	a=a%b
a+=b	a=a+b
a-=b	a=a-b
a<<=b	a=a<<b
a>>=b	a=a>>b
a&=b	a=a&b
a|=b	a=a|b
a^=b	a=a^b

The ternary operator ? :

As well as the unary and binary operators already described, C and C++ have a further assignment operator: ? :.

To see how this is used, consider the following fragment of code:

```
int a=6,b=7,c;
c = a>3 ? b : b*2;
cout << c;
```

The important line here is the one reading **c = a>3 ? b : 10**. Its operation is as follows:

First, the expression **a>3** is evaluated to see if it is true or false. Any of the logical operators described in Chapter Three can be used in this position; in this particular case, the test is simply to discover whether or not the value of **a** is greater than 3.

If the expression evaluates as true, then the value or expression which precedes the colon is assigned to the variable on the left of the statement – in this case, the variable **c**.

If the expression evaluates as false, then the value or expression which follows the colon is assigned to the variable on the left of the statement – the variable **c** again.

Working through our example, the expression **a>3** is found to be true; consequently the value of the variable **b,** which precedes the colon, is assigned to variable **c**. Had

a not been greater than 3, then the expression following the colon would be evaluated, and the resulting value would have been assigned to variable **c** – in this case, the result of **b*2**, which is 14.

Constants and variables

By definition, variables contain information which may change while a program is running. Constants, on the other hand, contain fixed values which cannot be altered by the program.

In the original C language, it was possible to declare a constant by means of the **define** macro, like this:

```
#define PI 3.14159
```

The effect of this is that before your program is compiled, the preprocessor replaces every occurrence of **PI** by **3.14159**. (Incidentally, note the convention that constants are entered in capitals.)

In C++ (and some more recent versions of C) the preferred way of declaring a constant is by means of the keyword **const**. The form of such a declaration is as follows:

```
const PI=3.14159
```

Now that **PI** has been declared to be a constant, any later attempts to modify it – by treating it as an lvalue, for instance – will be trapped by the compiler and reported as syntax errors.

Enumerated variables

In addition to the 'built in' data types such as int, char and float, C++ allows the programmer to create **enumerated** types.

Every variable type is subject to certain constraints which affect the range of values which it can contain. For instance, a variable of type signed char can hold any integer value between -128 and +127, but no other value.

The range of values which can be held in an enumerated variable are specified by the programmer, who can also associate each of these values with an **enumerated constant**.

A simple example may make this clearer. The following fragment shows how a simple enumerated variable type can be set up and used:

```
enum traffic_light{red,amber,green}first_set,second_set;
first_set=red;second_set=green;
```

In the first line of this fragment we have created a new data type **traffic_light** and specified that variables of this type can take any of the three values red, amber or green; no other values are available to them.

At the end of the first line we have declared two variables of type **traffic_light**, namely **first_set** and **second_set**.

The second line of code initialises the variable **first_set** to contain the value **red** and the variable **second_set** to contain the value **green**.

We could, of course, have initialised the variables at the same time as we declared them, like this:

```
enum traffic_light{red,amber,green}
 first_set=red,second_set=green;
```

Numerical equivalents of enumerated constants

Each of the enumerated constants red, amber and green is automatically associated with a numerical value. By default the compiler assigns the value zero to the first constant after the opening brace {, 1 to the next value, and so on. Thus in our example, red is associated with 0, amber with 1 and green with 2.

Assigning values to enumerated variables can be done by using either the enumerated constants (such as red, amber and so on) or by using the numerical equivalents of those constants. The following statements therefore have the same meaning:

```
second_set=red;
second_set=0; // these two lines have the same effect.
```

Assigning other values to enumerated variables: It is also permissible to assign specific numerical values to enumerated constants, instead of using the default values of zero for the first constant after the opening brace, 1 for the next and so on.

The following fragment shows how to assign numerical values when declaring an enumerated type:

```
enum traffic_light{red=6,amber,green=42}
```

Here red has been associated with the value 6 and green has been associated with the value 42; amber has not been associated with any value, and therefore automatically takes on the value 7, which is one higher than the value of the constant on its immediate left.

Using tag names

In the declarations we have seen so far, the reserved word **enum**, which always precedes the definition of an enumerated type, has been immediately followed by a **tag name**, namely **traffic_light**. In effect we have been making **traffic_light** into a new variable type, and later declaring variables of this type, such as **first_set** and **second_set**.

It is quite permissible to omit the tag name. However, if this is done, all the variables of the new enumerated type must be declared immediately after the closing brace surrounding the enumerated constants. Thus the following is quite legal:

```
enum {red,amber,green}first_set,second_set;
```

However, since the tag name has been omitted from this definition it is not possible at any later stage to define any further variables of the same type as **first_set** and **second_set**.

Where the tag name is omitted, the enumerated type is said to be **anonymous**.

Enumerated types without variables

It can sometimes be useful to create enumerated types even when no variable of that type is declared. For instance, consider the following:

```
enum {false,true};
```

Here we have neither a tag name nor any variables. However, we have associated the enumerated constant **false** with the value zero and the enumerated constant **true** with the value 1, and so can make assignments and comparisons to the enumerated constants instead of to numbers.

For instance, the second line of the following code is more meaningful than the third line, although they both mean exactly the same thing:

```
enum{false,true};
result=false; // this line and the next one
result=0;  // both assign zero to result
```

Using enumerated variables

The major benefit of enumerated variables is that they make your code easier to understand and debug, simply because the enumerated constants are more immediately meaningful than their numerical equivalents.

You can output the numerical equivalents of enumerated variables, but not directly. For instance, the following is not permissible:

```
enum traffic_light{red,amber,green}first_set,second_set;
first_set=red;second_set=green;
cout << first_set << second_set; // this code is illegal!
```

To output the numerical value of an enumerated variable, you must first cast it to an integer, like this:

```
enum traffic_light{red,amber,green}first_set,second_set;
first_set=red;second_set=green;
cout << int(first_set) << int(second_set); // that's better!
```

Postscript to Chapter Two

By the time that you have finished reading this chapter and working through the sample code it contains, you should be able to write and compile some simple C++ programs on your own.

Remember that all variables must be declared before they are used; in C++, this can be done at the point of the first use.

C++ has a wide range of arithmetic operators. These can be divided into unary operators, such as ++ and --; binary operators, such as / and *; and the ternary operator ? :.

There are also several bitwise operators, including &, | and ~, which can be used to manipulate the individual bits within a byte.

Constants can be declared by means of the reserved word **const**; once so declared, they cannot then be changed in the course of a program.

You can use enumerated variables to create simple data types of your own. The major advantage of doing this is to make your programs easier to understand and debug.

Exercises to Chapter Two

1. If you haven't yet entered and run the programs in Chapter Two, do so now.

2. Rewrite Program 2.1 to convert temperatures from Fahrenheit to Celsius.

3. What output will each of the following fragments produce?

```
int a=3,b;
b=a++;
cout << b << a;
```

```
int a=3,b;
b=++a;
cout << b << a;
```

4. Perform a bitwise AND with these binary numbers:

```
01100110
11001100
```

3

Program Control

Both C and C++ are very rich in commands to control the flow of your programs. It's important that you should learn to use these commands proficiently, as you will then be able to write well-structured programs which you and other people can easily maintain and debug.

Incidentally, the program control statements in C++ are identical to those in C, and so virtually all the topics covered in this chapter apply equally to both languages. If you are already familiar with loop and conditional statements in C, then you can skip straight to the next chapter.

About program control

In most low level languages, the only way it which it is possible to change the flow of a program so that it will repeat a section of code several times, or branch to different sections of code depending on such factors as keyboard input, is by using an absolute or a conditional Jump instruction. This technique suffers from the important disadvantage that it makes the workings of even a moderately complex program very difficult to follow.

A similar problem occurs in certain high level languages. For instance, although both Basic and Cobol offer limited looping structures, it is almost impossible to write a complex program in either of those languages without having recourse to their equivalents of the Jump instruction. Programs written in this way have been aptly compared to a plate of spaghetti: it's virtually impossible to work out what is happening at any given point.

There is of course a place for the Basic GOTO statement and its equivalent in other languages; even C++ has a **goto** command which is described later in this chapter. However, the C++ **goto** command should only be used when it actually helps to clarify the program flow; there is *always* some other way of achieving the same result, and **goto** should only be used on those rare occasions when its use results in clearer code. You should notice that, outside the sections in this chapter where its use is described, **goto** is never used in this book.

Making choices with if

The simplest way of changing the flow of a program written in C++ is by means of the **if** statement. Program 3.1 should give you a general idea of how it works; type it in and run it yourself:

Program 3.1

```
#include <stream.hpp>
main()
{
  // declare a variable of type float
  // and then prompt for a value
  float number;
  cout << "Type in a number and press [RETURN]\n";
  cin >> number;
  // input value and output message if greater than 10
  if (number>10)
  cout << "The number was greater than 10\n";
}
```

The purpose of this quite trivial program is simply to prompt for and input a number. If the number is greater than 10, then the message **The number was greater than 10** will be displayed and the program will end; if the number was not greater than 10, then the program will end without displaying the message.

The if syntax: To put this a little more formally, the simplest form of the **if** statement comprises three elements, the first of which is the reserved word **if**.

The second element is the condition, which must be enclosed between parentheses. Any condition can be used provided that the program can determine that it is either true or false. A series or combination of conditions can be used, linked by the logical AND, NOT or OR operators; these are described later.

The final element of the **if** command consists of the action to be taken if the condition is found to be true. This can be either a single statement, as in Program 3.1, or a block of statements; in the latter case, the block must be enclosed between braces { }.

For instance, the following fragment will test whether or not the floating point variable **number** contains a value greater than 10; if it does, then the block of statements enclosed between { and } will be executed.

```
cin >> number;
if (number>10) {
   cout << "The number was bigger than 10\n";
   cout << "Isn't that interesting!\n";
}
```

Note that there is no semi-colon after the closing parenthesis of the condition (**number>10**); instead, the opening brace of the block of statements which will be executed if the condition is true is placed at the end of the same line.

The placing of the opening brace for a conditional statement is purely a matter of convention. Some programmers place it at the beginning of the next line of code, and the effect is just the same.

What is truth? Although in Program 3.1 we have taken the condition to be true in what we might call the every-day sense, C++ regards any condition as true if it consists of an expression which returns a non-zero value. For instance, the condition

```
if (number)
```

is treated as false if **number** is equal to zero, and true for every other value of **number**.

This may strike you as rather curious. In reality it is a very useful feature, and you will come across several places in this book where we use it in order to produce very compact code.

Although any non-zero value is treated as true, it is quite proper to regard true as returning 1 and false as returning zero. You can even use these values in assignment statements. For instance, consider the following fragment:

```
int a=1,b=2,c; // declare some integers
c=a<b; // a is less than b, so c is true
cout <<c; // so 1 is displayed
```

Since the relationship between **a** and **b** in the second line is true, **c** is assigned the value 1, and this is output in the third line.

Conversely, the value of **c** at the end of the following fragment would be 0, since the relationship between **a** and **b** in the second line is False:

```
int a=1,b=2,c;
c=a>b; // this time c is false
cout << c; // so 0 is displayed
```

Nesting if statements

It's possible to **nest** one **if** statement inside another. The following fragment contains a simple example of nesting:

```
cin >> number;
if (number>10) {
   cout << "The number was bigger than 10\n";
   cout << "Isn't that interesting!\n";
   if (number>100) {
      cout << "In fact it was bigger than 100\n";
      cout << "Which is even more interesting!\n";
   }
}
```

Because the second **if** statement is nested inside the first, it won't even be tested for if the first condition is found to be false. In our particular example, this is just what we want; if the number isn't greater than 10, there's no point in seeing whether it is greater than 100.

Remember the simple rule that where a number of **if** statements are nested, all those statements which follow a condition which is found to be false will be bypassed.

Inexperienced programmers often forget this. If you have a series of **if** statements one after the other which don't work as they ought, check them carefully to see that they are properly nested. This is even more important (and tricky) when you use the **else** keyword described in the next section.

Using else

It's often necessary to execute one statement or block of statements if a particular condition is true, and a different statement or statement block if the condition is false. In C++ this is done with the keyword **else**. Virtually every modern high-level language has some equivalent construction.

Program 3.2 shows how **else** works:

Program 3.2

```
#include <stream.hpp>
main()
{
   float number;
   cout << "Type in a number and press [RETURN]\n";
   cin >> number;
   if (number>10) cout << "It was bigger than 10\n";
   else cout << "It wasn't bigger than 10\n";
}
```

If the condition in parentheses is true, then the statement (or block of statements) immediately following it will be executed; if it is not true, then the statement following **else** (or a block of statements enclosed between braces { }) will be executed instead.

Incidentally, if you are used to programming in Pascal you may recall that it is incorrect in that language to place a semicolon before **else**. This rule does not apply in C or C++; in both of these languages, you *must* include the semi-colon at the end of the line preceding the **else** command.

Nesting else statements: Inexperienced programmers who have written code including several **if** and **else** statements nested together sometimes find it difficult to work out just which sections of code will be executed under which conditions.

For instance, look at the following fragment:

```
cin >> number;
if(number>10)if(number>100)
   cout << "The number was bigger than 100\n";
else cout << "What a dull number!\n";
```

It's obvious that the second **if** is nested inside the first one. But what about the **else**? Will the statement which follows it be executed if the first **if** is false or if the second **if** is false?

In C and C++, the following very simple rule applies: an **else** statement refers to the **if** which immediately precedes it, so long as that **if** does not have its own **else** statement.

In the fragment printed above, therefore, the message **What a dull number!** will be output if the first condition is true – **number** is greater than 10 – and the second condition is false – **number** is not greater than 100.

If this isn't what you want, you can force a different evaluation of the conditions with braces, like this:

```
cin >> number;
if (number>10)
{if (number>100)
   cout << "The number was bigger than 100\n";}
else cout << "What a dull number!\n";
```

The message **What a dull number!** will now be output only if the first condition is false; that is, if **number** is less than 10.

More about comparisons

So far, we have tested to see whether a variable is greater than a specified value, using the operator >. C++ has a wide range of such relational operators; the full list is as follows:

Operator	Example	Meaning
==	a == b	Equal to
!=	a != b	Not equal to
>	a > b	Greater than
<	a < b	Less than
>=	a >= b	Greater than or equal
<=	a <= b	Less than or equal

Note especially the forms == and !=; these forms are peculiar to C++ (and C), and often cause problems for programmers more used to the = and <> operators used in Basic and Pascal.

Unintended assignments: The following code fragment shows how the = operator might be incorrectly used instead of the == operator in a conditional statement:

```
if (number=10) cout << "Number was 10"; // this is wrong!!
```

When the Zortech C++ compiler meets this line it will issue the warning message **Possible unintended assignment**. If you ignore this warning, it will then continue to compile the code, treating the statement in parentheses as an assignment (giving the value 10 to the variable **number**) rather than as a condition.

Not all compilers are so friendly, and even the Zortech compiler will not give this warning if you are compiling with the **-w** compiler flag set, as this turns warning messages off. The moral is clear: = is not the same as ==, and you must not use = in conditional statements.

Logical operators

As well as the relational operators described in the previous section, C++ has three logical operators, namely **&&**, which is logical AND, **||**, which is logical OR, and **!**, which is logical NOT.

Logical AND: The logical AND is used when it is necessary to check whether two different conditions are both true; that is, whether both one condition AND the other condition are true.

For instance, you might want to establish whether a particular variable contains a value between two numbers: greater than 10, for example, and less than 100. The following fragment will do this:

```
cin >> number;
if(number>10 && number<100) cout << "It was between 10 and
  100\n";
```

The condition will only be true – and the message will therefore only be displayed – if the variable **number** contains a value which is both greater than 10 AND less than 100; if one section of the condition is True but the other section is False – if **number** contains a value of 200, for example – then the message will not be shown.

There's no need to restrict yourself to just two conditions linked by **&&**, nor for all the conditions to refer to the same variable. The following line, for example, is quite acceptable:

```
if (a==10 && b < 6 && c > 42) cout << "True\n";
```

Only if all three of the conditions are satisfied will the message **True** be shown.

Logical OR: Logical OR is used when you want to test that at least one part of a condition is true.

Consider the following fragment:

```
if (number>10 || number <100) cout << "True\n";
```

The message **True** will appear either if **number** is greater than 10, OR if **number** is less than 100. It will also appear if both parts of the condition are true: that is, if **number** contains a value between 10 and 100.

Logical NOT: The **!** operator can be used to negate any relationship.

For instance, we have already seen that the relationship shown in the following fragment returns the value false, or 0, and then assigns this to variable **c**:

```
int a=1,b=2,c;
c=a>b;
cout << c;
```

Compare this with the following:

```
int a=1,b=2,c;
c=!a>b;
cout << c;
```

The relationship between **a** and **b** still returns the value false. However, the **!** operator has the effect of NOTting this; and since whatever is not false must be true, the result is that **c** takes on the value true, or 1.

Order of precedence

Where several logical operators occur either together or mixed with arithmetic operators, it is necessary to know the order of precedence which applies.

Consider the following statement:

```
6<4+3;
```

This evaluates as true because in C++ the logical and relational operators are given a lower position in the order of precedence than the arithmetic operators and consequently **4+3** is evaluated first. The line is thus equivalent to

```
6<(4+3);
```

The order of precedence of the various relational and logical operators is as follows, beginning with the highest:

```
    !

    >  >=  <  <=

    ==  !=

 &&

 ||
```

Building an if ladder

It's frequently useful to be able to check which of a variety of keys has been pressed. For instance, when a menu has been displayed, the program will have to monitor the keyboard to determine which of the various options has been selected. The simplest, though not the most elegant, way of doing this is by means of a construction called an **if-else-if** ladder.

To show how this works, look at the following code:

```
int keypress;
cout << "Press 1, 2 or 3 and [RETURN]\n";
start: // This is a label
cin >> keypress;
if (keypress==1) cout << "You pressed 1\n";
else if (keypress==2) cout << "You pressed 2\n";
else if (keypress==3) cout << "You pressed 3\n";
else goto start; // Go round again if not 1, 2 or 3
```

The way in which this code works is simple enough. If the variable **keypress** contains the value 1, then the first condition will be satisfied and the message **You pressed 1** will be output. If **keypress** contains the value 2, then the second message will be displayed, and so on.

The purpose of the last line is to trap any other responses; if **keypress** is not equal to 1, 2 or 3, then the **goto** in the last line forces a jump back to the place marked by the label **start**, and you have another chance to type in a number in the correct range.

The goto command

Our **if-else-if** ladder uses the **goto** statement to 'go round again' if any key other than 1, 2 or 3 is pressed. We shall now briefly consider the way in which the **goto** statement works.

First of all, you should understand that **goto** is strictly optional; it can always be replaced by a different construction, and usually should be. However, it does have a few legitimate uses, as we will see in a later section.

The **goto** command requires a label, which marks the position to which control of the program should be transferred. Labels are not defined beforehand, as they have to be in Pascal, and jumps can be made either backwards (to an earlier part of the program) or forwards.

A label must begin with either a letter or an underline character, followed by one or more letters, numbers or underlines, or a combination of these. It is followed by a colon :.

Program 3.3 uses a simple loop with **goto** to output the numbers from 1 to 20:

Program 3.3

```
#include <stream.hpp>
main()
{
   int counter=0;
   start:
   cout << ++counter < "\n";
      // increment counter then display it
   if (counter!=20) goto start;
      // go round again if counter!=20
}
```

The variable **counter** is initialised to zero. Then it is incremented – and the new value output – each time the loop is repeated. If **counter** is not equal to 20, then control returns to the label **start** and the loop is executed again.

We shall see several variations on this 'count up to 20' program in the remainder of this chapter; all of the other versions are preferable to this one because they avoid the use of the **goto** command.

The switch command

The **if-else-if** ladder which we met earlier is one way of handling the situation where a series of tests have to be made one after the other, but it certainly isn't the most elegant. Although the code looks straightforward enough at first glance, complex ladders can be difficult to debug, and so the technique is best avoided.

Fortunately, C and C++ provide a special command which can be used instead of the **if-else-if** ladder. It is **switch**, and it works in a very similar way to the Basic ON .. GOTO and ON .. GOSUB commands and the Pascal CASE command.

Using **switch**, our ladder code would look like this:

```
int keypress;
cout << "Press 1, 2 or 3 and [RETURN] \n";
start: // This is a label
cin >> keypress;
switch(keypress) {
   case 1: cout << "You pressed 1\n"; break;
   case 2: cout << "You pressed 2\n"; break;
   case 3: cout << "You pressed 3\n"; break;
   default: goto start; // Go round again if not 1, 2 or 3
}
```

There are several things to note about the way in which the **switch** command works.

case: After the reserved word **switch**, every line in which a comparison is to be made begins with the word **case** followed by a constant and a colon. The **switch** variable – in this case **keypress** – is checked for equality with this constant, and if this condition is satisfied, the statement immediately following is executed.

In some ways, the **case** command is much more restrictive than **if**. Most important, **case** can only test for equality, and can only be used for a comparison with a constant; **if**, on the other hand, can also test whether a variable is less than or greater than a particular value, and the comparison can be with either a constant or a variable.

Empty case statements: It is permissible to have empty **case** statements, like this:

```
start:
switch(keypress) {
   case 1:
   case 2: cout << "You pressed 1 or 2\n"; break;
   case 3: cout << "You pressed 3\n"; break;
   default: goto start; // Go round again if not 1, 2 or 3
}
```

In this case, if **keypress** is equal to either 1 or 2, then the message **You pressed 1 or 2** will be displayed.

Much the same thing can be done using alphabetical characters instead of numbers; the use of empty **switch** statements makes it possible to treat shifted and unshifted letters identically, like this:

```
#include <conio.h>
char keypress;
start:
keypress=getch();
switch(keypress) {
   case 'A':
   case 'a': cout << "You pressed a\n"; break;
   case 'B':
   case 'b': cout << "You pressed b\n"; break;
   default: goto start; // Go round again if not a,A,b,B
}
```

This example makes use of the function **getch**(), which requires the header file conio.h to be 'included'. This function fetches a character from the input stream (normally the keyboard) without waiting for [RETURN] to be pressed and without echoing the character to the output stream (normally the screen).

break: The last three examples have used the new reserved word **break** at the end of each of the lines in which a test is carried out. The purpose of this command is to force control to be transferred to the next statement after the closing brace } of the **switch** block.

Had **break** been omitted in each line, and assuming that the variable **keypress** contained the value 1, the output from the first **switch** code above would have looked like this:

```
You pressed 1
You pressed 2
You pressed 3
```

and control would then have been transferred back to the label **start**.

Unless **break** is included after each **case** statement, then when that condition has been satisfied, all the conditions which come after it – including the **default** condition – will be regarded as having been satisfied as well.

Because Basic has no equivalent of this use of **break**, many programmers who are moving up to C++ from Basic forget to use it, and then wonder why their programs don't work.

default: The final point to note about the **switch** statement is the reserved word **default**, followed by a colon. If the **switch** variable is not equal to the constant in any of the **case** statements, then the statement following **default:** will be executed.

Because **default** occurs after all the other elements in the **switch** ladder, it does not need to be followed by **break**.

The **default** statement is optional; if it (and its attendant **goto**) are missing then the program will not loop back to the **start** label if no match is found in any of the **case** statements.

The do while loop

We said earlier that it is always possible to avoid using **goto** in C and C++. One important way of doing so is by using the **do while** loop.

The **do while** loop is a useful way of allowing a series of statements to be repeated until a particular condition has been met. For instance, we could force the **switch** section of code to be repeated until a suitable number has been input without resorting to the awkward **label/goto** combination.

The **do while** form of the code would look like this:

```
int keypress;
cout << "Press 1, 2 or 3 and [RETURN]\n";
do { // beginning of the do while block
   cin >> keypress;
   switch(keypress) { // beginning of the switch block
      case 1: cout << "You pressed 1\n"; break;
      case 2: cout << "You pressed 2\n"; break;
      case 3: cout << "You pressed 3\n"; break;
   } // end of the switch block
} // end of the do while block
while(keypress<1 || keypress>3);
   // condition for do while loop
```

As you can see, the basic form of the **do while** looks like this:

```
do {block of statements} while (condition);
```

The loop begins with the reserved word **do**, followed by either a single statement or a block of statements enclosed between braces { }. The statement or block of statements will be repeated until the condition at the foot of the loop is satisfied. The condition itself appears in parentheses after the reserved word **while**.

Because the condition in a **do while** loop is at the bottom, such a loop is always performed at least once. The **do while** loop is therefore particularly useful when you need to validate keyboard input, or to read a disc file until the end-of-file character has been reached.

However, the **do while** loop can be used in many other places as well. For instance, note how it allows us to replace the **goto** and its associated label in the following version of our 'count up to 20' loop.

```
int counter=0;
do cout << ++counter << "\n"; while(counter!=20);
```

Because this **do while** loop contains only a single statement, the braces { } can be dispensed with. It should be immediately obvious how much more readable this form of the program is than the earlier one using **goto**.

The while loop

The **while** loop is very similar to the **do while** loop. It differs in that the condition is placed at the top of the loop. Consequently, a **while** loop will only be performed if the condition is true, while a **do while** loop will be performed once regardless of whether the condition is true or not.

The basic form of a **while** loop is like this:

```
while (condition) {block of statements}
```

As is the case with the **do while** loop, a block of statements may consist either of several statements between braces { } or of a single statement. The block or single statement will be repeated as long as the condition enclosed in parentheses is true (or has a non-zero value).

Our 'count up to 20' fragment could be rewritten using **while** instead of **do while**; it would then look like this:

```
int counter=0;
while(counter!=20) cout << ++counter << "\n";
```

Infinite loops: It is often necessary to set up **infinite loops** (sometimes called **forever loops**), and one way of doing this is to use **while** in conjunction with a condition which can never become false, like this:

```
while (1) { // block to be repeated in infinite loop }
```

Since the value in parentheses is not zero, the block will be repeated for ever. Remember, though, that even an infinite loop can be left by means of a **break** command included within it which will force control to be transferred to the next statement after the loop's closing }.

Infinite loops using enumerated variables: In Chapter Two we showed how anonymous enumerated variables can contain numeric values. For instance, the following line will associate the value 0 with the enumerated constant **false** and the value 1 with the enumerated constant **true**:

```
enum{false,true};
```

We can now write an infinite loop like this:

```
while (true) { // block to be repeated in infinite loop }
```

which is a little clearer.

Infinite loops can be set up in other ways as well, as we shall see later in this chapter.

Choosing between do while and while: As you can see, there are many situations where it makes no practical difference whether you choose to use a **do while** or **while** loop.

The only difference to bear in mind is that in a **while** loop, the condition is tested at the top of the loop, whereas in a **do while** loop, the condition is tested at the bottom. In the interests of writing code which doesn't behave in unexpected ways, therefore, follow this rule of thumb: if a loop must be executed at least once, you must use a **do while** loop; otherwise, prefer a **while** loop.

The for loop

Both **do while** and **while** loops are really intended for situations where it is not known how often a particular block of code will need to be repeated; typically, a block will be repeatedly executed until a particular keypress is detected or until a predetermined character is read from a file. Of course, both types can also be used to create 'counting' loops, as in our simple 'count up to 20' examples. However, C++ and C have a specific structure which is intended for this purpose, and which is analogous to the FOR-NEXT Loop in Basic or the Fortran DO Loop.

The C++ command is arguably much more powerful than its near equivalents in other languages. Look at the following version of our 'count up to 20' code; like the others, this will display the numbers from 1 to 20:

```
int counter;
for (counter=1;counter<=20;counter++)
   cout << counter << "\n";
```

The loop control parameters

You have probably realised already that the number of times that the loop is executed is controlled by the three statements enclosed in parentheses after the reserved word **for**:

```
(counter=1;counter<=20;counter++)
```

The three statements can be described as follows: first comes the *initialiser*; then the *condition*; and finally the *increment*. A semi-colon is placed between the initialiser and the condition, and another one between the condition and the increment.

Initialising the loop

In a **for** statement, the initialising statement always comes immediately after the opening parenthesis.

There is, however, no need for the initialising statement to confine itself to initialising a single variable, nor for the variable(s) to be initialised to 1. You could, for example, use two (or more) different variables to control a loop, separating them from each other with the comma operator , . For instance, the following fragment would initialise two variables, **counter1** and **counter2**:

```
(counter1=1, counter2=12;...)
```

It's also possible to move the initialising statement completely outside the parentheses, thus:

```
int counter =1;
for (;counter<=10;counter++)
```

Because the initialiser is missing from the **for** statement, the first semi-colon now comes immediately after the opening parenthesis.

The loop condition

The second part of the **for** statement after the opening parenthesis contains the condition; the loop will be repeated for as long as this condition remains true.

The condition in a **for** loop is tested at the 'top' – before the loop is executed for the first time – and it is thus possible for a loop not to be executed at all if the condition is false when the loop is entered.

For instance, consider the following loop:

```
for (int counter=1;counter<1;++counter) cout << "Hello\n";
```

When we run the code, the message **Hello** will be printed as long as the condition that **counter** is less than 1 is true; however, this condition can never be met since **counter** is initialised to 1 and then incremented. Consequently, the loop will not be executed (or the message output) at all.

Just as the loop variable can be initialised outside the parentheses of the **for** statement, the condition too can occur outside the parentheses. This can be done either by omitting the condition altogether, creating an infinite loop, or by including it within the body of the loop itself.

Another form of infinite loop: Omitting the condition results in an infinite loop:

```
for (int counter=1;;++counter) cout << "Hello\n";
```

Since the condition here is absent, it can never be false! If you incorporate this fragment in a full program, you can stop it by pressing [CTRL]/[C].

An easier way of programming an infinite loop involves leaving out everything between the parentheses except the semi-colons, like this:

```
for (;;) cout << "Hello\n";
```

This is the shortest and simplest way of creating an infinite loop in C++, and we will be meeting it repeatedly from now on.

Putting the condition in the loop body: Instead of putting the condition inside the parentheses, we can instead include the *reverse* of the condition inside the body of the loop. For instance, the following loop will execute twenty times:

```
for (int counter=1;;counter++){
   cout << counter << "\n";
   if (counter>20) break;
}
```

Here **break** forces the loop to be immediately abandoned; control then passes to the first statement after the closing brace.

Character variables in for loops: It's quite permissible to use variables of type char as loop control variables. For instance, the following is perfectly legitimate:

```
for (char letter='a';letter<='z';letter++) cout << letter;
```

and will output the sequence of lower-case characters between 'a' and 'z' inclusive.

Loop control with non-integers: It is also possible – but very much not recommended – to use real variables as loop counters.

For instance, the following code will work, but shouldn't be imitated:

```
for (float counter=1.1;counter<=1.4;counter+=.1)
  cout << counter;
```

The reason why it is unsafe to use floating point variables as loop counters is that it's impossible to guarantee that they are being held with sufficient accuracy in memory; rounding errors could easily result in the condition which should terminate the loop never being met, so that the loop becomes in effect an unwanted infinite loop.

Nesting loops

It is often necessary to write code in which one loop is placed 'inside' another. A simple example of this is shown in Program 3.4.

Program 3.4

```
#include <stream.hpp>
main()
{
  for (int counter1=1;counter1<=10;++counter1){
  // outer loop starts
    cout << counter1 << " ";
    for (int counter2=1;counter2<=10;++counter2){
    // inner loop starts
      cout << counter2 << " ";
    } // end of inner loop
  } // end of outer loop
} // end of main()
```

The output from this program will be

1 1 2 3 4 5 6 7 8 9 10 2 1 2 3 4 5 6 7 8 9 10 3 1 2 3 4 5 6 7 8 9 10

and so on. The first **1** represents the value held in **counter1**; this is then followed by **1** to **10** representing the values of the variable **counter2** as the inner loop is repeated 10 times.

When the inner loop has been executed 10 times, control is passed back to the outer loop; **counter1** is incremented and its value **2** is output, followed once more by **1** to **10** representing the values of **counter2** as the inner loop is again repeated 10 times, and so on.

All the different types of loop described above can be nested together.

Nested loops and break

Remember that the **break** command transfers control to the first statement after the closing brace } of the block in which **break** is found.

Usually this is what you want, but there may be occasions when it isn't enough. Consider the following rather artificial situation:

```
for (outerloop=1;outerloop<=10;++outerloop){
   for (middleloop=1;middleloop<=10;++middleloop){
      for (innerloop=1;innerloop<=10;++innerloop){
      if (innerloop==5) break;
      } // end of innerloop
   } // end of middleloop
} // end of outerloop
```

When the variable **innerloop** contains the value 5, the condition in the **if** line will be satisfied and the **break** will be executed. However, instead of transferring control right out of the three nested loops, it will only transfer control to the next loop out, namely the middle one.

It would be possible to get round this by inserting the line **if (innerloop==5) break;** in each loop, like this:

```
for (outerloop=1;outerloop<=10;++outerloop){
   for (middleloop=1;middleloop<=10;++middleloop){
      for (innerloop=1;innerloop<=10;++innerloop){
         if (innerloop==5) break;
      } // end of innerloop
      if (innerloop==5) break;
   } // end of middleloop
   if (innerloop==5) break;
} // end of outerloop
```

Here, each successive **break** command serves to transfer control one layer further out of the loops; when **innerloop** contains the value 5, the successive **break** commands are executed one after the other, like tumbling dominos.

Although this will work, it is inelegant and ugly, and certainly doesn't make debugging any easier. A much more intelligent solution is to use **goto**, like this:

```
for (outerloop=1;outerloop<=10;++outerloop){
   for (middleloop=1;middleloop<=10;++middleloop){
      for (innerloop=1;innerloop<=10;++innerloop){
         if (innerloop==5) goto end;
      } // end of innerloop
   } // end of middleloop
} // end of outerloop
end: // target of the goto command
```

We said earlier that it was permissible to use **goto** if it resulted in clearer code, and the above example is a case in point. However, in real life such cases are rare, which is why the example printed here looks so artificial.

Continue

C++ has one more loop command; this is **continue**. It has no direct equivalent in most other high level languages, though something like it can be constructed in Basic with GOTOs.

To see how **continue** works, look at Program 3.5. This prompts for a numeric input **daily_temperature**. The value input is added to the contents of variable **running_total**, which is initialised to zero at the beginning of the program.

There is also an integer variable **counter**, which is also initialised to zero; this is incremented every time the **do while** loop is executed, and thus shows how many temperatures have been input.

Program 3.5

```
#include <stream.hpp>
main()
{
   float running_total=0;
   float mean_temperature;
   float daily_temperature;
   int counter=0;
   do{
      cout << "Type in a temperature, or zero to quit\n";
      cin >> daily_temperature;
      if (!daily_temperature) continue;
      running_total+=daily_temperature;
      ++counter;
   } while (daily_temperature);
   mean_temperature=running_total/counter;
   cout << "The average temperature was "
      << mean_temperature << "\n";
}
```

The section of the code which prompts for the input, adds the latest value to **running_total**, and increments **counter**, is contained inside the **do while** loop; the loop condition **while (daily_temperature)** makes the loop repeat as long as the variable **daily_temperature** is true; that is, as long as it contains a value other than zero, which is the value we are using to act as a rogue value to terminate the program.

Since we are using zero as a rogue value, we clearly don't want it to be treated as if it were ordinary data and added to **running_total**; nor do we want **counter** to be incremented after a zero has been input. To prevent either of these events happening, we must check the variable **daily_temperature** after it has been input to see if it is zero, and if so we must jump straight to the end of the loop.

In Basic and some other languages this would have to be done using a GOTO statement. C and C++ offer the much more elegant **continue** statement; this forces the condition statement at the end of the loop to be executed at once, bypassing all the intervening code.

When **daily_temperature** contains the value zero, the condition **while (daily_temperature)** is no longer true, and the program is accordingly terminated.

The statement

```
if (!daily_temperature) continue;
```

is exactly equivalent to

```
if (daily_temperature==0) continue;
```

If you don't see why, you should re-read the section on the use of the **!** operator earlier in this chapter.

Because code containing **continue** can be difficult to debug, it's best to use it sparingly.

Postscript to Chapter Three

You should now be familiar with the very rich variety of control structures which are available in C and C++.

The simplest structure is provided by the commands **if** and **else**, and these can be expanded into an **if else if** ladder; however, the **switch** and **case** statements are easier to use and debug.

The **do while** loop tests for the truth of the loop condition at the end of the loop, and the contents of such a loop are thus always executed at least once; in **while** and **for** loops, on the other hand, the truth of the condition is tested at the beginning, so such loops will not be executed at all if the condition is false when they are first entered.

The material in a loop can consist of several statements enclosed between the { } operators, or of a single statement; in the latter case, the braces are not necessary.

break forces a premature exit from a loop, and **continue** forces the loop condition to be tested immediately.

Since **break** only forces an exit from the current loop, it may occasionally be helpful to use **goto** to exit from deeply nested loops.

Exercises to Chapter Three

1. If you haven't yet entered and run the programs in Chapter Three, do so now.

2. Use the **switch** statement to write a program to input any of the characters listed below from the keyboard and then display the appropriate response; if any other character is entered, display the message "Wrong!":

Input	Response
1	z
2	y
3	x
4	w
5	v
6	u

3. Which of the following expressions are True and which are False?

a 15==10+5   *d* int x=10,y=12; x>y || y>x;
b 0 && 0
c 15 || 0

4. Write three programs to count from 1 to 10 on the screen, using a different type of loop in each program. Don't use **goto**.

5. Write a program to input an integer value from the keyboard and print the message "Hello world" that many times. If a negative number is input, the program should display a suitable message and then end.

4

Introducing Arrays and Pointers

Like Basic, Pascal and other high level languages, C and C++ have a mechanism for handling **arrays** as well as simple variables. Where C and C++ differ from most other high level languages is in the variety of techniques which they provide for array manipulation. In C and C++, array handling is generally done by means of pointers, rather than by direct reference to array elements. The advantages of this approach are that the resulting code is very fast and compact; the disadvantage is that beginners often find it confusing.

Unfortunately, this isn't one of those places where you can simply forget about the difficulties; if you are going to become even a moderately proficient C++ programmer, then you will absolutely have to become familiar with pointers sooner or later. But be assured that the introduction to pointers in the second half of this chapter has been written with the complete beginner in mind.

About arrays

Ordinary variables can contain only a single value at any given time. Although this is perfectly adequate for many situations, there are occasions when it would be very useful to be able to allow a variable to contain a whole range of different values; this is particularly likely to be the case when a set of closely related variables needs to be input or output or manipulated in some other way.

Program 3.5, which we met in the previous chapter and which is printed again here as Program 4.1, does a perfectly good job of inputting a temperature for every day and adding each number to a variable called **running_total**. When the rogue value zero is input, the value of **running_total** is divided by the number of values which have been input, and the mean temperature thus calculated is output.

Program 4.1

```
#include <stream.hpp>
main()
{
   float running_total=0;
   float mean_temperature;
   float daily_temperature;
   int counter=0;
   do {
      cout << "Type in a temperature, or zero to quit\n";
      cin >> daily_temperature;
      if (!daily_temperature) continue;
      running_total+=daily_temperature;
      ++counter;
   } while (daily_temperature)
      mean_temperature=running_total/counter;
   cout << "The average temperature was "
      << mean_temperature << "\n";
}
```

Although this program works perfectly well, it seems a shame that the value of the variable **daily_temperature** is lost every time that a new value is input. This could be avoided if we could somehow allow **daily_temperature** to contain more than one value. If, for instance, **daily_temperature** could hold up to 31 different values, then it could contain the temperature readings for a complete month. This can in fact be done by declaring it to be an array variable; this will allow it to hold a number of different values simultaneously.

Declaring array variables

To declare an array variable, use the following format:

```
float daily_temperature[31];
```

The notation **[31]** after the variable name shows that **daily_variable** is an array variable which can hold up to 31 different values; that is, its **size** is 31. These values can be referred to as **daily_variable[0]**, **daily_variable[1]** and so on, up to **daily_variable[30]**.

Arrays start from 0, not 1: Note that although the array can hold 31 different values

– or, put another way, it has 31 **slots** – the highest-numbered slot is 30 and not 31 as you might have expected. This is because in C and C++ the total number of slots is calculated from 0, and not from 1 as seems more natural to non-programmers; the lowest-numbered slot in any array is thus [0] and not [1], and the subscript of the highest-numbered slot is always one less than the declared size of the array.

This is an important difference between the way in which C++ works and the usual operation of Basic. As a matter of fact, if you use the Basic statement DIM FRED(20) you are actually creating an array with a size of 21, because slot zero is in fact available, but most Basic programmers either do not know this or choose to ignore it.

Pascal allows you to specify the index of the lowest slot of an array using the form FRED[1..20] if the lowest slot is to be number 1 and the form FRED[0..20] if the lowest slot is to be number zero. C and C++ do not give you this choice.

A one-dimensional array – that is, an array with a single index enclosed – can be represented in tabular form like this:

```
slot[0]    slot[1]    slot[2]    slot[3]    slot[4]    ...
12         14         13         12         16
```

The value 12 is stored in slot[0], 14 in slot[1] and so on.

Some useful terms:

Note that arrays are **homogenous**; that is, all the items that they contain are of the same type; it isn't possible to create an array which holds a mixture of values of different types.

Arrays are also **aggregative** variables; that is, they consist of several different values all of which are identified by a single variable name.

A simple example: Program 4.2 shows one use for a simple array; the program reads in a series of five numbers, stores them in the array **set** and then outputs them in reverse order.

Program 4.2

```
#include <stream.hpp>
main()
{
    int set[5]; // declare an array variable
    cout << "Type in five numbers\n"; // and prompt for 5 values
    // move up the array inputting values
    for (int count=0;count<=4;++counter) cin >> set[count];
    // and then move down outputting them in reverse order
    for (count=4;count>=0;--count) cout << set[count];
}
```

The mechanism for reading in the various values and storing them in the different slots of the array variable **set** is quite straightforward: on the first pass through the first **for** loop, the loop variable **count** is equal to zero, and so **set[count]** refers to slot 0 of the array, and the first value input is stored in that slot. The next time through the loop, **count** has been incremented and now equals 1, so the second number input is stored in **set[1]**. This procedure continues until five values have been input.

The second loop outputs the numbers in the reverse order by simply starting at the highest-numbered slot (**set[4]**) and working down to **set[0]**.

Checking array bounds

In Program 4.2, the array **set** had five slots, numbered 0 to 4, and these were accessed by two **for** loops, one counting up and one counting down. Nowhere in the program was any attempt made to access any slot outside the **bounds** of the array – that is, an array slot greater than the declared dimension of the array, such as **set[25]** for instance.

If you are used to Basic or Pascal, or indeed to virtually any other high-level language, this probably won't surprise you very much, since all of these languages have inbuilt safeguards to prevent you from even trying to access an out-of-bounds array slot.

C and C++ are different. In the interests of speed, no bounds checking is carried out; consequently in Program 4.1 you could if you wished attempt to access **set[5]**, or even **set[200]**, without the compiler objecting.

The consequences of attempting to access out-of-bounds array slots depend on whether you are reading or writing to that location. If you try to read and display the value of a non-existent slot, your program at least won't crash, but the answer will be meaningless because the area of RAM which you've read will contain either a different variable, or part of your program code, or possibly even a portion of the operating system.

On the other hand, the consequences of trying to assign a value to a non-existent slot are quite likely to be fatal to your program, since you may overwrite a part of the program code or the operating system.

All sorts of intermittent and hard-to-find bugs can be caused by failing to check the bounds of array-handling operations. The moral is simple: always double-check that you aren't trying to access an array slot that doesn't really exist.

Initialising and assigning values to arrays

Values can be assigned to arrays by listing the values inside braces, separated by commas. For instance, the line

```
int set[3] = {1,2,3};
```

will insert the number 1 in slot 0, 2 in slot 1, and 3 in slot 2 of the array **set**.

If the braces do not contain sufficient values to initialise the complete array, then values will be assigned to individual slots starting at the beginning of the array; when the available values are exhausted, the remaining slots will be initialised to zero.

Arrays of unspecified size: When an array is declared and initialised at the same time, it's perfectly proper to leave out the reference to the size of the array between the [ ] operator-pair. For instance, the following is perfectly correct:

```
int set[] = {1,2,3};
```

It has the effect of assigning the number 1 to slot 0, 2 to slot 1, and 3 to slot 2 of the array **set**, which has the size 3.

String arrays

We have seen how Program 4.2 could input a set of five numbers and then output them in reverse order. Our next program will do the same thing with alphanumeric characters instead of numbers.

In C and C++, an array of characters which is terminated by a **null** is known as a **string**. In C++, and in most (though not quite all) implementations of C, the null is Ascii character 0, usually represented as **\0**. Generally speaking, you won't need to concern yourself about ensuring that the null is present at the end of the string as both **cin** and the C function **gets()** automatically add the null to the end of a string which has been input at the keyboard.

Because C++ and C strings are terminated by a null, they can be of any length, and the length of a string can change during the execution of a program.

Program 4.3 shows how Program 4.2 might look if changed to manipulate a character string rather than a set of integers.

Program 4.3

```
#include <stream.hpp>
main()
{
   char string[6];
   int count;
   cout << "Type in five characters and [RETURN]\n";
   cin >> string;
   for (count=4;counter>=0;--count) cout << string[count];
}
```

The first thing to notice about this version of the program is that although like the earlier version it expects five characters to be input, the array **string** has six slots instead of five, and these are numbered from 0 – 5.

The reason for this is that the array needs an additional slot to contain the final null which is added when it is input. *All string arrays must be one slot longer than their apparent maximum size* to allow room for the final null value.

Second, a string array can be input 'in one go' rather than by using a **for** loop; the line **cin >> string;** will assign the five characters typed in to slots 0 – 4 of the array **string** and then automatically add the null in the next slot.

A string can also be output directly; thus the line **cout << string;** would display the five characters which comprise **string** in the order in which they were input.

Initialising string arrays: String arrays can be initialised very simply, like this:

```
char string[6]="Hello";
```

This declares and initialises an array **string** of size 6.

It's also possible to assign values directly to individual slots of string arrays as we did earlier with numeric arrays. To store the individual characters which comprise the string **Hello** in the array **string**, you would use the following code:

```
string[0]='H';string[1]='e';string[2]='l';
string[3]='l';string[4]='o';string[5]='\0';
```

Note that the individual characters are enclosed in single quotation marks and that in this case the final null \0 has to be explicitly included.

String arrays of unspecified length: String arrays, like their numeric equivalents, can be declared and initialised without specifying their size. The following, for instance, is perfectly valid:

```
char string[]="Hello";
```

Like the previous version of the declaration, this creates an array of size 6, initialised to hold the word Hello and a final null.

Initialising arrays in other versions of C++: Although it is quite proper in Zortech C++ Version 2 to initialise arrays of any type as described above, this may not work with some other compilers. Some compilers will only allow global arrays (those declared outside any function including **main()**) to be initialised. Global variables are described in more detail in Chapters Five and Six.

Arrays of two dimensions

It's often necessary to construct arrays of more than one dimension. This is very easy to do in C++, though there are some important differences between the way in which C++ (and C) handle multi-dimensional arrays and the way in which they are used in other high-level languages.

You will remember that towards the beginning of this chapter we saw how to declare the one-dimensional array variable **daily_temperature** using the code **float daily_temperature[31]**.

An equivalent two-dimensional array would allow temperatures to be stored for every day of every month for several months. For instance, the following declaration will set up a two-dimensional array of 31 by 12 slots, covering all the months of the year:

```
float daily_temperature[31][12]
```

This construction is quite different from its Basic or Pascal equivalents, where the two dimensions are separated by a comma. Thus the Basic equivalent of the above line would be something like DIM DAILYTEMP(31,12).

Programmers who are used to the syntax of Basic or Pascal often fall into the trap of writing something like **float daily_temperature[31,12]** in C and C++. Unfortunately, this error will not be caught during compilation because it is in fact syntactically correct; it just doesn't mean what the programmer intends. It will in fact have the effect of creating a one-dimensional array **daily_temperature** of type float with a size of 12. (This is because of the way in which the comma operator , works in C and

C++; the expression to the left of the comma is first evaluated and then replaced by the value to the right of the comma.)

A small two-dimensional array can easily be represented in tabular form:

```
slot[0][0]    slot[0][1]    slot[0][2]    slot[0][3]
12             14            13             12

slot[1][0]    slot[1][1]    slot[1][2]    slot[1][3]
22             31            14            16

slot[2][0]    slot[2][1]    slot[2][2]    slot[2][3]
21             15            8             11

slot[3][0]    slot[3][1]    slot[3][2]    slot[3][3]
22             13            13             32
```

The first subscript of each slot refers to the row – row 0 is at the top, row 1 is below it, and so on. The second subscript refers to the column – the left-hand column is column 0, the second is column 1 and so on. Any value in the table can thus be uniquely identified by means of its column and row 'address', so that **slot[0][0]** contains the value 12 while **slot[3][2]** contains the value 13.

In reality, of course, a two-dimensional array is represented in the computer's memory in a linear form just like an array of only one dimension. **slot[0][0]** occupies the first location in memory set aside for the array, followed by **slot[0][1]**, **slot[0][2]** and **slot[0][3]**; this is followed by **slot[1][0]**, **slot[1][1]** and so on.

Because the subscript for the first dimension – the row – changes more slowly than the subscript for the second dimension – the column – C and C++ arrays are said to be **row-major** arrays.

Arrays of three or more dimensions

There is no need for arrays to be restricted to two dimensions. For instance, a four-dimensional array **large** of type float can be declared as follows:

```
float large[10][10][10][10];
```

For most practical purposes, you are unlikely to need to create arrays with more than two dimensions.

Should you ever need to create a large multidimensional array, you should bear in mind that it may require a very substantial amount of memory; for instance, since variables of type **float** each occupy four bytes, the array **large** declared above will require 40000 bytes. If you try to create such an array, you will be warned that you are declaring a *Very large automatic*.

Arrays with such a large number of dimensions not only consume large amounts of memory, but they are also very cumbersome to handle; moreover, if the individual slots of multidimensional arrays are to be accessed by means of subscripts as described above, this is substantially slower than accessing single-dimension arrays of the same total size.

Using sizeof(): To work out how many bytes of memory are required by an array, simply multiply the various dimensions together and then multiply the result by the number of bytes required by the data type of which the array consists.

You can find out how many bytes each data type requires by using the **sizeof()** operator; for instance, the following line will output **1**, which is the number of bytes occupied by a variable of type char:

```
cout << sizeof(char);
```

sizeof() can also be used to display the amount of space required for a complete array:

```
float large[10][10][10][10];
cout << sizeof(large);
```

will output **40000**.

Introducing pointers

Earlier in the chapter, we suggested that although there is nothing wrong in accessing array slots by means of their subscripts, as you would have to do in Basic, greater speed can almost always be obtained by the use of pointers. In the remainder of the chapter, we shall discover just what pointers are, and learn how to use them for work with ordinary variables and simple arrays.

Before we start looking at pointers in detail, a word of warning: pointers are not actually very difficult – although they frequently cause a lot of confusion to beginners – but if they are mishandled, they will sooner or later make your programs crash. This problem is exacerbated by the fact that absolutely no checks are carried out on pointer operations, any more than they are on array bounds, so that a misbehaving pointer can wreak all kinds of havoc.

What is a pointer?

First and foremost, a pointer is a kind of variable. Like all other types of variable, a pointer contains a value which may change during the execution of a program; however, the value which a pointer holds is the address – the location in the computer's memory – of some completely different variable; specifically, this is the address of the variable to which it 'points'.

A brief example will make this concept easier to understand. Look at the following fragment of code; the lines have been numbered to simplify the explanation which follows:

```
int number=55;                              // line 1
int *p1;                                    // line 2
p1=&number;                                 // line 3
cout << "p1 is pointing to the value " << *p1 << "\n"; // line 4
cout << form("p1 is pointing to address %x ", int(p1)); // line 5
```

In Line 1, an ordinary integer variable **number** has been declared, and has been initialised to 55.

In Line 2, a pointer variable **p1** has been declared. The type declaration **int** states that **p1** is a pointer to an integer variable; the asterisk * which prefixes the variable name specifies that this is a pointer variable.

In Line 3, variable **p1** is given the value **&number**. The & operator means *The address of*, and so the line can be read as "Assign to integer pointer variable **p1** the address of integer variable **number**". Until this assignment statement is reached, the pointer variable **p1** won't contain any meaningful value.

In Line 4 we output the contents of the variable which is pointed at by pointer **p1**. The meaning of the operator * is *The contents of a location*, and so the whole line can be read as "Output the contents of the variable held at the location to which **p1** is pointing". The variable concerned is **number**, and this contains the value 55, and so the output will be **55**.

Finally, Line 5 prints the hexadecimal equivalent of the value stored in pointer variable **p1**; this is, of course, the address in RAM at which the variable **number** is stored.

For most purposes, the address which a variable occupies is of no interest at all; indeed, there are no guarantees that a given variable will be stored in the same location during successive runs of the same program. However, the inclusion of this line may help you to understand that what a pointer actually contains is an *address* which represents the location in memory occupied by the variable to which the pointer is pointing.

Remember that when the * operator is used in the declaration of a variable, it stipulates that that variable is a pointer variable; when the * operator is used elsewhere, such as in an assignment statement, it means the contents of the memory location which is being pointed at by a previously declared pointer variable.

The & operator is often referred to as the **address operator**, and the * operator is called the **dereferencing operator**. When a pointer makes it possible to access the contents of a particular variable, that variable is said to be dereferenced by the pointer.

Note, by the way, how we have used the function **form**(), introduced in Chapter Two, to print out the address in hexadecimal. You will see that the pointer **p1** has been cast to an integer before being output.

Why use pointers?

The example which we have given of pointer use is quite artificial, and intended only as a demonstration. No programmer would ever in real life use a pointer as we have done, since the resulting code is no easier to debug or write than it would be to use the variable name in the ordinary way, and it's no faster either.

Although some situations do exist when it is helpful to be able to use pointers to ordinary variables, pointers are most often used in conjunction with arrays. Indeed, in C and C++ the connection between arrays and pointers is of crucial importance. Before looking at specific instances of array pointers, we'll first introduce some important points which you need to understand.

The pointer operators

The two pointer operators which we have just met – * and & – sometimes cause problems for newcomers because they have the same form as two completely different operators: * is also used to mean **multiply** and & is used to mean **bitwise AND**.

The way to tell the two different uses of these operators apart is this: if they are used as binary operators – with operands on both sides of them, as in **a*b** or **a&b** – then they mean **multiply** and **bitwise AND** respectively; if they are used as unary operators – preceding a variable but not appearing between two variables – then they are functioning as pointer operators.

Declaring pointers

Because pointers are variables, they must be declared just like other variables. The declaration must indicate the type of data to which the pointer will point, and the name of the pointer must be preceded by an asterisk. Thus if variable **p1** is a pointer to an integer, it must be declared by the line

```
int *p1;
```

Similarly if variable **fpoint** is a pointer to a floating point number, it must be declared by the line

```
float *fpoint;
```

As you can see, the convention is to leave no space between the * operator and the name of the variable to which it refers.

A pointer can be declared in the same line as ordinary (non-pointer) variables of the type to which it points. For instance, the line

```
int *p1, number1, number2, *p2;
```

will declare two integer variables **number1** and **number2** and two pointers to integers **p1** and **p2**.

This doesn't mean than a pointer to an int is itself of type int, any more than a pointer to a float is of type float or a pointer to a char is of type char. A pointer is simply a pointer, regardless of the type of variable to which it points.

Initialising pointers

Once a pointer has been declared, it must be given an initial value before it can be used. Global and static pointers (described below) are automatically initialised to zero, but will have to be reinitialised before they can be meaningfully used; automatic pointers – those declared inside any function including **main()** – are not initialised to any particular address.

It is vital that all pointers must be properly initialised before you try to use them; the consequence of using an pointer which has not been initialised will probably be that the computer will lock up and have to be reset.

How to initialise a pointer: Pointers can be initialised in any of three ways.

First, they can be pointed to the memory address of a variable of the appropriate type, like this:

```
int number=55;
int *p1;
p1=&number;
```

p1 has now been initialised so that it points to the address of **number**.

Second, a pointer can be given the value of another pointer of the same type, like this:

```
int number,*p1,*p2;
p1=&number;
p2=p1;
```

p2 has now been initialised to the value contained in **p1**, which is the address of variable **number**.

If you try to make a pointer to a variable of one type equal to a pointer to a variable of a different type, you will encounter problems of the sort described in the section on mismatched pointers below.

Finally, you can initialise a pointer by means of the reserved word **new**. This is described in Chapter Seven.

Mismatched pointers: The following fragment illustrates the sort of mistake which you should avoid:

```
float number=55.678;      // a number of type float
int *p1;                  // and a pointer to type int
p1=&number;               // don't go together
cout << *p1;              // and so produce garbage
```

Here **number** is of type float, while **p1** is a pointer to an integer.

Zortech C++ Version 2 will report a syntax error if you try to compile this; Version 1 would display an error message but would still compile.

Void pointers

C++ also has a **void** pointer type which can be used to point to variables of any type. A void pointer is declared like this:

```
void *vp1;
```

The only way in which a void pointer can be initialised is by pointing it at another pointer (of any type); it can only be dereferenced by using a cast or, more commonly, by assigning its value to a conventional pointer and then dereferencing that.

For instance, the following code fragment shows how a void pointer **vp1** is first pointed at the integer pointer **p1**; then the value at which it points is retrieved and displayed by pointing another integer pointer, **p2**, at it and dereferencing that:

```
int num1=25,*p1,*p2;
// declare an integer and two int pointers
void *vp1; // declare a void pointer vp1
p1=&num1; // point p1 at the address of num1;
vp1=p1; // point the void pointer at p1
p2=vp1; // point p2 at vp1
cout << *p2; // and dereference p2
```

Void pointers enable you to write more generalised code. We shall look at this in more detail in Chapter Six when we consider the implementation of the library function **quicksort()**.

Pointers and arrays

We have already suggested that C++ pointers are mostly used for handling arrays rather than simple variables. In the next section we shall see some simple examples of this use.

First of all, consider Program 4.4.

Program 4.4

```
#include <stream.hpp>
main()
{
   // version of the program using array subscripts
   char string[]="Hello there"; // declare and initialise
   int counter=0;
   while (string[counter]) {
      cout << string[counter];
      ++counter;
   }
}
```

This program begins by initialising the character array **string** so that it holds the value **Hello there**; remember that it isn't necessary to specify the size of an array which is simultaneously declared and initialised.

The integer variable **counter** is set to zero and then the individual characters which make up **string** are output one at a time in the **while** loop, using conventional loop indexing of the sort you may be familiar with in other high-level languages. The loop continues until **string[counter]** is false – that is, until it contains the null value marking the end of the string. Compare this program with Program 4.5, which uses a pointer to achieve exactly the same result.

Program 4.5

```
#include <stream.hpp>
main()
{
   // version of the program using pointers
   char string[]="Hello there";
   char *p1; // declare a pointer to char
   p1=string; // and initialise it to the start of string
   while (*p1) cout << *p1++;
}
```

The pointer **p1** is declared to be a pointer to a variable of type char, and is then pointed at the first location in the array **string**. **p1** is then dereferenced, and the value at which it points is displayed; then it is incremented to point at the next location, which contains the next character in **string**. This process continues until **p1** points at the null marking the end of the string, at which point the loop ends.

Remember that it isn't wrong to use subscripts as shown in Program 4.4; however, pointers are almost always faster than subscripts, and in many programming situations, speed is an important consideration. There are in any case other problems which can't be solved without the use of pointers, so you should become familiar with their use as soon as possible.

Initialising pointers to arrays

We've already stressed the importance of making sure that every pointer is initialised before it's used. If a pointer is pointing to a single item of data, the form **p1=&number** is used, where **p1** is a pointer and **number** is the variable to which **p1** is to point.

You might expect that when a pointer is initialised to point to the first slot in an array – which is slot zero, of course – the command would look something like this:

```
p1=&arrvar[0]
```

where **arrvar** is an array variable and **p1** is a pointer to it. In fact such a declaration is perfectly legal, but you will rarely if ever see it used outside a book on programming. Instead, you will find the form:

```
p1=arrvar
```

The reason for this is a rather subtle one; it is that in both C and C++, the name of an array variable on its own – that is, without the [ ] operators – is actually a pointer to the beginning of the array. If you want for any reason to find out just where an array **arrvar** resides in memory, you can actually do so with the command

```
printf("%x",int(arrvar))
```

This line will output the address in hexadecimal, though in practical terms this is not likely to be of much value.

You will remember that one of the ways in which a pointer can be properly initialised is by giving it the value of another pointer. That is exactly what is being done in the command **p1=arrvar**.

Incidentally, once your program has been compiled, **arrvar** will refer to a fixed location in memory. Consequently you can't change it by using an instruction like **arrvar++**.

Pointer arithmetic

In Program 4.5, the characters contained in the array **string** were output by initialising the pointer **p1** to the start of **string** and then outputting the character at which **p1** points. Then **p1** is incremented to point to the next character, and this too is duly output. The loop continues until the character pointed to is the null which marks the end of the string array.

Incrementing and decrementing pointers: We have seen in Program 4.5 that pointers can be incremented using the ++ operator, and they can of course also be decremented with the -- operator. When incremented, they point at the next slot in the array; when decremented, they point at the preceding slot.

As with all array work in C and C++, no bounds checking is carried out to ensure that you don't move your pointers outside the confines of the array. This is a frequent source of errors. Be very careful that your pointers aren't incremented or decremented to a position where they will point to something other than the array at which they ought to be pointing, or you will find that you are reading garbage.

Pointer addition and subtraction: As well as ++ and --, it is also possible to use the ordinary + and – operators with pointers. This often provides the most convenient way of accessing individual array slots without using subscripts.

For instance, if you want to output the fifth slot of array **arrvar**, you can either do so with subscripts, like this:

```
cout << arrvar[4]
```

or with a pointer **p1** (and assuming that the pointer is pointing to the beginning of the array to start with), in which case the code would look like this:

```
p1+=4;cout << *p1
```

The pointer has now been moved to a position four slots towards the end of the array; in the same way, the command **p1–=4** would move it four slots towards the beginning of the array.

Using pointers in for loops

We've already seen in Program 4.5 that the simplest way of using pointers to output a character string one letter at a time is by means of the **while** construction, like this:

```
while (*p1) cout << *p1++;
```

As long as the pointer **p1** is not pointing at a null, then the character at which it is pointing will be output and then the pointer will be incremented to point at the next address. Since every string by definition ends in a null, this provides a very convenient way of outputting a string one character at a time without knowing its length beforehand; similar techniques can be used for sending a string to a disc file or a printer.

We shall now see how pointers can be used to access the elements of an array whose length is already known, using a **for** loop. Both of the following fragments of code will produce the same output, but the first, which uses subscripts, will execute a little more slowly than the second, which uses pointers:

```
// Code using subscripts
int arrvar[]={1,2,3,4,5,6};
   // declare an array and output it one slot at a time
for (int counter=0;counter<6;counter++)
cout << arrvar[counter];

// Code using pointers
int arrvar[]={1,2,3,4,5,6},*p1;
   // declare an array and pointer
   //and output by incrementing the pointer
for (p1=arrvar;p1<&arrvar[6];p1++) cout << *p1;
```

The condition section of the **for** loop parameters reads **p1<&arrvar[6]**. This has the effect of causing the loop to be repeated until pointer **p1** is pointing at the address in which **arrvar[6]** is stored. You could also write this as **p1<arrvar+6**; the effect would be the same.

A curiosity: An important feature of C and C++ is that both languages provide the user with several different ways of achieving the same goal. You should understand that the effect of the following two expressions is identical in terms of the output they achieve:

```
cout << arrvar[counter];
cout << *(arrvar+counter);
```

Both of these expressions will output whatever value is stored in the slot of the array variable **arrvar** which is referenced by **counter**.

Surprisingly, the following expression has exactly the same effect:

```
cout << counter[arrvar];
```

However, this final idiom is unconventional, and we don't recommend that you make a habit of using it, though you can certainly try it out to prove to yourself that it works.

Arithmetic you can't do with pointers: Integer addition and subtraction are the only operations that may be performed on pointers; you can't add variables of type float to a pointer, for instance. Nor can you multiply or divide pointers or carry out any bitwise operations on them.

Two pointers of the same type can be compared to each other, but the result will only make sense if they are pointing at the same array. For instance, the following fragment is meaningless:

```
char array1,array2,*p1,*p2;
p1=arr1;p2=arr2;
if(p1<p2) ....
```

Since you have no idea where **array1** and **array2** will be stored in memory, or even if they will be stored in the same places in successive runs of the program, there will be no benefit in comparing pointers to them.

It is unsafe to assume that arrays or other items of data will be placed adjacent to each other in memory, and that you can therefore move a pointer 'off the end' of one item and into the next. The following code is based on just this mistaken assumption; there are two string arrays, **jack** and **jill**, and a pointer **p1** which starts off pointing to the beginning of **jack** and which is intended to be incremented until it has output the contents of both **jack** and **jill**.

```
char jack[10],jill[10],*p1;  // two arrays and a pointer
     // move the pointer through one
     // array and onto the next. This
     // won't work!
for (p1=jack;p1<&jill[10];p1++) cout << *p1;
```

The programmer has assumed that **jill** will be placed in memory immediately after **jack** and has attempted to move the pointer from one array to the next. This is almost guaranteed to fail, so don't try it.

In each of these cases, the warnings would not apply if you happened to know just where each variable was placed in RAM. However, unless your application is a very unusual one, this is unlikely to be the case.

Two pointers to a single array: Where two pointers are pointing at the same array, it's possible to make meaningful comparisons between them. Program 4.6 shows one situation in which this may be useful:

Program 4.6

```
#include <stream.hpp>
main()
{
   // declare a string and two char pointers
   char word[20],*p1,*p2;
   int length; // and an integer variable
   // prompt for a word
   cout << "Type in a word and press ENTER\n";
   cin >> word; // and input it
   p1=p2=word;
   // both pointers point to the start of the string
   // and p2 is incremented to the end of the string
   while (*p2) p2++;
   length=p2-p1;
   // the string length is calculated by comparing
   // the pointers, and then output
   cout << "\nthe length of the word is " << length << "\n";
}
```

This program prompts the user to input a word which is stored in the array **word**. Two pointers of type char, **p1** and **p2**, are pointed at the beginning of **word**.

The **while** loop has the effect of incrementing **p2** until it is pointing at a null value;

remember that false has the value zero, so when **p2** is pointing at a null value, the expression ***p2** evaluates as false and the while loop terminates.

Next, the length of the string is calculated by subtracting **p1** from **p2**; this is perfectly acceptable since both pointers are of the same type and are pointing at the same array. Finally, the length of the word (excluding the final null) is output.

A version of this program is supplied with your C++ compiler, as the standard function **strlen()**. We shall look at it in a little more detail in Chapter Six.

What pointer arithmetic means

When a pointer to an array is incremented, this means that it points to the next slot in the array. This remains true regardless of the number of bytes which each slot requires.

Most of our work in this chapter has involved arrays of type char. Since characters occupy a single byte, it follows that if a pointer which points at the first slot in the array is incremented so that it points to the second slot, the address which it contains will be that of the next byte.

If you are using arrays of other types, this will no longer be true. To see why, look at the following code, which outputs the address of the ten characters held in array **arrvar** and the characters themselves:

```
char arrvar[11],*p1; // declare an array and a pointer
p1=arrvar; // initialise the pointer to the array
   // and output the contents and address
   // of each element in turn
while (*p1) cout << *p1 << " address "
   << int (p1++) << "\n";
```

Assuming that **arrvar** contains the letters of the alphabet in order starting with **a** and continuing to **j**, typical output for this code might be as follows:

```
a 8178
b 8179
c 8180 ...
```

and so on. (Your own PC might store the variables in completely different addresses, of course) Each character occupies one byte, and so the full array of 11 characters occupies just 11 bytes.

If the code is adapted to handle variables of type int, and the array variables contain the numbers from 0 – 9 inclusive, the output might look like this:

```
0 8162
1 8164
2 8166 ...
```

and so on. The pointer variable **p1** now moves forward by two bytes instead of by one each time that it is incremented, because the compiler makes allowance for the fact that integers occupy two bytes as opposed to the single byte used by variables of type char.

Finally, if the code is changed yet again to handle an array of type float – and again assuming that the variables contain the numbers from 0 – 9 – the output might look like this:

```
0 8146
1 8150
2 8154 ...
```

and so on, because variables of type float require four bytes each.

Outputting values and incrementing pointers

It's very easy to become confused when using the ++ and -- operators in conjunction with pointers; when are you incrementing or decrementing the pointers, and when are you incrementing or decrementing the contents of the address to which they are pointing?

The following examples should help to clarify matters:

```
cout << ++*index;
```

This has the effect of incrementing what is stored at the location pointed to by the pointer variable **index** and then outputting it.

Compare this with the following:

```
cout << *++index;
```

This has the effect of incrementing the address to which **index** is pointing and then outputting the value contained in the address to which **index** is now pointing.

Finally, look at this:

```
cout << *index++;
```

This outputs the value contained at the address to which **index** is pointing and then increments the address.

Don't worry if you find this confusing at first. When you have gained some experience with pointers, you will find that the various expressions begin to come to you quite naturally; until then, just look them up when you need to.

Pointer arrays

Because many newcomers to C and C++ find the concept of pointers difficult to understand, they tend to lose sight of the important fact that pointers are just a special type of variable. In this section and the next we will underline this fact by mentioning two features of pointers which stress the fact that they are in many ways similar to other kinds of variable.

First, just as it is possible to have arrays of type int, float, char and so on, it is also possible to have arrays of pointers. One important use of them in C and C++ is to handle sets of character strings of different lengths.

Imagine that you are writing a program in the course of which any of a number of messages will need to be displayed on the screen. One way of doing this would be to create a two-dimensional array of characters, like this:

```
char messages[4][30]
```

You can then have up to 4 messages, each of which can be up to 29 characters long – remember that you must reserve one byte for the null \0 which ends each string. The array of messages could be initialised like this:

```
char messages[4][30]={"Insert a disc\n",
"The printer is busy\n",
"Processing - please wait\n", "Press any key\n"};
```

This is quite workable, but it suffers from two disadvantages. The first is that you have restricted yourself both as to the number of messages you can have and the amount of space that each one can occupy – you can't have any message longer than 29 characters plus the null. The second disadvantage is that some of your messages may be very much shorter than the 29 characters you have allocated, and this will result in a considerable waste of memory.

A more sophisticated approach is to use code like the following to initialise an array of pointers which point to strings which can be of varying lengths:

```
char *messages[] = {"Insert a disc\n",
"The printer is busy\n",
"Processing - please wait\n",
"Press any key\n"};
```

This creates an array of pointers – not an array of strings – with the first pointer pointing at "Insert a disc", the second at "The printer is busy", and so on. The actual array is only eight bytes long: each pointer occupies two bytes and there are four of them in the array. The character strings themselves are stored in the same area of memory as global variables.

Because it is not necessary to stipulate the number of elements in the array, there is no restriction on either the number of messages you can have or on the length of each one, and no memory space is wasted.

Program 4.7 will display all the messages one after the other:

Program 4.7

```
#include <stream.hpp>
main()
{
    char *messages[] = {"Insert a disc\n",
    "The printer is busy\n",
    "Processing - please wait\n",
    "Press any key\n"};
    for (int counter=0;counter<4;counter++)
    cout << *(messages+counter);
}
```

Pointers to pointers

In both C and C++ it is possible to have pointers which point not to the addresses at which data is stored, but rather to other pointers. In effect they function as pointers to pointers. This can be very confusing if you don't understand exactly what is going on, so look at this code very carefully:

```
int number,*p1,**p2;
number=42;
p1=&number;
p2=&p1;
cout << **p2;
```

In this fragment, **number** is a variable of type int; **p1** is a pointer to type int; and **p2** is a pointer to a pointer of type int. This technique is properly known as **multiple indirection**.

The third line of this fragment causes **p1** to contain the address of variable **number**.

The fourth line causes **p2** to contain the address of pointer variable **p1**.

Finally, the last line outputs the value pointed to by pointer **p1** which is itself pointed to by **p2**; in other words, it outputs the number **42**.

There's no need to stop here; you can go on to pointers to pointers to pointers if you wish. However, there is almost never a need to do this, and obviously such code is difficult to debug and maintain. The technique is mentioned here only in order to show the lengths to which it is possible to take the use of pointers in C and C++.

Postscript to Chapter Four

You should by now have a clear understanding of the basic operation of both arrays and pointers in C++. If anything is still confusing you, read back through the chapter, paying careful attention to all the examples, until you completely understand what is happening. It is particularly important that you should understand how simple pointers work, because nearly everything else in C and C++ depends on their use, and if you are unable to handle them confidently, you will find that your programming range is severely restricted.

Arrays must be declared using the form **int arrvar[100]**, which declares an array **arrvar** of type int; storage is set aside for 100 slots, which will be numbered 0 – 99.

Arrays can be of more than one dimension; two dimensional arrays are stored as arrays of one dimension. The first subscript refers to the 'row' and the second to the 'column', and the rows are in effect stored sequentially.

The fastest way to access array slots is by means of pointers. All pointers must be declared using the * operator, and they should only be used to point at variables of the type for which they are declared. Thus the declaration **char *p1** states that **p1** is a pointer variable which can only be used to point at variables of type char.

Pointers must be initialised; if a pointer is to be initialised to point to an ordinary variable, the idiom **p1=&variable** should be used. If a pointer is to be initialised to point to the first slot in an array, use the form **p1=arrvar**.

To access, or dereference, the contents of the address to which a pointer refers, use the form ***pointer**.

Exercises to Chapter Four

1. If you haven't yet entered and run the programs in Chapter Four, do so now.

2. Write a **Marks** program to input twenty integers representing examination marks and then output the average mark, the lowest mark, and the highest mark. Use array indexes.

3. Rewrite the **Marks** program using pointers instead of indexes.

4. Write a program that uses pointers to detect whether or not a word is a palindrome.

5

Introducing C++ Functions

This chapter describes the construction and use of simple functions in C++. The way in which C++ uses functions differs in subtle but important ways from the way in which they are used in the original C language, and also from the way in which they are used in Pascal.

About Functions

First of all, a little theory! Like Pascal and Algol (but unlike most versions of Basic), C and C++ are **block structured** languages; that is, they enable the programmer to build up complete applications from a set of self-contained 'building blocks'.

It is good programming practice to make these blocks as generalised and reusable as possible. In the programs we have constructed so far we have used only one of these blocks – the one called **main()**, which every program must include – but most C++ programs contain many more.

The great advantage of using functions is that once they have been devised and tested, they can then be used in a variety of different situations without the programmer having to worry about the fine details of how they work. This is commonly called the **black box** approach to programming; it allows you to save a great deal of time when creating programs by simply 'plugging in' functions which you or other people have created, and so avoid the need to 'reinvent the wheel'.

If you are used to Pascal, you will already be familiar with this approach. However, there are important differences in the way in which the building block approach is implemented in Pascal and its use in C++.

One of these is that in Pascal, the basic block of code is the procedure; in C++ it is the function. The code which belongs to a C++ function is enclosed between a pair of braces, { and }; these have the same purpose as the keywords BEGIN and END in Pascal.

All functions are named, and each name is followed by a pair of parentheses (). You will remember that these parentheses also occur in the definition **main()**. In the case of most functions, these brackets enclose the **argument list**, which details the values which may be passed to the function. The arguments are the **formal parameters** to the function, and inside the function they behave like variables. The parentheses after **main()** have been left empty because so far we have been passing no values to that function. It is in fact possible to pass values to **main()**, and we shall see how this can be done later in this chapter.

Incidentally, it is quite common in Pascal to create procedures inside other procedures. It is not possible in C and C++ to create functions inside other functions.

A simple example

The following program consists of two short functions. One of them is the compulsory **main()**; the other, which contains only one assignment statement, is **divide()**.

As its name implies, the purpose of the function **divide()** is to receive two floating point values from **main()**; to divide the first number by the second; and then to return the resulting floating point value to **main()**, which displays it.

Program 5.1

```
#include <stream.hpp>
float divide(float x, float y) // Declaring the function
{                              // Function opening brace
   return x/y;                 // This returns the result
                              // of the division
}                              // Function closing brace
main()
{
   float first_no, second_no, answer;
   cout << "Type in two floating point numbers\n";
   cin >> first_no >> second_no;
   // Next line calls function and receives returned value
   answer=divide(first_no, second_no);
   cout << "The result of the division is "
      << answer << "\n";
}
```

There are several features about this program which deserve some attention.

Locating functions

C++ functions can be placed anywhere in the source code, or even in a completely different file. In this book **main()** will almost always be placed after every other function, and you will find that most other books follow the same convention, but there is nothing to stop you from putting **main()** first and following it with other functions. However, before you do so, you should read the detailed section on function placement later in this chapter.

Declaring the function

Every function must be **declared** before it can be used: that is, the compiler must know its name, what type of value (if any) it returns to **main()** (assuming that it was invoked from **main()**), and how many values, and of what type, are to be passed to the function.

In Program 5.1, the function **divide()** is declared like this:

```
float divide(float x, float y)
```

This shows that the function **divide()** expects two values of type float to be passed to it, and that the value which the function will return will also be of type float.

Functions without argument: It's perfectly possible to write functions to which no arguments at all are passed, and which will themselves return no values. For example, consider the following short function **bell()**, which will sound the computer's 'bell' or loudspeaker:

```
void bell()
{
   printf("\a");
}
```

The reserved word **void** placed before the name of the function shows that the function returns no value; the empty parentheses after the name of the function signify that it expects no values to be passed to it.

To sound a tone from the speaker, simply include the function printed above in your programs and then include the function-call **bell()** at those places in your code where you want the speaker to sound.

In C, the use of empty parentheses after the name of a function can be understood to mean that an unspecified number of values will be passed to the function; if no values are to be passed, then **void** is placed in the parentheses like this:

```
void bell(void)
```

This is also acceptable in C++, but it is not the recommended usage.

Automatic variables in functions

When the function **divide()** is invoked – that is, when the statement in **main()** reading

```
answer = divide(first_no, second_no);
```

is executed – the value which is contained in the variable **first_no** is copied into the function's variable **x**, and the value contained in **second_no** is copied into the function's variable **y**.

About the scope of variables: Except for the fact that values are copied from **first_no** into **x** and from **second_no** into **y**, no other connection exists between the variables **x** and **y** in the function **divide()** and the variables **first_no** and **second_no** in **main()**. They occupy different locations in the computer's memory, and any changes which you make to the values stored in **x** and **y** in **divide()** will have no effect at all on the contents of the variables **first_no** and **second_no** in **main()**. This would remain true even if the variables in the function **divide()** happened to have the same names as the corresponding variables in **main()**.

In C++, variables which are created in functions are known by many different names; the terms **local** and **automatic** variables are the most common. In this book we shall generally use the term **automatic variables** to describe variables which are created within functions.

Automatic variables are created on the computer's stack; they are pushed onto the stack at the moment of their creation and they remain there until the closing brace of the function in which they exist is reached; the stack pointer is then moved up and the variables declared in that function are said to 'go out of scope' and become inaccessible.

Two things follow from this. The first is that it is impossible to access an automatic variable outside the function in which it has been declared, or even inside the same function until it has been declared.

The second point, which is a little more subtle, is that if a function is called several times in the course of a program, then any variables which are local to that function will be recreated – and then destroyed – each time that the function is entered and subsequently left. An automatic variable cannot therefore directly refer to any previous value that it might have had in an earlier incarnation.

Under certain circumstances this may cause programming difficulties; we shall see how to avoid them later.

Dynamic variables: It is also possible in C++ to create **dynamic variables** on the 'heap' of free memory rather than on the stack. Creation and destruction of these variables is entirely in the hands of the programmer, and the normal scoping rules do not apply. Dynamic variables are introduced in Chapter Six.

Register variables: It is legal to declare integer-type variables (those of type int, char or long) as **register variables**. These are variables which reside in a CPU register. The reason for using them is that they allow certain types of code to run more quickly than ordinary variables; for this reason register variables are often used in the original C language as loop counters and the like.

The code to declare a register variable **reg_1** would look like this:

```
register int reg_1;
```

In C++ Version 2, the declaration that a variable is a register variable will be taken only as a recommendation to the compiler, and there are few if any advantages to be gained from such a declaration.

Global variables: C and C++ allow you to create **global** variables which will remain in scope during an entire program. Global variables are created by declaring them outside any function, including **main()**. In theory they can be declared at any time; however, it is customary to declare them at the very beginning of a program.

For instance, to declare a global integer variable called **counter**, you would include the following line at the very beginning of your program, and before the opening brace of either **main()** or any function:

```
int counter;
```

Don't forget the semi-colon at the end of the statement.

Global variables are automatically initialised to zero when they are created.

We mentioned in Chapter Four that some versions of C++ do not allow arrays to be initialised unless they are global arrays. In Zortech C++ Version 2, both global and automatic arrays can be initialised.

Scope resolution: If a function declares an automatic variable which happens to have the same name as a global variable, then within that function it is the automatic local variable which will be referenced and not the global one. This is an important point, and if you forget it, you will find that your programs may suffer from mysterious bugs.

If you want to reference a global variable when the program would otherwise reference an automatic variable, you can do this in C++ (though not in C) by using the **scope resolution operator** which is ::.

Imagine, for instance, that you have a global variable called **first_value** and an automatic variable, declared inside a function, with the same name. Normally within that function the statement

```
old_value = first_value*2;
```

would reference the automatic variable called **first_value** – the one which is local to the function – and not the global one. However, the statement

```
old_value = ::first_value*2;
```

using the scope resolution operator will reference the global variable rather than the automatic one.

More about function declarations

If you have some experience of programming in the original C language, the form of the function declaration in Program 5.1 may look rather strange to you. However, if you are used to programming in Pascal, it may not seem so unusual!

You will remember that the C++ form of the function declaration looked like this:

```
float divide(float x, float y)
{... // and so on
```

The common form of an equivalent function declaration in most versions of C would be like this:

```
float divide(x,y)
float x,y; // the parameter types are declared here
{... // after the opening brace the function is the same
```

You can see that the type of the formal parameters has not been declared inside the parentheses of the declaration statement, but on the next line (though still before the function's opening brace).

This style is also permitted in C++ Version 2 to allow compatibility with old code, but you are strongly advised not to use it in new programs as it may not be supported in future versions.

Void functions

We mentioned earlier that if a function does not return any value at all – like **bell()** – it should be prefixed with the reserved word **void** to declare the fact.

It would be possible to rewrite Program 5.1 so that instead of returning the result of the division to **main()** to be displayed, it is actually displayed inside **divide()**. The program would then look like this:

```
#include <stream.hpp>
void divide(float x, float y) // No value returned
{ // Function opening brace
   cout << "The result of the division is "
      << x/y << "\n";
} // End of the function
main()
{
   float first_no, second_no;
   cout << "Type in two floating point numbers\n";
   cin >> first_no >> second_no;
   divide(first_no, second_no); // Nothing to return
}
```

Because the function **divide()** returns no value, it isn't necessary to put a **return** statement before the closing brace. The program simply 'falls off the end' of the function when it reaches the final brace, and control is returned to the calling program.

Where a value has to be returned from a function, it is perfectly proper to provide several different **return** statements, choosing the appropriate one by means of if statements. There is thus no need for a **return** statement to be the last statement in a function.

Where a function does not return a value, many programmers feel that it is better practice to place a **void return** before the closing brace. The function **divide()** would then look like this:

```
void divide(float x, float y)
{
   cout << "The result of the division is "
      << x/y << "\n";
   return; // no value is returned
}
```

This convention has not been used in this book.

Using static variables

The fact that an automatic variable ceases to exist when it goes out of scope is generally very useful; it means, for example, that different functions, written perhaps by different programmers, can use the same (automatic) variable names without worrying about possible interference between them.

However, there can be occasions when it would be useful to preserve the value of a variable between successive calls to the same function.

For instance, you may be writing a program which contains a function to create and return numbers in the Fibonacci sequence 1, 1, 2, 3, 5, 8 ... where each number is calculated by adding together the two previous numbers in the series. Each call to the function should return the next number in the sequence.

Although techniques exist to establish the value of any number in the series without reference to the two previous numbers, in the discussion that follows we will assume that you have decided not to use one of these methods. Consequently, each call to the function, which we will call **fibon()**, will require the new value to be calculated by reference to the two previous values.

Obviously this can't be done using ordinary automatic variables, as they provide no mechanism by which the previous values can be retained from one function call to the next.

One way around the problem would be to declare the appropriate variables to be global, enabling them to retain their value between successive calls to **fibon()**. Attractive though this appears, it is not an ideal solution because it denies you the security from external interference that automatic variables give.

A more sensible alternative is to use **static variables**. This is done by placing the keyword **static** in front of the type declaration of the appropriate variables. The following fragment shows how this can be done:

```
float fibon()
{
   static int val1, val2, val3;
   val3=val2+val1;
   val1=val2;
   val2=val3;
   return val3;
}
```

Even after the function **fibon** has gone out of scope, the values in **val1**, **val2** and **val3** will be preserved because they have been declared to be static variables; however, because they are automatic variables within the function **fibon()**, they retain the advantage that they can't be accessed or changed by any other part of the program once **fibon()** has gone out of scope.

Incidentally, if you're tempted to try to build this function into a complete program of your own, you should know that it has a bug in it. Static variables, like global variables, are automatically initialised to zero. This is fine for **val1**, but **val2** needs to be set to 1, not 0.

There are several possible solutions to this; however, none of them is elegant. One solution would be to use a global variable **fibonflag** which is initialised to 0 at the beginning of the program. If **fibonflag** is equal to 0, then **val2** can be initialised to its starting value; once this is done, the value of **fibonflag** can be changed to ensure that **val2** isn't reinitialised next time that **fibon** is called. The complete code for this would look something like this:

Program 5.2

```
#include <stream.hpp>
int fibonflag;      // global variable
int fibon()         // beginning of function
{
   static int val1, val2, val3;// automatically
                    //initialised to 0
   if (fibonflag==0) val2=1;// initialise to 1 first
                    //time round
   val3=val1+val2;  // calculate values for
   val1=val2;       // the Fibonacci sequence
   val2=val3;
   fibonflag=1;     // set fibonflag
   return val3;
}                    // end of function
main()
{
   int answer;
   for (int counter=0;counter<10;++counter)
     cout << fibon() << "\n";
}
```

We recommend that you type this program in and try it out. Since **fibonflag** is a global variable, it can be accessed both inside the function **fibon()** and inside **main()**. You could even use this fact to reset the Fibonacci sequence to the beginning by putting the statement **fibonflag=0** somewhere in the body of your program.

All the same, no-one could pretend that using the global variable **fibonflag** is an elegant solution to the problem of setting **val2** to 1 the first time that the function **fibon()** is called.

Fortunately C++ does offer more elegant ways of handling problems of this sort. One is to use recursion.

Recursion

In Basic, the only way in which it is possible for a subroutine to be executed several times in succession is for it to be invoked repeatedly from either the main program or from a different subroutine. This is called **iteration**. C and C++ offer an additional way in which a function can be repeatedly executed by allowing a function to call itself; this is called **recursion**.

Many routines can be written either recursively or iteratively. For instance, Program 5.3 is an iterative version of our Fibonacci sequence program:

Program 5.3

```
#include <stream.hpp>
    // This is an iterative version of the program
void fibon()
{
   int val1, val2, val3;
   val1=0;
   val2=1;
   for (int counter=0;counter<10;++counter){
     val3=val1+val2;
     val1=val2;
     val2=val3;
     cout << val3 << "\n";
   }
}
main()
{
   fibon();
}
```

The only difference between this program and the one which we printed as Program 5.2 is that instead of **main()** using a **for** loop to invoke the function **fibon()** 10 times, generating a new number in the Fibonacci sequence each time the function is invoked, the function **fibon()** itself contains the **for** loop. **fibon()** is thus called only once.

Compare this program with Program 5.4, which generates exactly the same output by using recursive techniques:

Program 5.4

```
#include <stream.hpp>
    // This is a recursive version of the program
int counter; // counter is a global variable
void fibon(int val1,int val2)
{
  int val3;
  if (counter++==10) return;
  val3=val1+val2;
  cout << val3 << "\n";
  fibon(val2,val3); // The function calls itself
}
main()
{
  fibon(0,1); // The first call to the function
}
```


In this second version of the program, instead of a single call to the function **fibon()** from **main()**, there are several calls: the first is from **main()**, but instead of using a **for** loop within the function **fibon()** to generate a set of numbers in the sequence, the numbers are instead generated by letting the function make successive calls to itself. This program therefore uses a recursive function, whereas Program 5.3 uses a slightly different form of the function which works iteratively.

In Program 5.4, each call to the function **fibon()** generates a new set of automatic variables **val1**, **val2** and **val3**, none of which is the same as any of the similarly-named variables which were created the last time the function was called. Thus if the function **fibon()** is called 10 times, there will be 10 different sets of automatic variables bearing the names **val1**, **val2** and **val3**.

This fact means that we don't need to bother to include the following lines of code which were used in Programs 5.2 and 5.3:

```
val1=val2;
val2=val3;
```

Instead, we can get exactly the same effect more easily by passing the values stored in **val2** and **val3** into the new automatic variables **val1** and **val2** which are created when **fibon()** is called recursively. If you don't see how this works, 'walk through' the code manually, writing down the values of each variable as you go. Don't be surprised (or disheartened) if you find it tricky; some people seem to find recursive code very easy to understand, while others find it difficult at first.

Notice that in the recursive version of the program we have used the global variable **counter** in order to keep track of the number of times that the function **fibon()** has called itself.

Compared to iterative code, recursive code suffers from two disadvantages: first, it is often harder to understand; and second, the fact that new automatic variables are created every time a recursive call is made may result under certain circumstances in stack overflow problems. This won't arise with a short program like this, but it's as well to be aware that the problem can occur.

You may therefore wonder why anyone would bother to write recursive code. The reason is that there are certain problems which are relatively simple to solve recursively, but much more difficult to solve iteratively. One classic example of a recursive program is the Quicksort sorting technique. (Quicksort is described in more detail in Chapter Six.) Anyone who aspires to a high standard of programming should be able to write and understand recursive code.

Inline functions

Every call to a function slows down the execution of your program to some extent. The delay is generally very slight and can thus usually be ignored, but in certain time-sensitive applications, you may wish to avoid it altogether.

C++ allows a function to be compiled **inline**. This means that instead of the compiled code containing a single machine code version of the function which can then be invoked from different parts of the program, there will instead be a complete copy of the function code at every place from which that function can be invoked. Thus if an inline function is called from 10 locations, the compiled program will contain 10 copies of the code for that function.

It is possible to recommend to the compiler that a function should be compiled inline; the final decision will be made when the code is compiled. In general only very short functions will be compiled inline, as otherwise the price to be paid in the increased length of the compiled program will more that outweigh the benefits to be gained from increased speed. With very short functions, inline code may actually be shorter as well as faster.

The following fragment of code shows the use of the inline specifier for the **bell()**

function which we met earlier:

```
inline void bell() {printf("\a");}
```

Because this function is so short, everything has been placed in a single line of code. This isn't obligatory; we've done it here merely to show that it is possible.

Arguments to main()

We mentioned earlier that it is possible to pass values to **main()**. Since by definition no function can be called before **main()**, you may wonder where these values can come from; the answer is that they can be included as part of the command to run the compiled program; in other words, they form the DOS command tail.

You may recall that when running the Zortech ZED editor you can optionally specify the name of the file which you wish to edit, like this:

```
ZED PROGRAM.CPP
```

In this example, the command tail PROGRAM.CPP represents the name of the file which will be loaded as soon as ZED is ready.

The two main advantages of using the command tail to input information directly into **main()** are that it looks much more professional and – more important – that it simplifies the incorporation of programs into batch files. A typical use for command line arguments is to pass to your program the names of files with which it must work; several examples of this technique are included in Chapter Eleven.

The various elements in the command tail must be separated from each other by spaces, *and not by commas*; thus, for example, the command

```
MOVE PROG1 PROG2
```

has two arguments (PROG1 and PROG2), while the command

```
MOVE PROG1,PROG2
```

has only a single argument (PROG1,PROG2).

Look at the following simple program which shows how information contained in the command tail can be used inside a C++ program, shown on the next page.

Program 5.5

```
#include <stream.hpp>
#include <stdlib.h>
main(int argc, char *argv[])
{
   if (argc!=2){ // check for number of arguments,
              // exit if wrong
     cout << "Enter the day as the command tail!\n";
     exit(1);
   }
   cout << "Today is " << argv[1] << "\n";
}
```

Type in this program under a name like DAY.CPP and then compile it. When it has finished linking and ZED prompts for **Program parameters (or Esc):** type in the day of the week and press [RETURN], and the program will respond with the message **Today is Thursday** or whatever day you have typed in.

You can get the same effect from the DOS prompt by typing in

DAY THURSDAY

If you forget to type in the day of the week after the name of the program – or if you just press [RETURN] when asked for **Program parameters (or Esc):** – the program will terminate with the message **. Enter the day as the command tail!**

We will now analyse the program to see how the trick is done. The answer lies in the two special variables **argc** and **argv**, which must always be used exactly as you see them in the example.

argc must be declared as an integer. It contains the number of arguments found on the command line. The name of the program itself counts towards the total, so the value of **argc** will always be at least 1; if the command line consists of the name of the program plus one argument, as in our example, then **argc** will be equal to 2.

argv must be defined as a pointer to an array of strings; the empty brackets [] show that it is an array of unspecified length; we have already met this construction in Chapter Four. **argv[0]** then points to the name of the program; **argv[1]** points to the first element in the command tail; and so on.

The way in which pointers are used to pass arguments to functions is described in detail in Chapter Six; for the moment, you can use **argv** without knowing exactly how it works.

When you write a program which takes arguments from the command tail, it's always worth checking at the beginning of **main()** that the correct number of arguments have been entered. This explains the lines:

```
if (argc!=2){
    cout << "Enter the day as the command tail!\n";
    exit(1);
}
```

Note in passing how we have used the library function **exit()** to abort the program if the wrong number of arguments have been entered in the command line. This is why we had to include the line **#include <stdlib.h>** at the beginning of Program 5.5.

Using numbers in the command tail

The command tail almost always contains one or more strings – typically the names of files on which an operation is to be performed – but there may be occasions when you need to use numbers in the command tail. Since C++ regards the command line arguments as consisting of strings, we clearly need a way of turning them into numbers. This can easily be done with the standard library function **atoi()**. Its name, by way, stands for Ascii TO Integer.

Imagine, for example, that you wanted to adapt the Fibonacci sequence program printed as Program 5.2 so that instead of merely printing out the first 10 numbers in the Fibonacci sequence, it would print out however many numbers you wanted. One way of doing this would be to prompt with a question like *How many numbers do you want to see?* and then to call the function **fibon()** the appropriate number of times.

A more professional way of achieving the same result would allow you to type in the command **FIBONACCI 30**, for example, at the DOS prompt, assuming that you wanted to see the first 30 numbers of the sequence. The following version of the program (on the next page) will achieve just that:

Program 5.6

```
#include <stream.hpp>
#include <stdlib.h>
int fibonflag;
int fibon()          // the Fibonacci function
{
   static int val1, val2, val3;
   if (fibonflag==0){
     val1=0;
     val2=1;
   }
   val3=val1+val2;
   val1=val2;
   val2=val3;
   fibonflag=1;
   return val3;
}
main(int argc, char *argv[]) // one argument is required
{
   int answer;
   if(argc==1){
     cout << "Type in a number as a command-line tail\n";
     exit(1); // abort if argument not given
   }
   for (int counter=0;counter<atoi(argv[1]);++counter)
   cout << fibon() << "\n";
}
```

As in Program 5.5, if no command tail is present, the program aborts with a suitable message. In the **for** loop in the penultimate line of **main()**, the value of **counter** is checked to see if it is less than the integer value of the string **argv[1]**, which is the number typed in as the command tail.

Overloading functions

In C++ (though not in C) it is possible to **overload** functions; that is, more than one function within the same program can be given the same name, and the correct one will automatically be called during the running of the program.

You may be asking yourself why on earth anyone would wish to have several functions sharing the same name. The answer is that it can often help to make a program more readable by allowing you to give the same name to different functions which all have the same general effect, even though they may involve different data types or different numbers of arguments.

At the beginning of this chapter, Program 5.1 showed how a simple function might be used to calculate the result of a division between two numbers. In the same vein, Program 5.7 below includes two functions whose purpose is to add together either two or three numbers entered as a command tail, and then output the total of these numbers together with a suitable message.

Program 5.7

```
#include <stream.hpp>
#include <stdlib.h>
void add(int a, int b, int c) // First function add()
{
   cout << "Three values were input and totalled "
     << a+b+c;
}
void add(int a, int b) // Second function add()
{
   cout << "Two values were input and totalled " << a+b;
}
main(int argc, char *argv[])
{
   int a,b,c;
   a=atoi(argv[1]); // first value assigned to a
   b=atoi(argv[2]); // second value assigned to b
   if (argc==3) add(a,b); // Call 2nd function
   if (argc==4){ // if three values ...
     c=atoi(argv[3]); // third value assigned to c
     add(a,b,c); // and call 1st function
   }
} // finish
```

When the program is run, the number of arguments in the command tail is checked using **argc**. If the value of **argc** is 3, then two values were input and the first **add()** function is invoked; if the value of **argc** is 4, then three values were input, and so the second **add()** function is invoked.

Which of the two basically similar functions is actually used will depend on how many arguments are being passed to it: if only two arguments are passed, then the second function will be called, but if three arguments are passed, then the third function will be called. To show that this really does happen, a message identifying the function used will also be displayed.

Overloading is most often used in conjunction with special functions called **constructors** which we will meet in Chapter Seven.

The reserved word overload

Zortech C++ Version 1 required that when functions which were not member functions of a class or structure were overloaded, that the reserved word **overload** was placed at the beginning of each function declaration. Thus the first **add**() function in Program 5.7 would be declared like this:

```
overload void add(int a, int b, int c)
```

The use of **overload** is not required in Version 2, and it is recommended that it should not be used.

Finding the correct overloaded function: When functions are overloaded, the correct function to be invoked in any particular case is determined by checking the number and type of the arguments which are being passed to the function in any given function call. *The return value – if any – is not taken into account when the compiler selects the appropriate function.* All functions overloaded with the same name should therefore have the same return type, or should all return void.

Functions with default arguments

In the examples we have looked at so far, the number of arguments that are required by a function has been set in the function declaration; any attempt to call a function using fewer arguments than are called for in the declaration will result in the program failing to compile. (The only exception to this is in the case of overloaded functions, where different functions sharing the same name may require different numbers of arguments, as in the example in Program 5.6.)

In C++ (though not in C), it is possible to set up a function prototype in such a way that default values will be supplied if fewer than the correct number of arguments is supplied to a function.

Consider the following program, which is a new version of the recursive Fibonacci sequence Program 5.4, and which avoids all the problems which we encountered earlier:

Program 5.8

```
#include <stream.hpp>
void fibon(int val1,int val2,int counter=0)
// a default argument
{
   int val3;
   if (counter++==10) return; // quit when done
   val3=val1+val2;
   cout << val3 << "\n";
   // Recursive call passes three arguments
   fibon(val2,val3,counter);
}
main()
{
   fibon(0,1); // First call passes two arguments
}
```

Here, the function **fibon()** can be called with either two arguments or three. The third argument is **counter**; the effect of the assignment **int counter=0** in the function declaration is that if the third argument is missing when the function is called, then the value 0 will be assigned to that variable by default.

The effect of this is that we have eliminated any need to use **counter** as a global variable. Instead, it becomes an automatic variable within **fibon()**, taking the default value of zero when that function is called from **main()**, but overriding that default when the function is called recursively using three arguments, with **counter** as the last argument.

Ordering default arguments: The only point which you need to watch when using default arguments is that they must be placed after all the other arguments in the argument list.

Consider this function declaration:

```
void func(float a, int b=16, char letter = 'F')
```

The function **func()** can be invoked with either three arguments, two arguments, or only one argument; default values will be provided for **b** or **letter** if required, but no default value will be provided for **a**.

Functions with an unspecified number of arguments

C++ allows you to declare a function with arguments whose numbers and types are unknown at compilation time. This is done by using the special ellipsis operator **...** in the function declaration as follows:

```
void fcall(...)
```

This declares a function returning no value, taking an unspecified number of arguments of unspecified type.

If some but not all of the arguments are known, the known arguments must be listed first. For instance, if the argument list is known to contain an integer **a** and a floating point number **b**, it might look like this:

```
void fcall(int a, float b, ...)
```

The use of the comma to separate the list of known arguments from the ellipis operator **...** is not compulsory in Zortech C++ Version 2, but is strongly recommended.

In most cases where a function may expect to receive arguments of varying numbers or types, the situation is best met by function overloading as described above. However, this cannot deal with all circumstances, and so the following brief description of the use of functions with unspecified arguments may be helpful.

The stdarg.h library

Included with the compiler is the **stdarg.h** library which contains several functions and macros which are intended to be used in conjunction with functions taking unspecified arguments. Their use is best understood by means of the sample code in Program 5.9.

Program 5.9

```
#include <stream.hpp>
#include <stdarg.h>              // includes the necessary
                                 // functions & macros
int total(int no_in_list,...) // a function with
                                 //unspecified arguments
{
   int running_total=0;
   va_list v1;      // v1 is a variable of type va_list
```

```
    va_start(v1,no_in_list);// va_start() points v1 to
                            // first argument. Extract an
                            // argument and repeat, adding
                            // each value to running_total
    for(int counter=0;counter<no_in_list;counter++)
        running_total=running_total+va_arg(v1,int);
    va_end(v1); // close down the operation
    return running_total; // and send back the result
}
main()
{
    cout << "First with two arguments...\n";
    cout << total(2,1,2);
    cout << "\nThen with three arguments...\n";
    cout << total(3,1,2,3);
    cout << "\nThen with four arguments...\n";
    cout << total(4,1,2,3,4) << "\n";
}
```

As you can see, **total()** has been declared as a function which can take a variable number of arguments. The first argument is obligatory; this is an integer, and it is used to inform **total()** of the number of additional arguments which will be passed to it.

The automatic variable **running_total** is then declared and initialised to zero. This will be used to calculate the cumulative total of all the values passed as additional arguments to **total()**.

Next the variable **v1** is declared to be of the special type **va_list**; this type is defined as a macro in the stdarg.h library. Variable **v1** will then be passed to the library functions **va_start()** and **va_end()**.

The function **va_start()** is then called with the arguments **v1** and **no_in_list**; this initialises **v1** to point at the beginning of the list.

The **for** loop then uses the function **va_arg()** to extract one argument from the list at a time, and adds its value to the variable **running_total**. This continues until all the arguments have been extracted.

The function **va_end()** then closes the operation, and the value stored in **running_total** is duly returned to **main()** and displayed.

Don't worry if you find this hard going. The occasions on which you will need to use a function which takes a variable number of arguments will be very few and far between. Remember too that the technique of using functions which take unspecified arguments is inherently risky because it is not possible to carry out any checks on the types of the arguments being passed. For this reason, other techniques should be used wherever possible.

Locating functions

So far, all our examples have placed **main**() at the end of the program; the functions which it calls have preceded it. It is quite possible, however, to call a function before the function code has been supplied.

If you do this, you must provide a **prototype** – sometimes called a **header** – before the function is invoked. The prototype to a function generally looks exactly the same as the function declaration, except that it ends in a semi-colon.

Program 5.10 is a reworking of Program 5.4, placing the function code after **main**() but including the function prototype before **main**().

Program 5.10

```
#include <stream.hpp>
int counter;
void fibon(int val1, int val2); // function prototype
main()
{                                   // beginning of main()
   fibon(0,1);
}                                   // end of main()
   // beginning of function fibon()
   void fibon (int val1, int val2)
{
   int val3;
   if (counter++==10) return;
   val3=val1+val2;
   cout << val3 << "\n";
   fibon(val2,val3);
} // end of function fibon()
```

As you can see, the function prototype is exactly the same as the function declaration, except for the final semi-colon. It is permissible to simplify the prototype slightly by omitting the variable names in the argument list; they are in any case ignored by the compiler. If this were done, the prototype for **fibon**() would look like this:

```
void fibon(int, int); // no variable names given
```

It is probably better to include the variable names in a function prototype as this simplifies debugging. In any case you must include the variable names when actually declaring the function.

The reserved word extern: Some C++ compilers expect function prototypes to be prefixed by the reserved word **extern**. This is not required in Zortech C++ Version 2, and **extern** should not be used in this context. It does however have another use, which is described in the next section.

The modular approach

Something which many newcomers to C++ find very confusing is that it is possible to split their programs between several different files. Books generally don't do it this way because it is much easier to show examples of code where everything – variables, functions, **main**() and all – are all jammed together into a single file; but when you are creating 'real' programs of your own, it can be extremely helpful to keep your functions in separate files, so that you can incorporate them in the finished code of many different programs. This is all part of the black box approach which we mentioned at the beginning of the chapter: once you have a function working, you can then 'plug it in' to as many other programs as you like; you can even use functions which other people have written.

Using #include files

The simplest way of splitting your programs between different files is to use the **#include** facility. The effect of this is simply to find the file specified by the preprocessor directive **#include** and to add it to your file at the point where the **#include** command is found.

For instance, you could break down Program 5.4 into two files, naming them (for example) FIBON.CPP and MAINCODE.CPP. The code for FIBON.CPP would then look like this:

```
#include <stream.hpp>
int counter;
void fibon(int val1,int val2)
{
   int val3;
   if (counter++==10) return;
   val3=val1+val2;
   cout << val3 << "\n";
   fibon(val2,val3);
}
```

and the code for MAINCODE.CPP would look like this:

```
#include "fibon.cpp"
main()
{
    fibon(0,1);
}
```

As you can see, all we have done here is to divide Program 5.4 'down the middle', with all the code belonging to the function **fibon()** in the first section, which we have called FIBON.CPP, and everything else in the second section, MAINCODE.CPP. The only substantial change is the addition of the line **#include "fibon.cpp"** to the beginning of MAINCODE.CPP. When you compile MAINCODE.CPP, the entire text of FIBON.CPP will be loaded in at the position of the **#include** statement, and the compiler will generate the necessary .OBJ and .EXE files (one of each).

Notice that in the directive **#include "fibon.cpp"** we have placed quotation marks instead of the usual chevrons < > around the name of the file to be included. The chevrons are used to identify a file from the \INCLUDE directory, while the quotation marks identify a file which has been stored in the default program directory. If you wish, you can specify a complete DOS path inside the quotation marks of the **#include** directive.

Creating separate .OBJ files

A more common way of handling a program which consists of several functions is to compile each function into a separate .OBJ file and then to link them all together. This makes it possible to use functions written by other people for which you do not even have the original source code; as long as you have an .OBJ file and an appropriate **header** file for each function, you can build a complete program out of a number of separate .OBJ modules. In effect this is exactly what you do when you incorporate library functions such as **printf()** and **gets()** in your own programs.

Saving the header: To break down your code into a number of separate .OBJ files, you must first save the prototype for each function (except **main()**) as a header file, giving it the extension .HPP if it is a C++ file or .H if it is a C file. For instance, we could create a file called FIBON.HPP containing just the following header:

```
void fibon(int, int);.
```

Compiling the functions: Next, the source code of each function must be loaded into ZED and compiled, giving it a name with a .CPP extension. The code for our example, FIBON.CPP, would look like this:

```
#include <stream.hpp>
int counter;
void fibon(int val1,int val2)
{
    int val3;
    if (counter++==10) return;
    val3=val1+val2;
    cout << val3 << "\n";
    fibon(val2,val3);
}
```

This file must have an **#include** directive for any file which it uses during compilation; in our case we obviously need **stream.hpp** as **fibon()** uses **cout <<**; in some cases – particularly when dealing with classes, which are described in Chapter Seven and subsequently, there may be information in the header file which is also needed, so that file may also need to be included.

The file containing the function must now be compiled into an .OBJ file; it can't in any case be converted into an .EXE file since it doesn't have any **main()**. If you are doing this from ZED, enter the -c compiler flag when prompted; if you are working at the DOS command line, type in the command

```
ZTC -c filename.ext
```

where *filename.ext* represents the name and extension of the file which you wish to compile. A message will be displayed to inform you that the compilation was successful.

Compiling the main program: The third step is to compile the code incorporating **main()** into an .OBJ file. We shall be call it MAINCODE.CPP, and it ought to look like this:

```
#include "fibon.hpp"
main()
{
    fibon(0,1);
}
```

Once again, we must have an **#include** directive for any files which are needed during compilation. Specifically we must include the header file FIBON.HPP, as this will provide the compiler with the information it needs about the workings of **fibon()**.

Compilation is carried out as before, using the -c flag to generate an .OBJ file.

Linking the completed .OBJ files: When you have finished compiling the various modules into .OBJ files, you can link them together into a working .EXE program.

This can be done from inside ZED with the MAKE utility, but where only a small number of files is involved it is simpler to invoke the Zortech linker BLINK.EXE directly from the DOS command line. The command takes the form

```
BLINK filename+filename+filename...,exefile
```

where *filename* represents the name of an .OBJ file (excluding the file extension, which will always be .OBJ) and *exefile* represents the name to be given to the final .EXE file; if this is omitted, the .EXE file will be given the same name as the first .OBJ file in the list. For instance, to link together FIBON.OBJ and MAINCODE.OBJ to create FIBON.EXE, you would enter the command

```
BLINK FIBON+MAINCODE
```

A DOS path can be placed in front of each filename if required. BLINK will then link the named files together and create the finished .EXE file.

There are a couple of points to watch about using BLINK. The most important is that you must leave no spaces anywhere in the command line. You must also be careful that all the files being linked together were compiled using the same memory model.

Using global variables in separately compiled files

When separately compiled modules are linked together to form a single program, any global variables which are declared in any of the modules will not be recognised in any other module.

This can sometimes be an advantage, as it allows different modules to have their own global variables which will not conflict with each other even if they happen to share the same name. More commonly, however, global variables will need to be truly global, capable of being accessed from within every module.

To achieve this, every module which needs to access a global variable which has been declared in another module must contain a special **extern** declaration to that variable.

Imagine, for instance, that we wished to access the global variable **counter** inside MAINCODE.CPP, although it was originally declared in FIBON.CPP. To do so we would need to include the following declaration in MAINCODE.CPP before the beginning of **main**():

```
extern int counter;
```

The original declaration of this variable in FIBON.CPP would not be affected.

The purpose of the declaration **extern int counter** is to inform the compiler that the integer variable counter exists and can be found in another file; no space is reserved for the variable as a result of the **extern** declaration, and the connection between the actual global variable **counter** from FIBON.CPP and the module MAINCODE.OBJ will not be made until the two modules are linked into a single .OBJ file.

extern and global arrays: If you wish to access a global array in a module other than the one in which it was declared, you must use the reserved word **extern** like this:

```
extern array_name[];
```

where *array_name* is the name of the global array declared in another module. Note the use of the empty [] operator pair; the compiler does not need to know the size of the array, only that it can be found in another module.

Postscript to Chapter Five

When you write a program in C++, you should as far as possible break it up into small 'building blocks' or functions. This helps to make the code more readable, and thus easier to debug and maintain.

You should by now understand how to prototype a function, how to pass arguments to a function, and how to return a single value from a function. You should also be aware of the important differences between global, automatic and static variables, and understand that when arguments are passed to a function, only *copies* of their values are actually passed over, allowing them to be modified *ad libitum* by the function without affecting the original values.

Short functions may be declared **inline** if speed of execution is important; however, there may be a penalty to pay in overall code size.

You should know how command line arguments may be passed to **main()**, using **argc** and **argv**.

Functions may be overloaded; that is, two or more functions which perform similar operations on different types of data or on different numbers of arguments may all be given the same name.

It is possible to split a long program up into a number of separate .OBJ modules which can then be linked together to create a single .EXE program. If this is done, global variables which are to be accessed in modules other than the one in which they were declared must be declared anew as **extern**.

Remember that functions exist to make your code easier to read. They do this by hiding complexities within themselves, making the overall flow of your program easier to understand.

Exercises to Chapter Five

1. If you haven't yet entered and run the programs in Chapter Five, do so now.

2. Write a program which expects a single integer number **x** in the command tail and then passes it to an iterative function. The function then displays the numbers from **x** down to zero on the screen.

3. Rewrite this program using a recursive function.

4. Rewrite the program again, putting the function and the main program in separate modules; the function prototype should be in a header file. Compile the modules separately and then link them together into an executable program.

6

Pointers and Functions

We have seen in Chapter Four that there is a very close relationship between arrays and pointers. In this chapter, we shall see that a similar close relationship exists between pointers and functions. We shall also learn how to allocate memory dynamically while a program is running, rather than when the program is created and compiled.

Returning several values from functions

In Chapter Five, we looked at three basic forms of C++ function.

The first, and simplest sort, is the type to which no values are sent and from which no values are returned. Such a function is declared as:

```
void function_name()
```

where *function_name* is the name of the function. You will remember that the reserved word **void** before the function name declares that the function will not return any value to the calling program (which may be either **main()** or another function, of course).

Our short inline function **bell()** was of this type; it required no values to be passed to it, and returned none. It was coded as follows:

```
inline void bell() {printf("\a");}
```

The second type of function expects to receive one or more arguments, but does not return any value to the calling program. Such a function is declared as:

```
void function_name(argument_list)
```

where *function_name* is the name of the function and *argument_list* is a list of the arguments being passed to the function.

Finally, there are functions which return a single value to the calling program. Such functions generally receive one or more arguments from the calling program, but this is not essential. Such a function is declared like this:

```
return_type function_name(argument_list)
```

where *argument_list* is a list of the arguments being passed to the function and *return_type* is the type of the value being returned to the calling program.

Restrictions affecting C++ functions

C++ functions as described above suffer from two restrictions which can seriously limit their usefulness.

The first restriction is that it is not generally possible for C++ functions to modify variables which are not local to that function (with the exception of global variables). Passing arguments to functions actually involves passing *copies* of variables rather than the variables themselves, thus ensuring that a function cannot improperly alter variables which are outside its scope. Normally the fact that variables in **main()** are immune from unauthorised and unexpected interference in any function is a useful safeguard against programming errors. However, there may be occasions when we actively want a function to change the values of a series of variables in the calling program.

A second and related, restriction is that there is no direct way in which a C++ function can return more than one value to the calling program. In this regard, C++ functions are much more limiting than Pascal procedures or Fortran subroutines, both of which can return several values.

There is, however, a simple solution to both problems. Instead of working on its own copy of the variables passed to it as arguments by the calling program, a function which is to modify one or more variables in the calling program can be induced to do so by passing it the *addresses* of the arguments rather than their values. You will probably not be surprised to learn that this is done by means of pointers.

A worked example

Consider the situation in which two variables of type int, **var1** and **var2**, contain values which must be swapped over, so that at the end of the operation **var2** contains the value that had previously been in **var1** and *vice-versa*. Program 6.1 will accomplish this:

Program 6.1

```
#include <stream.hpp>
main()
{
   int var1,var2,temp;
   cout << "Type in a value for var1\n";
   cin >> var1;
   cout << "Type in a value for var2\n";
   cin >> var2;
   cout << "Swapping ....\n";
   temp=var1;var1=var2;var2=temp; // this is the swap routine
   cout << "var1 now contains " << var1 << "\n";
   cout << "and var2 contains " << var2 << "\n";
}
```

Note the use of the variable **temp** which is used to hold the contents of **var1** during the exchange of values.

It isn't difficult to imagine circumstances in which it would be useful to use the swap routine **temp=var1;var1=var2;var2=temp** as a function. In a bubble sort, for instance, every number in turn in a list to be sorted is compared to its neighbour and swapped with it if necessary; this process is repeated until the entire set of numbers is sorted. Clearly it would be easiest to do this by means of a function call which might look something like this:

```
swap(var1,var2);
```

However, we have already seen that this can't be done using the normal C++ 'pass by value' technique, since to be effective it would involve the function changing the values of both **var1** and **var2** in the calling program.

The solution is to use the address operator **&** in the function declaration, so that instead of making copies of the values being passed, the function instead takes the addresses of the original values. This is known as **passing by reference**, as the function refers directly to the addresses of the variables in the argument list. Our simple **swap()** function would then look like the listing overleaf.

```
void swap(int &firstvar, int &secondvar)
{
    int temp=firstvar;firstvar=secondvar;secondvar=temp;
}
```

The function is declared to be **void** because it passes no values back to the calling program with a **return** statement. Because the *addresses* of the variables have been passed rather than the values which the variables contain, you may think that the declaration **int &firstvar, int &secondvar** in the function header would suggest that **firstvar** and **secondvar** are some kind of pointer variable rather than ordinary variables.

This is in fact almost exactly the case; they are in fact a special kind of variable called a **reference variable**. Reference variables partake of some of the features of pointers and some of the features of ordinary variables.

One very important difference between reference variables and pointer variables is that reference variables, once declared, can be treated exactly like ordinary variables; that is, the values to which they refer can be accessed directly, without the need to use the dereferencing operator *, as you would have to do with ordinary pointers. That is why it is possible to use them in an expression which is as easy to read and code as **temp=firstvar;firstvar=secondvar;secondvar=temp**.

Reference variables are described in more detail towards the end of this chapter.

Using call by reference in a program: Putting the function **swap()** into a simple program would result in the following:

Program 6.2

```
#include <stream.hpp>
void swap(int &firstvar, int &secondvar)
{
int temp=firstvar;firstvar=secondvar;secondvar=temp;
}
main()
{
int var1,var2;
cout << "Type in a value for var1\n";
   cin >> var1;
   cout << "Type in a value for var2\n";
   cin >> var2;
   cout << "Swapping ...\n";
   swap(var1,var2);
   cout << "var1 now contains " << var1 << "\n";
   cout << "and var2 contains " << var2 << "\n";
}
```

A different technique

The idiom outlined above is the best way to implement function calls using pass by reference. However, an alternative technique is also available, and this is described here briefly for the sake of completeness. This involves using the address operator & in the actual function call rather than in the function declaration; pointer variables must then be used within the body of the function. Program 6.3 shows what Program 6.2 would look like if this technique were used.

Program 6.3

```
#include <stream.hpp>
void swap(int *firstvar, int *secondvar)
{
   int temp=*firstvar;*firstvar=*secondvar;*secondvar=temp;
}
main()
{
   int var1,var2;
   cout << "Type in a value for var1\n";
   cin >> var1;
   cout << "Type in a value for var2\n";
   cin >> var2;
   cout << "Swapping ....\n";
   swap(&var1,&var2);
   cout << "var1 now contains " << var1 << "\n";
   cout << "and var2 contains " << var2 << "\n";
}
```

As you can see, this is much more complicated than the previous version of the program. However, in the original C language, this provided the only technique for pass by reference function calls, and you may accordingly meet it. The C++ version (in Program 6.2) is generally to be preferred on the grounds of simplicity.

Using the const specifier when passing by reference

Where speed of execution is particularly important, a little time can be saved by using the pass by reference technique even when the values of the original variables are not going to be altered by the function to which they have been passed. This is because no time is spent in making extra copies of the variables which are being passed to the function.

However, this is a potentially dangerous way of doing things because you might have made some programming or logical error in the function which would have the effect of changing the original values when they should have been left unaltered. This cannot occur when you use the pass by value technique, because any alterations to the automatic variables within the function will not affect the values of the variables in the calling program.

To prevent any possibility of errors in the code of a function changing values which have been passed to that function by reference, use the **const** specifier in the function declaration. This has the effect of making it impossible within the function to alter the values of any variables passed into the function by reference, and so there can be no danger of inadvertently changing the value of such a variable.

For instance, the following function will accept two variables passed by reference from the calling program, will add them together, and then return the result of the addition.

```
int add(const int &firstvar, const int &secondvar)
{
    return firstvar+secondvar;
}
```

The use of the reserved word **const** ensures that any mistaken attempt to change the value of **firstvar** or **secondvar** within the function will be trapped when the program is compiled.

Remember that passing a variable into a function by reference is only compulsory when you wish to alter the original value of the variable rather than to copy it into an automatic variable and alter that. If you decide to pass a variable into a function by reference in order to speed up the execution of your code, but do not wish to alter the value of that variable within the function, the use of **const** to prevent unintended changes to it is strongly recommended.

Passing arrays to functions

As we have just seen, the normal way of handing arguments to functions is by means of the pass by value technique, which means that the function is working with copies of the variables rather than the variables themselves.

However, when an array is used as an argument to a function, the situation is subtly different. Because it would be very wasteful of both time and memory if a complete array – perhaps of considerable length – had to be copied every time that a function call was invoked, a different technique is used.

You should remember that the name of an array (without the operator-pair [ ] after it) is actually a pointer to the first slot in the array. Consequently, it is possible to pass an array to a function by using the name of the array on its own as an argument. We shall see some examples of this in the following sections.

Pointers or subscripts? By now you are probably familiar with the fact that C++ tends to provide at least two ways of carrying out most operations. You should therefore not be surprised to discover that there are two quite different ways of handling arrays in functions.

In the discussion which follows, we shall use the faster of the two techniques, which involves the use of pointers to access the array within the function. The second technique, which uses array subscripting methods within the function, will be described later in the chapter.

Handling arrays in functions with pointers

The pointer technique works on the basis that since the name of the array is itself a pointer, the function declaration must use a pointer of the appropriate type to refer to the array, and this pointer can then be manipulated in the ways described in Chapter Four to gain access to individual elements of the array.

Consider the following fragments of code. First, we shall declare a string – that is, an array of type char – and then call a function **screen()** – the purpose of which is to output the string to the screen – passing the string to it as an argument.

```
char string[30]; // declare a string of length 30
screen(string); // and hand it to function screen()
```

The declaration for the function **screen()** includes a pointer of type char to reflect the fact that a pointer to an array of char is being passed to it. It looks like this:

```
void screen(char *p1);// function declaration
```

The body of the function then uses a **while** loop to display the string one character at a time. The location at which the pointer **p1** points is incremented each time the loop is repeated, and the loop is left when **p1** is pointing at the null which marks the end of the string:

```
while (*p1) cout << *p1++; // display chars till done
```

The complete program is shown on the next page:

Program 6.4

```
#include <stream.hpp>
void screen(char *p1) // a pointer to char
{
    while (*p1) cout << *p1++;
}
main()
{
    char string[30];
    cout << "Type in a word\n";
    cin >> string;
    screen(string);
    // function call passes a pointer disguised as an array-name
}
```

More about const: You may remember that when the address of a variable is passed to a function, either by means of a pass by reference call as described earlier or when the address of the start of an array is passed as in Program 6.4, it is possible for an error in programming within the function to improperly alter the original value of the variable.

We have already seen that the **const** specifier can be used to trap any such unintended changes. **const** could also be used in Program 6.4 in order to ensure that the array **string** isn't altered in the course of the function **screen()**. The program would then look like this:

```
#include <stream.hpp>
void screen(const char *p1)
{
    while (*p1) cout << *p1++;
}
main()
{
    char string[30];
    cout << "Type in a word\n";
    cin >> string;
    screen(string);
}
```

Freezing values and freezing addresses: It's important to note that this use of **const** has the effect of 'freezing' the data which is stored at the address at which the pointer **p1** is pointing at any given moment, *but it does not freeze the address itself.* This is why it is possible to move **p1** through the array as we have done.

A technique is available which allows a programmer to freeze the address at which a pointer is pointing rather than the data which that address contains. For instance, if a function **funct()** has the header line

```
void funct(char *const p1)
```

then pointer **p1** is frozen at the address to which it is pointing; however, the data stored at that address can change.

Finally, it is possible to freeze both the data and the address, using this idiom:

```
void funct(const char *const p1)
```

Here pointer **p1** cannot be moved from the address at which it initially points; furthermore, the value contained in the address at which it points cannot be changed either.

These distinctions can be quite important, and if you get them wrong, then your program won't work. If you do use the **const** specifier, be certain that you haven't frozen the address at which a pointer is pointing rather than the value stored there, or *vice-versa.*

strlen() again

In Chapter Four we looked briefly at a way in which pointers could be used to determine the length of a string, and pointed out that a technique for doing this is available as a standard library function. The following code shows one way in which this function could be implemented:

```
int strlen(char *p1)
{
   char *p2;
   p2=p1;
   while (*p2) p2++;
   return p2-p1;
}
```

Because this function returns the integer value which represents the length of the string, it must be declared as **int strlen(char *p1)**.

The code to invoke this function might look something like this:

```
cout << strlen(string);
```

The actual mechanics of checking the string-length are identical to those described previously in Chapter Four.

Passing individual array members

Program 6.4 showed how an array-name can be used as an argument to a function. It is also possible to pass individual elements of an array to a function. In this case, the elements are treated like ordinary variables; that is, copies of the individual elements are passed instead of a pointer to the beginning of the array. Compare Program 6.5 which passes individual array elements to be output by the function **screen()** with Program 6.4 which passes the complete array and then outputs it with a **while** loop within the function **screen()**.

Program 6.5
```
#include <stream.hpp>
void screen(char letter)
{
    cout << letter;
}
main()
{
    char string[30];
    cout << "Type in a word\n";
    cin >> string;
    for (int counter=0;string[counter];counter++)
    screen(string[counter]);
}
```

Program 6.5 will execute more slowly than Program 6.4 because in the latter program, the entire array **string** is copied into the function **screen()** (one character at a time) whereas nothing at all is copied in Program 6.4.

In Program 6.4, the elements of the array **string** in **main()** are accessed by means of a **for** loop and subscripts. This has been done here to clarify the way in which the program works. It would be perfectly proper – and faster – to access the individual elements by means of a pointer; for an example of this, look ahead to the bubble sort program, Program 6.7.

Changing the contents of the array

Another important difference between Program 6.4 and Program 6.5 is that because in the former we were working with the original array (the address of which has been passed into the function **screen()**), any changes which we might make to that array in the function would be reflected if **string** were to be accessed again in **main()**.

On the other hand, where individual array elements are copied into the function, as in Program 6.5, any changes which might be made to them will be lost as soon as the function finishes executing and the automatic (local) variable **letter** goes out of scope.

Pass by reference for array elements

If you want individual array elements – but not the whole array – to be changed by a function, you can use the pass by reference technique described earlier.

Program 6.6 uses this technique to pass every second member of the array **string** into the function **caps()**. This function then makes use of the standard library function **toupper()** to turn each character passed to it into its upper case equivalent (non-alphabetic characters are unaffected). Then **string** is output, showing that those characters which were passed into the function **caps()** have been capitalised. The function **toupper()** requires the header file ctype.h to be included.

Program 6.6

```
#include <stream.hpp>
#include <ctype.h>
void caps(char &letter) // pass by reference to a char
{
   letter=toupper(letter); // and turn it into upper case
}
main()
{
   char string[30];
   cout << "Type in a word\n";
   cin >> string;
   for (int counter=0;counter<30;counter+=2)
   caps(string[counter]);
      // send alternate characters to caps()
   cout << string; // and then display the result
}
```

A simple sorting program

We will now use some of the techniques we have learned in this chapter to write a simple bubble sort program. This is printed as Program 6.7 on the next page.

Introducing the bubble sort: If you are unfamiliar with the way in which a bubble sort works, the following brief description should help you to understand it.

The **sort list** – the set of numbers to be sorted – is held in an array of type int. The first element is compared with the second, and if necessary they are swapped; then the second element is compared with the third, and swapped if necessary, and so on until the last element but one has been compared to the last element, and has been swapped if necessary.

Then the whole procedure is repeated again, starting once more at the beginning of the array. Each time that the operation is repeated, the list becomes more ordered. A flag is set whenever a swap has taken place, and reset at the end of each pass through the list; if a complete pass through the array occurs without any swaps being required, then the flag will be equal to zero, and the sort will be complete.

A bubble sort is not particularly fast; though it works very rapidly where relatively small amounts of data are being sorted, it becomes rapidly less efficient as the length of the sort list increases. However, it is easy to understand. Incidentally, it gains its name from the fact that high numbers which occur at the beginning of the sort list can be imagined to 'bubble' upwards as the sort proceeds.

Program 6.7

```
#include <stream.hpp>
void swap(int &first, int &second) // swap() function
   // values are passed to the function by reference
{
   int temp=first;first=second;second=temp;
} // end of the function
main()
{
   int array[20],*p1,maximum_number,flag;
   // First, prompt for how many numbers will be sorted
   cout << "How many numbers will you input (maximum 20)?\n";
   cin >> maximum_number;
      // Now a for loop to input the values and store them
      // in the array. Pointers access the elements
   cout << "Enter the numbers, pressing RETURN after each\n";
   for (p1=array;p1<&array[maximum_number];p1++) cin >> *p1;
      // A message to show the computer's still awake ...
   cout << "Sorting ....\n";
      // and we start passing through the sort list;
      // we continue passing as long as any swaps
      // have been made, as detected by the flag,
      // which is reset to zero at the beginning
      // of each pass, and set to 1 whenever
      // a swap has been made
```

```
do {
    flag=0;
    for (p1=array;p1<&array[maximum_number-1];p1++){
        if (*p1>*(p1+1)){
            // call function swap if necessary, and reset flag
            swap(*p1,*(p1+1));
            flag=1;
        }
    }
}
    // if flag is zero (false) the job is done;
    // otherwise go round again
while (flag);
    // And now output the sorted list
    for (p1=array;p1<&array[maximum_number];p1++) cout << *p1;
}
```

Enter the above program into your computer and work carefully through it to see how it works. In particular, note how pointers to elements in the sort list are used in the function call **swap(*p1,*(p1+1))**.

An awkward restriction: One restriction on the program as it appears here is that the sort list cannot hold more than 20 numbers, as this is the maximum size allocated to the array. It would be possible to increase the number of items that can be sorted by specifying a bigger array, but there is a penalty to be paid for this approach: if you reserve space in the program for an array of 500 elements and then on a particular occasion only want to sort a list of half a dozen numbers, then virtually the entire array will have been reserved for no purpose.

This probably wouldn't matter inasmuch as the program will still run, but it represents a highly inefficient approach to programming and memory management. It would clearly be better if we could allocate only as much memory as is actually required; since this will vary from one run of the program to the next, this means that the memory allocation will have to take place while the program is running. This is a very important concept, and we will see how it can be achieved later in this chapter.

Handling arrays in functions with subscripts

We have already mentioned that the preferred way of manipulating an array which has been passed to a function is by means of pointers. However, it is possible to use subscripts instead.

Earlier, we devised a function **screen**() to which an array of type char was passed.

The function declaration looked like this:

```
void screen(char *p1); // using pointers
```

Exactly the same goal can be achieved by using this function declaration instead:

```
void screen(char array[]); // using subscripts
```

The function call from **main()** would be the same in both cases:

```
screen(string);
```

Note that the size of the array isn't specified in the declaration; instead, we use empty square brackets [ ]. This isn't surprising if you think about it. Since the array has previously been declared, and space has been reserved for it, C++ already knows how big it is; and since no bounds checking is carried out, the onus is on the programmer to make sure that no attempt is made to access any elements beyond the end of the array.

Incidentally, it is quite in order to put in the size of the array between the [ ] pair if you want to do so. However, normal programming practice is to leave it out as there is no advantage to be gained from including it.

Once an array has been passed to a function using subscripts, the individual elements can be accessed by their subscripts.

This is in contrast to the method used in the function **screen()** in Program 6.4, which was designed to output the contents of the string which had been passed to it by moving a pointer along the array and outputting the character at which the pointer was pointing. It looked like this:

```
void screen(char *p1) // pointer version
{
   while (*p1) cout << *p1++;
}
```

The subscript version of the same function looks like this:

```
void screen(char array[]) // subscript version
{
   int counter=0;
   while (array[counter])
     cout << array[counter++];
}
```

As you can see, the subscript version is not only longer, but also clumsier, because it involves the use of the automatic variable **counter** which was not needed in the pointer version. The subscript version also runs more slowly than the pointer version. As you can see, there really are advantages to be gained by using pointers instead of subscripts!

The subscript version of the full program would look like this:

Program 6.8

```
#include <stream.hpp>
void screen(char array[])
{
   int counter=0;
   while (array[counter]) cout << array[counter++];
}
main()
{
   char string[30];
   cout << "Type in a word\n";
   cin >> string;
   screen(string);
}
```

Functions which return pointers

We have already met functions which return nothing – that is, their return value is **void** – and functions which return values of type int, float and so on. It is now time to meet functions which return pointers to values rather than the values themselves.

Consider the situation in which you wish to find out whether a particular character is contained within a string; if the character is present, then it will be displayed; if it is not present, then a suitable message will be displayed instead.

The conventional way of handling this problem in C++ would be to make the function return a pointer to the character if it exists in the string, and a null pointer – one which points to memory location zero – if it does not exist.

Program 6.9 shows how the job can be accomplished.

Program 6.9

```
#include <stream.hpp>
char* find(char *pt1, char symbol) // returns a pointer
{
   for (;*pt1!=0;pt1++) if (symbol==*pt1) return pt1;
      // search string for symbol, return pointer if found
   return pt1=0;
      // otherwise return null pointer
}
main()
{
   char word[20],*p1,letter;
   cout << "Type in a word\n"; // Prompt for a word
   cin >> word; // and input it
   cout << "Type in a letter\n"; // then prompt for a letter
   cin >> letter; // and input that too.
   p1=find(word,letter); // Call function find()
         // which returns a pointer to
         // the required character
         // if it is in the word, or
         // a null if it is not.

   if (p1) cout << *p1 << "\n"; // Display if not a null pointer
   else cout << "Not present in word\n"; // otherwise not found
}
```

The function **find()** receives a pointer **pt1** to the beginning of array **word**. In the function's **for** loop the pointer is moved through the array one character at a time, and the value at which it points is compared to the value of **symbol**. If a match is found, then the pointer is returned, containing the address of the matching character; if no match is found before the pointer reaches the null value at the end of the string, then the pointer is set to zero and returned.

In Program 6.9, **main()** is a simple driver to test that function **find()** works. It first prompts for a word and a single character, then calls **find()**. If pointer variable **p1** is returned as a null, then the single character has not been found within the word; otherwise, it points at the position of the character within **word**.

Pointers to functions

By now you should be used to the idea that variables have addresses in memory, and that it is often useful to be able to manipulate them by means of pointers. In the case of variable types which occupy more than one byte, the pointer holds the address of the first byte of the variable.

Functions also occupy an address in memory. This being so, it follows that it is possible to call a function by means of a pointer which holds the address of that function.

Declaring a function pointer: Just as it is necessary to use an int pointer to point to an integer and a float pointer to point to a floating point number, so also a pointer which will point to a function must match the type of function to which it will point. For instance, a function which returns no value and receives no arguments would be declared like this:

```
void funct();
```

and a pointer to such a function would therefore be declared like this:

```
void (*fp)();
```

Note the use of the parentheses in the expression **void (*fp)**; this means that **fp** is declared to be a pointer to a function which returns no value; if the parentheses were omitted, the expression **void *fp** would mean that **fp** is declared to be a function returning a void pointer.

Initialising a pointer to a function: Once a pointer to a function has been declared, it can then be pointed at a function of the appropriate type. This is done using the idiom

```
fp=funct;
```

This points the pointer **fp** at the starting address of function **funct**. Note that it would be incorrect to use () after the function name in this case; the only time when it is correct to omit () after the name of a function is when you are referring to the address of the function, as here.

Using a pointer to a function: Now that you have declared a pointer to a function, you can invoke that function either in the normal way using the name like this:

```
funct();
```

or by using the pointer like this:

```
(*fp)();
```

Actually, function calls are hardly ever carried out in this way, and the only time you are likely to see this idiom is when you have to pass the address of one function as an argument to a second function. A few of the functions in the library are written in this way; the most useful is the quicksort function, which we shall now examine.

Using quicksort

The quicksort function **qsort()** is contained in the stdlib.h library. With it you can sort the contents of any array into ascending order. (If you are not familiar with the quicksort algorithm, you need to know only that it provides the most rapid way of sorting large arrays, and that the sort is carried out 'in place'; that is, it requires no extra memory.)

The prototype of **qsort()** looks like this:

```
void qsort(void *base,int nel,int size,
   int comparison_function(void *,void *));
```

base is a pointer to the first element in the array to be sorted; the array name only is required, without the [] operator.

nel is an integer specifying the number of elements in the array.

size is an integer specifying how many bytes are required for each element. The simplest way of handling this is by means of the **sizeof()** operator, so that if you are sorting an array of type char, you would pass this argument as **sizeof(char)**.

Finally, *comparison_function* is the name of a function which the programmer must write which will compare two elements of the array and return a positive integer if the first element is larger than the second, a negative integer if the first element is smaller than the second, and a zero if both elements are equal. The prototype of the user-supplied function must look like this:

```
int comparison_function(void *,void *);
```

That is, it must accept two void pointers, and it must return an integer.

The advantage of doing things in this way is that it enables the **qsort()** function to work equally well regardless of the type of array which is passed to it; all that is required is that the user should provide a suitable comparison function for each type of array which will be passed in a particular program.

Once the name of the appropriate comparison function has been passed to **qsort()**, it is then called from within **qsort()** by means of the following code:

```
(*comp_fp)(a,b)
```

where *a* and *b* are void pointers to the items to be compared.

Some practical examples

For instance, if you wish to quicksort an array of 200 characters, you would first need to create a comparison function which would probably look something like this:

```
int comp1(const void *a,const void *b)
{
   strcmp((char*)a,(char*)b);
}
```

This uses the library function **strcmp()** to compare two characters and return 1 if the first character is 'larger' than the second (closer to the end of the alphabet), −1 if the second character is 'larger' than the first, and zero if they are the same.

The code **(char*)a,(char*)b** has the effect of casting the void pointers to pointers to char.

You would then call **qsort()** like this:

```
qsort(array_name,array_size,sizeof(char),comp1);
```

where *array_name* is the name of the array you are going to sort and *array_size* is the number of items it contains.

Sorting integers: Similarly, if you want to quicksort an array of integers then your comparison function might look like this:

```
int comp2(const void *a,const void *b)
{
   return *(int*)a-*(int*)b;
}
```

The idiom ***(int*)a** casts the void pointer to an integer pointer and then dereferences the result; thus the expression **return *(int*)a-*(int*)b** has the effect of subtracting the integer value pointed to by **b** from the integer value pointed to by **a** and returning the result. This will be positive if **a** is pointing to a number larger than that pointed to by **b**; negative if **a** is pointing to a number smaller than that pointed to by **b**; and zero if the numbers pointed to by **a** and **b** are equal.

Function **qsort()** will then be called like this:

```
qsort(array_name,array_size,sizeof(int),comp2);
```

Passing C++ function pointers to C functions

An additional problem about using the **qsort()** library function is that it isn't actually a C++ function at all, but a C function. Because of diferences in the way function calls are handled in C and C++, you *must* force your comparison function to be compiled as if it were a C function. This is done by inserting the code **extern "C"** in front of the declaration of the comparison function. If you do not do this, the program will not compile. You must do this whenever you declare C++ functions whose names will be passed to C functions.

The complete code for a program demonstrating the use of quicksort to sort an array of 10 integers is shown as Program 6.10.

Program 6.10

```
#include <stream.hpp>
#include <stdlib.h>

const int NUMBER_OF_ITEMS=10;

extern "C" int comp(const void *a,const void *b)
{
   return *(int*)a-*(int*)b; // comparison function
}

main()
{
   int numbers[NUMBER_OF_ITEMS];
   cout << "Type in 10 integers\n";
   for (int counter=0;counter<NUMBER_OF_ITEMS;counter++)
     cin >> numbers[counter]; // input an array of 10 ints
   cout << "\nSorting....\n\n";
   qsort(numbers,NUMBER_OF_ITEMS,sizeof(int),comp);
   for (counter=0;counter<NUMBER_OF_ITEMS;counter++)
     // display the sorted list
     cout << numbers[counter] << "\n";
}
```

More about reference variables

The original C language uses both ordinary variables and pointer variables, and we have already seen that both of these types are also available in C++. C++ also makes available the use of a new kind of variable, called a **reference variable**.

Reference variables are in some ways a cross between an ordinary variable and a pointer. Although we have not formally introduced this new type, we have in fact already met them briefly in functions to which values have been passed by reference; look back at Program 6.2 to refresh your memory of how this was done.

Declaring a reference variable

We have already seen that a function which uses reference variables is declared like this:

```
void function_name(int &firstvar, int &secondvar)
```

The names of the reference variables **firstvar** and **secondvar** in this function declaration are preceded by a declaration of their type, followed by the address operator **&**. You can create reference variables elsewhere using the same idiom. The only point to observe is that when a reference variable is declared outside a function declaration, it must be initialised at the same time as it is declared by pointing it at a location in memory. This may be an existing variable.

The following fragment may make this clearer:

```
int number=23; // int variable initialised to 23
int &new_one=number; // reference variable initialised
        // to 23 by pointing it at number
```

Two variables have been declared in this fragment. The first is an ordinary variable, **number**, of type int.

The second is a reference variable, also of type int, and the effect of the = operator is to point it at the ordinary variable **number**. From now on, you can refer to **number** either by means of its original name or by means of the reference variable **new_one** which refers to it. Consequently the two following lines have the same effect:

```
cout << number;
cout << new_one;
```

From now on, any changes that you make to **number** will be reflected in **new_one**, and *vice-versa*. This is known as an **alias**.

Reference variables on the heap: It is also possible to point a reference variable at a location on the heap of free memory. This is described in detail later in this chapter.

Dynamic memory allocation

All the variables we have used in all the programs printed in this book so far have been created by the compiler on the computer's stack, giving us very little control over them. (The operation of the stack is described in a little detail in Chapter Eight.)

We have already seen that this can result in memory allocation taking place on a very rough-and-ready basis. For instance, imagine a program which is intended to handle several hundred names and telephone numbers. Doing this by means of conventional arrays might work reasonably well – and if you were writing the program in Basic you would have no other real choice – but because the array dimensions would have to be fixed at compilation time, it would not be possible to increase the amount of data which your program could handle without changing the array sizes and recompiling it. Conversely, if the program was set up to handle 500 names and telephone numbers but you only wanted to work with 30, a vast amount of memory would be committed to arrays and this memory would never be fully used.

Another disadvantage of stack variables is that they will continue to occupy memory space until they go out of scope, even if they are no longer needed. Thus a large array which might be needed at the beginning of **main()** but which might never be used again in the entire program would continue to occupy space until the program ceased to run.

Fortunately, C++ offers a very simple technique for creating variables in a section of memory called the **heap**. Variables which are created here never go out of scope; the programmer can cause them to be created and deleted at any point in the program, and when they are deleted the memory which they occupy will be recovered.

The technique of creating and destroying such variables is known as **dynamic memory allocation**.

Creating heap variables

A heap variable is created by using the C++ operator **new**; this returns a pointer to the beginning of the memory allocated to the variable. The following fragment shows how easy this is:

```
char *word = new char[20];
```

This line reserves sufficient space on the heap for 20 values of type char, and returns a pointer to the first of them. **word** is thus both the name given to the array which we have just caused to be stored on the heap and a pointer to the first element of that array; this is the usual way in which arrays are treated. Once space for the string has been reserved and **word** has been pointed at the first element in it, the entire string can be output in the usual way with **cout << word**. Individual elements can be accessed by using either subscripts (**word[0]** to **word[19]**) or with pointers.

Testing for space: It's possible that as you allocate more and more space to heap variables during the running of a memory-hungry program, you may run out of heap memory altogether. When this happens, the operator **new** will return a null pointer.

You can thus test to see whether you have sufficient memory to create a new heap variable by trying to create it and then examining the pointer value returned to see whether it is null; if it is, then there is insufficient memory to create the variable you wish on the heap.

The following fragment of code will create a new heap variable **word**, reserving sufficient space in it for 20 characters; if sufficient memory is not available, a message will be displayed:

```
char *word = new char[20]; // reserve space on the heap
if (!word) cout << "Not enough memory\n"; // or warn
```

A careful programmer will always test that memory has been successfully allocated before proceeding. Any attempt to access a heap variable for which space was not available will almost certainly cause the computer to lock up.

Destroying heap variables

Once a heap variable has been created, it can be destroyed by using the operator **delete**. The space which was reserved by means of the command **new** is then returned to the heap, and this space can then be reallocated by means of further **new** commands as required. For instance, the character array **word** can be removed from memory by using the line

```
delete word;
```

Inexperienced programmers often forget to destroy variables which have been created on the heap when they are no longer required. The memory which such variables occupy is thus rendered inaccessible. As long as you are writing small programs which require little memory, this won't cause any practical problems, though it is certainly bad programming practice. However, in a large data-processing system, failing to destroy unwanted heap variables while at the same time continuing to create new variables on the heap may well cause the system to crash, unless you have remembered to test to see if you have sufficient heap memory available when using the operator **new**, as described above.

A difficult bug to catch: If you attempt to use the **delete** operator to destroy a heap variable which has already been destroyed, the error will not be detected by the compiler, and the bugs which will occur will be particularly difficult to track down. (The same error can be made with the **free**() function described briefly below.)

Freeing a specified number of bytes

It is possible to delete a fixed number of bytes; for instance, the command

```
delete [20] word;
```

will free 20 bytes beginning at the location pointed to by **word**.

A simple example

Program 6.11 is a new version of Program 6.9, using dynamic memory allocation techniques to create the array variable **word** on the heap. The space thus allocated is then freed at the end of the program. As you can see, the remainder of the program functions in exactly the same way as the previous version.

Program 6.11

```
#include <stream.hpp>
char* find(char *pt1, char symbol)
{
   for (;*pt1!=0;pt1++) if (symbol==*pt1) return pt1;
   return pt1=0;
}
main()
{
   char *p1,letter;
   char *word=new char[20];
   cout << "Type in a word\n";
   cin >> word;
   cout << "Type in a letter\n";
   cin >> letter;
   p1=find(word,letter);
   if (p1) cout << *p1 << "\n";
   else cout << "Not present in word\n";
   delete word;
}
```

Creating reference variables on the heap

It is possible to create reference variables on the heap. For instance, to create a reference variable **number** of type int on the heap, the code would look like this:

```
int &number = *new int;
```

Notice that when you do this, you must use the dereferencing operator ***** in front of the operator **new**. The reason for this is that **new** normally returns an address to a pointer; however, a reference variable is not an ordinary pointer.

Once such a reference variable has been created on the heap, values can be assigned to it just as if it were an ordinary variable. For instance, the following code will create a reference variable of type int, prompt for a value to be put into it, double that value, and finally output the result.

```
int &number = *new int;
cout << "Type in a number\n";
cin >> number;
number*=2;
cout << number;
```

Deleting reference variables on the heap

Since **delete** needs to know the address of the first byte of the range which is to be deleted, deleting a reference variable requires that you cast the reference variable to a pointer of the appropriate type. The code to delete the reference variable **number** from the previous fragment looks like this:

```
delete (int*)(&number);
```

Remember that using reference variables on the heap is entirely voluntary; most users find it more natural to use pointers. The code which is generated by the compiler is identical whichever technique you use.

A different way of proceeding

The operators **new** and **delete** do not exist in the original C language. Consequently, you may come across code which has been written using the original C functions **malloc()** and **free()**, which are found in the stdlib.h library.

To allocate heap memory for an array of char of size 20 the following form would be used:

```
word=malloc(20*sizeof(char))
```

This will allocate sufficient bytes for the storage of 20 characters, returning a pointer to the beginning of the memory thus allocated. Should sufficient memory not be available, a null pointer will be returned.

To free heap memory allocated with **malloc()**, use the **free()** function like this:

```
result=free(word);
```

where **result** is of type int. You should then test **result**; if it has the value 0, then the memory has been successfully freed; if it has the value -1, then the heap has been corrupted or a serious bug has occurred, and the program should be aborted before the system crashes.

When to use dynamic memory allocation

There are no fixed rules which will tell you for certain whether a particular variable should be placed on the stack or in the heap; the choice is up to you as the programmer, and in many cases a program may run equally well regardless of whether you use the stack, the heap, or a mixture of both. However, the following suggestions may be helpful.

Variables which are needed for 'housekeeping' while a program is running – loop counters, flags and the like – should be treated as ordinary stack variables. Variables which contain the user's data – arrays and the special types described later in this book – are best treated as dynamic (heap) variables; this is especially true if the amount of space that they will require cannot be foretold during compilation.

Postscript to Chapter Six

This chapter has covered a great deal of ground, all of which you will need to understand before you can confidently handle the more complex aspects of pointers and function calls.

Where a function returns either a single value or no value at all, the simplest and safest way of proceeding is by using the technique of passing by value. The function makes its own copy of the values which are being passed to it, and any modifications which are made to these values are not carried back to the calling program.

Where it is necessary for a function to pass back more than a single value, or where it must modify the arguments which have been passed to it, the technique of pass by reference must be used instead. This has the additional advantage of being somewhat faster than passing by value, since there is no need to make local copies of the values passed. If you are using pass by reference techniques only to gain speed, and not because you want to alter the arguments which have been passed to the function, the use of the keyword **const** will ensure that these values are not changed inadvertently.

Complete arrays are always passed to functions by reference. The array elements can be accessed within the function either by pointers or by subscripts; the former technique is faster. Arrays of more than one dimension can always be treated as if they were arrays of one dimension.

It is possible to create and destroy variables dynamically, using the operators **new** and **delete**. **new** returns a pointer to the beginning of the heap memory which has been reserved, and **delete** frees the heap for further use.

Exercises to Chapter Six

1. If you haven't yet entered and run the programs in Chapter Six, do so now.

2. Write a program which contains a function which accepts two integer arguments. If the first argument is bigger than the second, swap the arguments around. Use pass by reference.

3. Rewrite the program using the & operator in the function call rather than pass by reference.

4. Write a version of Program 6.10 to sort strings of characters into alphabetical order.

7

Introducing Structures

One of the most powerful features of C++ is that it allows the programmer to create purpose-built variable types; these new types can then be handled in exactly the same way as the inbuilt types such as float, int, char and the like.

For instance, a common programming problem is to have to create a database in which information of various types will be stored. A simple example might be a file containing a list of, say, a hundred names and telephone numbers. In a language such as Basic, the most obvious way of proceeding would be to create a couple of arrays, one for the names and the other for the telephone numbers: NAME$(20) might contain the name of the 20th person in the file, and NUMBER$(20) might contain that person's telephone number. (NUMBER$ would need to be a string array because telephone numbers may contain non-numeric characters, such as brackets.)

In more sophisticated languages such as C and Pascal, the facility exists to create specific structures for containing information of this sort. In Pascal, such a structure is called a **record**, and a Pascal record might contain a field for an individual's name and another for his telephone number.

In C, a similar construction is called a **structure**. Like its Pascal equivalent, a C structure can contain a number of fields each of which may hold such information as a name and a telephone number. Each record is known as an **instance** of the structure, or alternatively as an **object** of the type of the structure. These usages will become clearer as we proceed.

Where C++ differs from both C and Pascal is that it allows structures to contain **member functions** as well as data; member functions of a structure are functions which manipulate the data contained in that structure. (C++ structures and classes have many other powerful features as well, but the concept of structures and their member functions is enough to be getting along with at the moment.)

Creating a simple structure

To show how structures work, we shall begin by creating a very simple one to hold names and telephone numbers. Such a structure can easily be developed into an extremely complex affair, using linked-list techniques and the like, but for the moment we shall consider only the simplest form.

Structure data fields

When you devise a new structure, the first decision which you must make concerns the number and type of the variables (or **elements**) which you will need. In our first simple structure, we shall use only two data elements, **name** and **tel_number**. In the real world, both of these would be of type char, because, as suggested above, telephone numbers often contain non-numeric characters. However, we shall treat the **tel_number** field as a long int, so that we can see later how different types of structure elements can be passed to functions.

A simple structure to incorporate these two elements might look like this:

```
struct phone_directory
{
   char name[20]; // up to 19 characters in the name
   long int tel_number; // only numerals in the number
};
```

There are several things to notice here. First, note that the structure is declared using the reserved word **struct** followed by the **tag-name** name of the structure which we are creating – in this case **phone_directory**. Remember that we are declaring a structure, not a variable; in due course we shall be able to create as many variables of type phone_directory as we wish, in just the same way as we can create variables of type float, int, char and so on.

Second, the structure declaration is followed by its definition. This includes the declaration of the individual data elements which form part of the new structure (and may include other features as well, as we shall see later). The data elements which are being declared must be enclosed between a pair of braces { }. Data elements cannot be initialised in the same way as ordinary variables which are not elements of a structure; thus the syntax

```
long int tel_number=12345;
```

is not available. Initialisation is normally carried out by means of a **constructor**, as described later in this chapter.

Third, a semi-colon is used after the closing brace. As far as C++ is concerned, a structure definition is a statement, and like every other statement it must be terminated by a semi-colon.

Finally, a structure is often placed in a separate file of its own; in this way, it can be made available to any number of different programs which might need to use it. This parallels the way in which functions can be compiled to .OBJ files, allowing them in due course to be linked together to produce a single .EXE file as described in Chapter Five.

For the moment, we shall jam everything – structures, data elements, member functions, and **main**() – into the same file. Later in this chapter we shall show how to split them into a number of different files which can be compiled separately and finally linked together.

Creating objects

Now that we have defined the structure **phone_directory**, we can declare some objects (or instances) of that type. Each object is analogous to a single record in a database.

There are two ways in which objects can be declared. The simplest is to use the same technique as we have already used to declare variables of pre-defined types such as int and float. Thus to declare two objects **first** and **second** of type phone_directory, you would use the following code:

```
phone_directory first,second;
```

Much the same thing can be done in the original C language, but the code would then be slightly different:

```
struct phone_directory first,second;
```

This slightly more complex form is also syntactically acceptable in C++, but we suggest that you do not use it. C++ puts user-defined types such as our **phone_directory** on the same footing as those which are a native part of the language, and it makes sense to treat them as such, without the addition of **struct** whenever a new object is declared.

Another way of creating objects: It is also possible to create objects by listing their names immediately after the closing brace of the structure definition, and before the semi-colon. Thus to define the structure **phone_directory** and simultaneously create two objects of that type, **first** and **second**, you would use this code:

```
struct phone_directory
{
    char name[20];
    long int tel_number;
}first,second;
```

Anonymous structures: The tag-name of a structure can be omitted if all the objects of the structure will be declared before the semi-colon which marks the end of the structure definition (though the compiler will warn you that there is *no tag-name for struct*.) Thus the following code will create the objects **first** and **second** without actually specifying a tag-name:

```
struct
{
    char name[20];
    long int tel_number;
}first,second;
```

As you can see, the way in which structures are declared is very similar to the declaration of enumerated types as described in Chapter Two.

Referencing the data elements of individual objects

Let us assume that we have declared just two phone_directory objects, **first** and **second**. We now need to be able to insert a name into the **name** field and a telephone number into the **tel_number** field of each.

There are – as you may anticipate from your experience of C++ to date – two completely different ways of doing this. The way which is described in this section is the same as that used in C. Although it is adequate for a simple structure such as **phone_directory**, it is far less powerful than the more advanced methods available with C++.

Accessing the individual elements of an object is done by means of a special operator called the **dot operator**. The following code shows how this could be used to insert a name and a number into the **name** and **tel_number** fields of **first**:

```
cin >> first.name >> first.tel_number;
```

As you can see, the dot operator . is placed between the name of the structure variable **first** and the name of the data element, or field, which we want to access.

In the same way, we could display the contents of both the **name** and **tel_number** fields of the object **second** with this code:

```
cout << second.name << second.tel_number;
```

Arrays of objects

You can create an array of objects in much the same way as you can create an array of any other type; indeed, arrays of objects are very common.

To define the structure **phone_directory** and then create an array of 100 objects of this type, you would first declare and define the **phone_directory** structure and then (in **main**()) declare a suitable array of objects. The code might look like this:

```
#include <stream.hpp>
struct phone_directory // structure declaration
{
   char name[20]; // declare two data elements
   long int tel_number;
}; // and end with a semi-colon

main()
{
   // declare an array of 100 objects
   phone_directory phone_num[100];
}
```

This will create an array **phone_num** of 100 objects of type **phone_directory**, ranging from **phone_num[0]** to **phone_num[99]**.

Arrays of objects on the heap: Arrays of objects can be created on the heap using the operator **new**, using this construction:

```
phone_directory *phone_num=new phone_directory[20]
```

This will declare an array of 20 objects of type **phone_directory**.

When deleting such arrays, you must use this syntax:

```
delete [20] phone_num;
```

Failure to specify the number of objects to be deleted is not a syntax error, but it will result in none of the elements being deleted.

Referencing the elements of an array: The elements of an array of objects can easily be referenced with the dot operator. For instance, we can display all the names and phone numbers which the array **phone_num** contains using the code overleaf:

```
for (int counter=0;counter<100;counter++)
    cout << phone_num[counter].name
       << phone_num[counter].tel_number;
```

Note that the dot operator . comes after the subscript which identifies the array-element we want to access.

Structures and bit-fields

Where the range of values which will be held by a variable is small, it is possible to represent that data in a highly compressed form known as a **bit-field**.

To understand the advantages of using bit-fields, imagine that you wish to create a structure to contain a date. Such a structure might look like this:

```
struct date
{
    int day;
    int month;
    int year;
};
```

Since each integer variable requires two bytes, the complete structure **date** requires a total of six bytes.

Using bit-fields permits a much more compact arrangement:

```
struct date
{
    unsigned day : 5;
    unsigned month : 4;
    unsigned year : 7;
};
```

The declaration **unsigned day : 5** means that the data element **day** will be stored as an unsigned integer occupying just 5 bits; similarly **month** will be stored in 4 bits and **year** in 7 bits. Altogether only two bytes (16 bits) will be needed instead of the six bytes which would be required if ordinary integers were used.

You can declare an instance of the **date** structure and access the individual elements of the **date** structure with the dot operator in the usual way as shown on the next page:

```
date today;
today.day=23;
today.month=11;
today.year=91;
cout << today.day << "/" << today.month
   << "/" << today.year;
```

This will output the result **23/11/91**.

Restrictions governing bit fields: The data elements which comprise bit fields are conventionally **unsigned**, and some implementations of both C and C++ insist upon this.

Bit-fields do not have addresses and thus cannot be accessed by means of the **&** operator.

Although bit-fields can save space in memory, accessing them is generally slower than accessing ordinary variables; they should thus probably not be used in cases where speed is essential.

Unions

As we have seen, structures can contain several variables of different types simultaneously. As well as structures, C++ also provides a complex data type called a **union** which is similar to a structure in that it can incorporate variables of several different types, but with the important limitation that it can only hold one type at any given moment.

A union is declared in much the same way as a structure, except that the reserved word **union** replaces **struct**:

```
union example
{
   int i;
   float f;
};
```

This declares a union with the tag-name **example**; it contains one variable **i** of type int and one variable **f** of type float.

Just as with a structure, these variables can be given values using the dot operator as shown on the next page:

```
example sample; // declare an object of type example
cout << "Type in an integer\n";
cin >> sample.i; // input an integer
cout << "\n" << sample.i; // and display it
cout << "\nType in a float\n";
cin >> sample.f; // then input a real number
cout << sample.i; // then display it
```

However, the union **sample** cannot *simultaneously* contain both the floating point value and the integer value. The programmer must keep track of which data element in the union was most recently updated, and then work exclusively with that.

Unions are not described any further in this book.

The story so far

Putting together everything that we have learnt so far about structures, a program to create a new structure **phone_directory** and then use it to input and then immediately output 100 names and telephone numbers would look something like Program 7.1.

Program 7.1

```
#include <stream.hpp>
struct phone_directory
{
   char name[20];
   long int tel_number;
};

main()
{
   phone_directory phone_num[100];
   cout << "Type in a hundred names and numbers\n";
   for (int counter=0;counter<100;counter++)
   cin >> phone_num[counter].name
      >> phone_num[counter].tel_number;
   cout << "Here's the list...\n";
   for (counter=0;counter<100;counter++)
   cout << phone_num[counter].name << " "
      << phone_num[counter].tel_number<< "\n";
}
```

Complex elements in structures

In the structure **phone_directory**, we have used one simple data element – the long int **tel_number** – and one complex element – the character array **name**. In this section we shall look in a little more detail at how to access the individual elements of an array within a structure, and also see how it is possible to nest one structure within another.

Accessing array elements within a structure

The problem of accessing individual array elements in a structure is handled much as you might expect from what you have learned in earlier chapters.

For instance, if we wanted to display the third character of the string array **name** in an object called **first**, we could do so using the idiom

```
cout << first.name[2];
```

The same effect could also be achieved using a pointer; thus if **p1** is a pointer of type char which has been pointed at **first.name** using the code

```
p1=first.name;
```

then the third character of **name** could be output with the command

```
cout << *(p1+2);
```

Nesting structures

It is also possible to nest one structure inside another: that is, for one of the elements in a structure to consist of another structure. This seems confusing and awkward to many beginners, but because it permits simple structures to be 'reused' in more complex ones it can be a very useful way of improving the 'black box' aspect (modularity) of your code.

Let us imagine that in our **phone_directory** example we want to have everyone's first, second and last names instead of the single element **name**. One way to do this would be to rewrite the structure so that it contains three string array elements of suitable length – **first_name**, **second_name** and **third_name** – instead of the single element **name**.

However, we shall assume that we have already devised a suitable structure **full_name** which contains just the three string elements that we need. We can then use the ready-made structure **full_name** as an element inside the structure **phone_directory**.

The way to do this is as follows. First, you will need a suitable **full_name** structure, which might look like this:

```
struct full_name //declare a structure called full_name
{
  char first_name[20]; // these are all elements of
  char second_name[20]; // the structure full_name
  char last_name[20];
};
```

Next, define the structure phone_directory, giving it the data elements **tel_number** of type long int and **name** of type **full_name**. Notice that this allows us to treat our new type **full_name** just like the native C++ type long int. The code for the structure **phone_directory** might then look like this:

```
struct phone_directory
{
  full_name name; // name is an object of type full_name,
      // nested inside type phone_directory
  long int tel_number;
};
```

If you declare **sample** to be an object of the structure **phone_directory**, you can input data into the element **first_name** by using this code:

```
cin >> sample.name.first_name;
```

here we have used the dot operator twice: the first time to access the structure **name**, which is nested inside the structure **phone_directory**; and the second time to access **first_name**, which is an element within **full_name**.

This sort of thing can become quite complicated, and it is easy to become confused. It may help you to remember that the sequence is always from the outer elements towards the inner one; thus we move from **sample**, which is an object of the outer structure, to **name**, which is a data element within that structure, to **first_name**, which is a data element of the inner structure.

Using static elements

When several different objects of a structure are created, each object has its own individual copy of each element which makes up the structure. Thus in Program 7.1, each object had its own **name** and **tel_number**, and each one would normally contain different data. Any change which is made to the **name** element in one object would have no effect on the **name** element of any other object.

It is also possible to create **static elements**, in which case only a single version of that element is available to all the different objects, and any changes which are made to that element will affect its value in every other object. The contents of a static element are thus shared between all the objects.

The code to declare a static element **shared_value** of type int would look like this:

```
static int shared_value;
```

Initialising static elements: Unlike other data elements, static elements can be initialised directly. This is done using code like this:

```
struct sample // declare a struct
{
static int shared_value; // declare a static variable and
}int sample::shared_value=123; // initialise it after the
        // brace using the scope resolution operator
```

A better way of initialising a static element to a particular value is to use this code

```
int sample::shared_value=123;
```

independently of the structure and outside any function, as if it were a global variable. In fact, of course, it is *not* a global variable – its scope is not global but limited to its own structure – which is why the name of the structure and the scope resolution operator :: must be used.

We shall not be using static elements just yet; however, in Chapter Eight we shall show how useful they can be for implementing linked lists and some other data structures.

Structures and functions

Passing individual object elements to functions is very straightforward. The dot-operator is used for this. For instance, to pass the contents of field **tel_number** which is part of the object **first** to a function **funct()**, you would use this code:

```
funct (first.tel_number);
```

Since **tel_number** is of type long int, this is the type of value which **funct()** should expect to receive. Since this is an ordinary pass by value, and the function is working with a copy of the argument rather than with the argument itself, any change which is made within **funct()** will not be reflected in the calling program.

Passing arrays from objects to functions: To pass the character array element **name** to **funct()**, you would pass the array name, which functions as a pointer to the beginning of the array in the usual way:

```
funct (first.name);
```

The function declaration would read:

```
funct (char *p1);
```

where **p1** is a character pointer to the beginning of **first.name**.

Remember that because the address of the beginning of the array **name** has been passed to the function **funct()**, any changes which this function makes to this array will be reflected in the calling program.

Passing object elements by reference Object elements can also be passed by reference. For instance, if **first.tel_number** is to be passed into function **funct()** by reference, the function declaration would look like this:

```
funct (long int &phone_number);
```

Because a pass by reference involves giving the function the address of the argument which is being passed, any changes which are made to the argument in the course of the function will be reflected in the calling program.

Passing complete objects to functions

It is sometimes necessary to pass complete objects to functions. This is done by passing the address of the beginning of the object, rather than by copying over the whole object. You should remember that much the same situation occurs when an array is passed as an argument to a function. Because the address of the object will be passed, the function will be working with the original data rather than with a copy of it.

Imagine that in our telephone number program we have a function **display()** which outputs both the name and telephone number of an object which is passed to it. Such a function might look like this:

```
void display(phone_directory *p1)
{
   cout << (*p1).name << " " << (*p1).tel_number;
}
```

and the object **first** would be passed to it by the line

```
display (&first);
```

There are several things to notice here. The first is that the header line of the function declares a pointer **p1** of type phone_directory.

Secondly, notice the parentheses around the dereferenced pointer before the dot-operator **(*p1).name**.

Third, note that the function call must explicitly pass the address of the object using the address operator **&**. This is an important difference between the way in which structure objects and arrays are passed to a function.

The arrow operator

Actually, few programmers would ever use such a complicated idiom as **(*p1).name** to access an element of an object which has been passed to a function. This is because C++ has a special operator which is intended for this exact purpose. It is usually called the **arrow operator**, and it is made up of a minus sign followed by a 'greater than' symbol, like this: **->**. When this is used, you can dispense with both the dereference and dot operators ***** and **.** as well as with the brackets. The expression **p1->name** has exactly the same effect as **(*p1).name**, and is much easier to read. Our **display()** function would now look like this:

```
void display(phone_directory *p1)
{
   cout << p1->name << " " << p1->tel_number;
}
```

When to use the arrow operator

You can use the arrow operator whenever you have passed a complete object of a structure to a function and you wish to access an individual element of that structure, such as **name** or **tel_number**. You can also use the arrow operator when an object of a structure (or an array of objects) has been created on the heap, because items created on the heap are accessed by means of pointers.

Program 7.2 shows how this would work:

Program 7.2

```
#include <stream.hpp>
struct phone_directory
{
   char name[20];
   long int tel_number;
};
```

```
main()
{
  phone_directory *book = new phone_directory[10];
  phone_directory *p1;
  cout << "Type in ten names and numbers\n";
  for (p1=book;p1<&book[10];p1++)
    cin >> p1->name >> p1->tel_number;
  cout << "Outputting...\n";
  for (p1=book;p1<&book[10];p1++)
    cout << p1->name << " " << p1->tel_number << "\n";
}
```

First of all, a structure **phone_directory** is declared. Then, in **main()**, an array of ten objects of the structure is created on the heap, using the operator **new**. These can be thought of as **book[0]** to **book[9]** respectively.

Then a pointer **p1**, of type **phone_directory**, is created. In the first **for** loop this pointer is stepped through the **book** array, inputting **name** and **tel_number** for a single object on each pass through the loop.

When ten names and numbers have been input, the second for loop resets the pointer **p1** back to the first object; it then steps through the array once more, this time displaying the names and telephone numbers.

Using member functions

Although the system described above works quite well – it is indeed all that is available in C – the fact that structure elements have to be manipulated by means of functions which don't 'belong' to the structure means that the code is often clumsy and difficult to debug and maintain. Fortunately, C++ provides a far better and simpler system of proceeding, based on the concept of **member functions**.

So far, we have thought of a structure merely as a way of gathering together various types of data under a single umbrella. In reality, it is much more than this, for it can include also a set of functions – which we shall refer to as **member functions** – appropriate for use with that structure. Such member functions are sometimes referred to as **methods**.

Using member functions will enable us to access the data elements which form part of the structure **phone_directory** without needing to use code which doesn't belong to the structure.

An additional advantage of using member functions is that the 'black box', or modularity, aspect of our code becomes even stronger. This is because, unlike ordinary functions, member functions don't exist 'outside' the structures to which they belong. This fact makes program construction and maintenance much more straightforward; once you have got a member function to work inside a structure, it will always work because the nature of the structure means it is completely isolated from all the other code that you write.

Adding member functions to a structure

We shall now add simple member functions to our familiar **phone_directory** structure to replace the global input and output functions which we have used up to this point.

The first part of the structure declaration and definition don't change:

```
struct phone_directory
{
    char name[20];
    long int tel_number;
```

With the data elements declared, we can now add prototypes for the member functions; the actual code – the **action section** – will follow later, after the semi-colon which ends the structure definition. (Very short functions can be included in the structure definition in full as **inline** code, but for the purposes of simplicity we shall not do this here). The two prototypes of the two functions will look like this:

```
void get_data(); // this one will input data
void put_data(); // and this one will display it
```

Member functions are very easy to write because there is no need to pass values to them or return values from them, since all member functions have completely free access to the data elements in the structure to which they belong.

This completes the structure definition, so we can round it off with the usual closing brace and semi-colon. The whole thing should look like this:

```
struct phone_directory
{
    char name[20];
    long int tel_number;
    void get_data();
    void put_data();
};
```

Coding the member functions

The next task is to write the action code for the two member functions. The first of them, **get_data()**, might look something like this:

```
void phone_directory::get_data()
{
   cout << "Enter the name\n";
   cin >> name;
   cout << "Enter the phone number\n";
   cin >> tel_number;
}
```

There are a couple of interesting things to notice here. The first is that the function declaration specifies both the structure name **phone_directory** and the function name **get_data()**, separating them with the :: operator. We have met this operator earlier; it is the scope resolution operator, and its function here is to make it clear which structure the function **get_data()** belongs to. After all, you might have several different structures, each one of which has a different **get_data()** member function, and the use of the :: operator preceded by the structure name makes it plain just where each member function belongs.

Because the data elements of a structure have global scope as far as the member functions of that structure are concerned, the member functions can refer freely to those elements without needing to pass any values back and forth.

Another example: The **put_data()** function looks pretty much the same; it is actually even simpler than **get_data()**, since it uses no prompts. A very short function like this is a natural candidate for inline coding, and we shall see later how this would work.

```
void phone_directory::put_data()
{
   cout >> name >> "\n";
   cout >> tel_number >> "\n";
}
```

Putting it together

So far we have created a structure, **phone_directory**, which has two data elements and two member functions. The code for the whole thing should look like this:

```
struct phone_directory
{
   char name[20];
   long int tel_number;
   void get_data();
   void put_data();
};
```

```
void phone_directory::get_data()
{
   cout << "Enter the name\n";
   cin >> name;
   cout << "Enter the phone number\n";
   cin >> tel_number;
}
void phone_directory::put_data()
{
   cout >> name >> "\n";
   cout >> tel_number >> "\n";
}
```

The next task is to write a program that will create a couple of objects of this structure, and then use the member functions to input and output data to these objects. The following is a simple example of such a program:

```
main()
{
   phone_directory first,second; // create two objects
   first.get_data(); // put data in one
   second.get_data(); // and then in the other
   second.put_data(); // and then take it
   first.put_data(); // out of each again
}
```

As you can see, the member functions are called by giving the name of the object you are using, followed by the dot operator . and then the function name.

The entire program would now look like this:

Program 7.3

```
#include <stream.hpp>

struct phone_directory
{
   char name[20];
   long int tel_number;
   void get_data();
   void put_data();
};
void phone_directory::get_data()
```

```
{
   cout << "Enter the name\n";
   cin >> name;
   cout << "Enter the phone number\n";
   cin >> tel_number;
}
void phone_directory::put_data()
{
   cout << name << "\n";
   cout << tel_number << "\n";
}

main()
{
   phone_directory first,second; // create two objects
   first.get_data();
   second.get_data();
   second.put_data();
   first.put_data();
}
```

Making modular code

You can if you wish divide Program 7.3 into sections for separate compilation. The first section, incorporating the structure declaration and definition, is the header file, and this should be stored on disc with the extension .HPP:

```
// save this as PHONE.HPP
struct phone_directory
{
   char name[20];
   long int tel_number;
   void get_data();
   void put_data();
};
```

The second section is the 'action section':

```
// compile this file as PHONE.CPP
#include <stream.hpp>
#include "phone.hpp" // include structure header file
void phone_directory::get_data() // first member function
```

```
{
  cout << "Enter the name\n";
  cin >> name;
  cout << "Enter the phone number\n";
  cin >> tel_number;
}
void phone_directory::put_data() // second member function
{
  cout << name << "\n";
  cout << tel_number << "\n";
}
```

Finally comes the program which actually uses the structure we have set up:

```
// compile this as MAIN.CPP
#include "phone.hpp"
main()
{
  phone_directory first,second;
  first.get_data();
  second.get_data();
  second.put_data();
  first.put_data();
}
```

When you have compiled PHONE.CPP and MAIN.CPP, you can link them together with the BLINK linker with the command

```
BLINK PHONE+MAIN
```

to produce a single .EXE file with the name PHONE.EXE

Accessing heap member functions

When objects of structures are created on the heap of free memory, their member functions are accessed by means of the -> arrow operator. Program 7.4 shows this in detail.

Program 7.4

```
#include <stream.hpp>
struct phone_directory
{
  char name[20];
  long int tel_number;
```

```
      void get_data();
      void put_data();
};
void phone_directory::get_data()
{
   cout << "Enter the name\n";
   cin >> name;
   cout << "Enter the phone number\n";
   cin >> tel_number;
}
void phone_directory::put_data()
{
   cout << name << "\n";
   cout << tel_number << "\n";
}
main()
{
   phone_directory *first = new phone_directory;
   phone_directory *second = new phone_directory;
   first->get_data();
   second->get_data();
   second->put_data();
   first->put_data();
}
```

As you can see, this program differs from Program 7.3 in only two details: the objects **first** and **second** have been created on the heap (by using the **new** operator) instead of on the stack; and their member functions **get_data**() and **put_data**() have been accessed using the arrow operator and the idiom

```
first->get_data();
second->get_data();
```

The rule is very straightforward: when an object has been created on the stack, use the dot operator . to manipulate a member function; when an object has been created on the heap, use the arrow operator -> instead.

Creating objects by reference

You should remember that it is possible to create reference variables on the stack. Objects can be created in just the same way, though not many programmers would trouble to do so.

You should recall that references are in fact addresses, but that they can be treated like ordinary variables; the dereferencing is carried out by the compiler without the dereferencing operator *****. You should also remember that when reference variables are created on the heap, the operator **new** has to be dereferenced, ***new**.

When objects are created as references, the member functions and elements are manipulated using the dot operator **.** instead of the **->** arrow operator. Thus if in Program 7.4, **main()** were rewritten to create **first** and **second** as references on the heap and then access their member functions, it would look like this:

```
main()
{
   phone_directory &first = *new phone_directory;
   phone_directory &second = *new phone_directory;
   first.get_data();
   second.get_data();
   second.put_data();
   first.put_data();
}
```

The compiled code produced by this would look exactly the same as that produced by **main()** in Program 7.4, so there are no advantages to be gained over using this system in place of the more conventional coding of Program 7.4

Using heap storage within a stack structure

One very common way of handling the storage of data elements within a structure which is itself created on the stack is to place at least some of the elements on the heap. If the structure **phone_directory** were to be implemented in this way, it might look like this:

```
struct phone_directory
{
   char *name;
   long int *tel_number;
   void get_data();
   void put_data();
};

void phone_directory::get_data()
{
   name=new char[20];
   tel_number=new long int;
```

```
    cout << "Enter the name\n";
    cin >> name;
    cout << "Enter the phone number\n";
    cin >> *tel_number;
}

void phone_directory::put_data()
{
    cout << name << "\n";
    cout << *tel_number << "\n";
}
```

The code you would write in **main()** would remain exactly the same as it was in Program 7.4, except that the dot operator . would be used to access the member functions instead of the arrow operator **->**.

Heap allocation within a member function

There are a couple of interesting points to notice about the way in which the heap storage has been handled. First, note that the operator **new** is used within the member function in which values are allocated to the elements – in this case **get_data()** – but that both elements are declared as pointers of the appropriate types at the beginning of the structure.

Because C++ treats **name** as a pointer to the beginning of a character array, it is possible to write lines such as

```
cout << name;
```

without using the dereferencing operator *****. However, this operator must be used when accessing the long int element **tel_number**.

Incidentally, note that although the code which we have written allows for the creation of elements on the heap, it doesn't provide any way in which these elements can be deleted when they are no longer needed. This is actually a serious failing, since if structure objects (such as **first** and **second**) go out of scope, the portion of them which exists on the stack will be destroyed, but the portion which has been created on the heap will continue to exist, but will be impossible to access. We shall see later how this particular problem can be very neatly handled using a special function called a **destructor**.

Variable length array storage: An interesting advantage of using the heap to store the data element **name** is that we no longer need to assign a fixed array length of 20 to it. Instead, we can use just as much memory as is necessary, and no more.

This is done by using the library functions **strlen()** and **strcpy()** (from the string.h library) to assign only as much room as is necessary for the name which has been typed in. The string typed in is stored temporarily in **buffer**; its length is calculated by means of the **strlen()** function, and the necessary amount of space is then reserved for **name** on the heap using **new**, and finally the contents of **buffer** are copied into **name** using the **strcpy()** function. **buffer** is a static element; we only need one copy of it, which can then be shared by all the objects of the structure.

This way of allocating space for **name** may seem like a lot of trouble to go to, but most programmers would consider it effort well spent to gain more efficient use of memory.

The code in **get_data()** would then look like this:

```
void phone_directory::get_data()
{
   static char buffer[20];
   cout << "Enter the name\n";
   cin >> buffer; // store the name in buffer
   // reserve the right amount of space
   name=new char[strlen(buffer)+1];
   strcpy(name,buffer); // and then copy buffer into name
   tel_number=new long int;
   cout << "Enter the phone number\n";
   cin >> *tel_number;
}
```

Using inline functions in a structure

You will remember that it often makes sense for very short functions to be declared **inline**. This suggests to the compiler that a new copy of the function should be inserted into the compiled code at every point where that function is called, so that there will be as many copies of the function in the compiled code as there are function calls; this has the advantage of speeding up program execution at the expense (normally) of slightly longer code.

Thus in Chapter Five, we created the inline function **bell()**, using the following code:

```
inline void bell() {printf("\a");}
```

Member functions can also be declared inline; indeed, this is one of the most common uses of the technique. It provides the important advantage that the code is much easier to read and understand.

When a member function is to be implemented inline, the reserved word **inline** is not required. Instead, the opening brace containing the function's code is placed immediately after the brackets containing the argument list (if any).

A simple example: We suggested earlier that the short member function **put_data**() could easily be implemented inline. If this were done, the entire code for the structure **phone_directory** would look like this:

```
struct phone_directory
{
   char name[20];
   long int tel_number;
     // implement get_data() in the usual way -
   void get_data();
     // and implement put_data() inline -
   void put_data() {cout >> name >> "\n"
     >> tel_number >> "\n";}
};

void phone_directory::get_data()
{
   cout << "Enter the name\n";
   cin >> name;
   cout << "Enter the phone number\n";
   cin >> tel_number;
}
```

Introducing constructors and destructors

So far in this chapter we have seen how to create a completely new data type of our own devising, and how to equip it with both its own data elements and member functions.

The data type which we have created – **phone_directory** – still doesn't look very much like the types which are built in to C++, such as int and char, though you will see as you read further on in the book that it is actually possible to create user-defined types which behave in ways which are very similar indeed to the predefined types.

For the moment, remember that there is no need to limit user-defined types to such database-like types as **phone_directory**. For instance, in Chapter Eight we shall devise a special class called **fibonacci**; this type will have permissible values 1, 2, 3, 5, 8 ... in the Fibonacci sequence. Objects of the **fibonacci** class will be restricted to these possible values, in just the same way as variables of type int are restricted to whole-number values.

Other types which you might devise include special types for screen windows; for serial output; for binary coded decimals; for octal numbers; or for dates. The list is virtually endless, and your imagination is the only limit to the range of types that you can create.

Automatic initialisation

It isn't hard to see that it can often be an advantage if certain actions are undertaken when an object of a particular structure is created. This is particularly useful when initial values must be assigned to the data elements which belong to a structure, either by means of direct assignment or by requesting information from the user.

For instance, in our **phone_directory** structure we could automatically collect a name and a telephone number from the user whenever an object of that type is declared. This is clearly a much better way of proceeding than having to call the **get_data**() function explicitly.

Further examples are easy to find. For instance, if we were creating a structure to handle serial output, we might well want to automatically initialise the serial port (or perhaps a modem); or if we were creating a special type of screen window, we might want to automatically save the current screen display to a buffer in memory, thus enabling it to be restored when the window which we are creating is later removed.

Automatic clear-up

As well as automatic initialisation, it can often be helpful to have some sort of automatic clear-up routine which can be invoked when a structure object goes out of scope.

One obvious task which could be carried out by such a clear-up routine would be to free any heap memory which had been allocated by the structure; other possible clear-up tasks include sending a shut-down sequence to the serial port, or any other device, and restoring a screen to its previous appearance after removing a window from it.

In C++, these tasks of automatic initialisation and clear-up are performed by special member-functions known respectively as **constructors** and **destructors**.

Creating a constructor

A constructor is a special type of member function. It differs in only two respects from other member functions: it is called automatically when an object is created, and thus doesn't need to be called explicitly; and it has the same name as the structure of which it is a member.

As with all member functions, it must first be declared within the braces which define all the other member functions and data elements of the structure. The declaration for a constructor in the structure **phone_directory** would look like this:

```
phone_directory();
```

A constructor of this sort, to which no arguments are passed, is called a **default constructor**. It is also possible for one or more arguments to be passed to a constructor, in which case they would be listed in the brackets after the name of the constructor. We shall see some examples of this in later chapters.

If the **phone_directory** constructor is to create the elements **name** and **tel_number** on the heap, and then prompt and input values for both these elements from the console, it would look like this:

```
phone_directory::phone_directory()
{
    static char buffer[20];
    cout << "Enter the name\n";
    cin >> buffer;
    name=new char[strlen(buffer)+1];
    strcpy(name,buffer);
    tel_number=new long int;
    cout << "Enter the phone number\n";
    cin >> *tel_number;
}
```

As you can see, this is identical to the 'heap' version of the function **get_data()** which we met earlier, complete with the facility to reserve only as much heap memory as is necessary for **name**. The only important difference is that whereas **get_data()** had to be called explicitly from **main()** whenever it was necessary to insert values into the elements **name** and **tel_number,** this constructor will be called automatically whenever a new object of the structure **phone_directory** is declared. If an array of structures is created, the constructor will be called once for every element in the array.

Adding a destructor

Having devised a constructor for **phone_directory**, we can now add a destructor. The only purpose of this will be to recover the heap space taken up by **name** and **tel_number**. This is a very typical use of a destructor, but as we have already pointed out, destructors can also be used for any other kind of clear-up operation which may be desirable.

Like the constructor, a destructor must be declared along with the other member variables and the data elements. The declaration would look like this:

```
~phone_directory();
```

Like the constructor, the destructor has the same name as the structure, but in this case it is preceded by the tilde operator ~. You may remember that this operator is used in bitwise operations to signify complementation. Since destruction is the complementary operation to construction, this seems a very apt choice of symbol.

The code for our destructor can be very simple; the only requirement is to reclaim the space on the heap, which can be done with **delete**. However, we shall on this occasion also display a suitable message, just to show that the destructor really has been called successfully. The destructor will look like this:

```
phone_directory::~phone_directory()
{
    delete name;
    delete tel_number;
    cout << "Destructor called\n";
}
```

You should remember that every kind of variable (except for a global variable) goes out of scope when the closing brace which corresponds to the opening brace preceding the declaration of the variable is encountered. Since we have been declaring the objects of **phone_directory** in **main()**, the destructor will be called when the final brace at the end of the program is encountered, as this is the point at which the objects go out of scope.

Deleting arrays of objects: Remember too that when you are deleting arrays of objects which have been created on the heap, you must specify the number of objects to be deleted. The code looks like this:

```
delete [20] objects;
```

where *objects* is the pointer which was returned when the objects were created with **new**.

Return values from constructors and destructors: You may have noticed that although neither constructors nor destructors appear to return any value, they are not preceded by the reserved word **void**.

The reason why **void** is not used is that both constructors and destructors do in fact return a value, but it is implicit rather than explicit. It is in fact the special pointer **this**, which means *the address of the object (structure or class) which I am currently in*.

Although every object of a structure has its own copies of all the data elements (except static elements), only one copy exists of a structure's member functions regardless of how many objects are created. The implicit **this** pointer provides a means by which a member function can know which object of a structure it is dealing with.

It is occasionally necessary to use **this** explicitly, especially when overloading operators, and we shall meet this usage in the following chapters. For the moment, you only need to know that both constructors and destructors *do* return a value, but that you do not need to declare this fact.

Are constructors and destructors really necessary?

Although constructors and destructors are extremely useful, there is no rule that says that they are absolutely necessary. Even where you have used a constructor, it may well not be necessary to use a corresponding destructor, and *vice-versa*.

If a structure needs any form of initialisation – especially if any part of it is created on the heap – then a constructor will probably be necessary. If any kind of tidying up is needed when the structure goes out of scope, and certainly if any part of it exists on the heap, then a destructor will be called for. But you will certainly find that there will be many structures for which neither a constructor nor a destructor are of very much value at all.

Putting it together

Program 7.5 contains the latest version of the telephone directory program.

Program 7.5

```
#include <stream.hpp>
#include <string.h>
struct phone_directory
```

```
{
    char *name;
    long int *tel_number;
    phone_directory();
    ~phone_directory();
    void put_data();
};
phone_directory::phone_directory() // the constructor
{
    static char buffer[20];
    cout << "Enter the name\n";
    cin >> buffer;
    name=new char[strlen(buffer)+1];
    strcpy(name,buffer);
    tel_number=new long int;
    cout << "Enter the phone number\n";
    cin >> *tel_number;
}
phone_directory::~phone_directory() // the destructor
{
    delete name;
    delete tel_number;
    cout << "Destructor called\n";
}
void phone_directory::put_data()
{
    cout << name << "\n";
    cout << *tel_number << "\n";
}
main()
{
    phone_directory sample[10]; // an array of ten objects
        // now output them...
    for (int counter=0;counter<10;counter++)
        sample[counter].put_data();
}
```

In this version of the program, we have used most of the features which we have described earlier in the chapter.

First, we have declared the structure **phone_directory**. This has a constructor, which automatically reserves space on the heap for the string array **name** and the long int **tel number** and then prompts for values for these elements.

We then created an array **sample**, which contains ten objects of type **phone_directory**.

Finally, the contents of the elements **name** and **tel_number** are output by means of the member function **put_data()**.

All manipulation of the elements is carried out by means of member functions. Although this is the preferred technique when working with structures, there will inevitably be cases when this won't be possible, and you can then access the elements directly using the dot and arrow operators.

Overloading constructors

We learned in Chapter Five that it is possible to **overload** functions; that is, two or more functions in the same program can share the same name, provided that they are distinguishable by the number and type of the arguments that are being passed to them. The use of overloaded functions was demonstrated in Program 5.7.

It was suggested in Chapter Five that overloaded functions were most commonly used with constructors, and so in this section we shall explore constructor overloading. We shall meet several more overloaded constructors in the chapters which follow.

So far, we have used only a single constructor, to which no values have been passed by the calling program. Instead, the constructor itself has prompted for the values which are to be given to the various structure data elements.

It would be possible to handle things differently. For instance, we might want to pass appropriate values for the data elements from **main()**, instead of prompting for them to be input.

Because of C++'s ability to overload constructors, it is actually possible to use both techniques in the same program. Program 7.6 shows how this could be done.

Program 7.6

```
#include <stream.hpp>
#include <string.h> // for the strcpy() library function

struct phone_directory
{
char name[20];
   long int tel_number;
   phone_directory();
   phone_directory(char *,long int);
   void put_data();
};
```

```
phone_directory::phone_directory()
{
        // This version of the constructor
        // expects no arguments to be
        // passed to it from main()
    cout << "Enter the name\n";
    cin >> name;
    cout << "Enter the phone number\n";
    cin >> tel_number;
}

phone_directory::phone_directory(char *p1, long int num)
{
        // This constructor expects two arguments
        // (a char pointer and a long int) to
        // be passed to it from main()
    strcpy (name,p1);
    tel_number=num;
}

void phone_directory::put_data()
{
    cout << name < "\n";
    cout << tel_number < "\n";
}

main()
{
    // This will call the first constructor
    phone_directory one;
    // This will call the second constructor
    phone_directory two("Peter",1234567);
    one.put_data();
    two.put_data();
}
```

In Program 7.6, we have created the structure **phone_directory** entirely on the stack. This isn't compulsory if you use overloaded constructors, of course; it might just as well have been created either partly or wholly on the heap.

There are two constructors, which share the same name. The first expects to be passed no arguments from **main()**, and the second expects to be passed a char pointer and a long int.

Notice the way in which we have used the library function **strcpy()** to copy the string from **main()** to the data element **name**. This is necessary because there is no direct way of making one string equal to another in C++.

Destructors are never overloaded: Because no heap storage was used in Program 7.6, and because no other form of clear-up was necessary, no destructor was used (though it would have been possible to use one to display a message, for instance, when the objects went out of scope).

Note that although it is perfectly proper to have overloaded constructors, provided only that their argument lists are sufficiently differentiated for the compiler to be able to decide which to use on any particular occasion, you can never overload a destructor. *A structure can never have more than a single destructor.*

Postscript to Chapter Seven

In this chapter, we have taken our first real steps towards object oriented programming by creating a new data structure, **phone_directory**, which contains both data elements and member functions.

In a C++ structure, the member functions have free access to all the data elements in the structure, without any scoping restrictions. If the data elements are to be manipulated directly from **main()** or from elsewhere in the program, this must be done by means of the dot operator **.** (or the arrow operator **->** if manipulating the elements by means of pointers).

A data element can be declared static, in which case there will be only one copy of it, shared between all the objects of that type. Otherwise, every object has its own copies of all the data elements, so that changes made to an element in one object are not reflected in changes to the contents of that element in other objects.

Constructors and destructors are special member functions. A constructor is called automatically when an object of a particular type is created, and a destructor is automatically called when an object goes out of scope. Typical uses for a constructor are to initialise values within the structure, or to prompt for information from the user; a destructor is most often used to restore the system to its prior condition, which may involve freeing heap memory or closing down an external device.

Constructors can be overloaded, enabling structures to be created in a variety of different ways. Destructors cannot be overloaded.

Exercises to Chapter Seven

1. If you haven't yet entered and run the programs in Chapter Seven, do so now.

2. Define a structure called **books** which will be able to store the following information:

```
book_title
author
publisher
```

3. Write a program which declares an array of 100 **books** and which includes suitable functions (in **main**()) to input and output data.

4. Rewrite the program using member functions.

8

Classes, Structures and Friends

In Chapter Seven we saw how structures can be used to contain both data elements and member functions. They thus go some way to satisfying the first of the requirements of object oriented programming, namely Abstract Data Typing. (The other features are Type Derivation and Polymorphism; we shall deal with these in later chapters.)

However, although C++ structures provide a powerful way of organising data and functions, and are a considerable advance on structures in C, which cannot have member functions but only data elements, they still suffer from some important disadvantages. Most of these can be overcome by using a similar but more advanced form of Abstract Data Typing called a **class**. In this chapter, we shall explore some of the important differences between C++ structures and classes.

Data hiding

The data elements of a C++ structure can be manipulated in either of two quite different ways: either from outside the structure, by means of the dot and arrow operators; or from within it, by means of the member functions.

For instance, if **phone_list** is an object of type **phone_directory** containing the data elements **name** and **tel_number**, then these elements can either be accessed directly from **main()**, using some idiom like **cout << phone_list.name**, or they can be accessed using member functions such as **put_data()**.

We have already seen that in general it is better to use member functions to access data elements rather than to do so directly from **main()**. However, the fact remains that it is still *possible* to access the individual elements from outside a structure, and sometimes this can lead to unwanted results.

The concept of data hiding

It can be beneficial to have some data elements concealed within an abstract data type so that they cannot be either read or altered from outside the type. We shall illustrate this concept by constructing a new abstract data type, **fibonacci**: objects of this type can have any of the values in the Fibonacci sequence 1, 1, 2, 3, 5, 8, 13...

The code for this structure would look like this:

```
#include <stream.hpp>
struct fibonacci
{
   unsigned long int var1, var2, result;
   fibonacci() {var1=0; var2=1; result=var1+var2; }
   void increment() {var1=var2; var2=result;
      result=var1+var2; }
   void display() {cout << result; }
};
```

As you can see, the structure contains three data elements, **var1**, **var2** and **result**, and three member functions. These are the default constructor **fibonacci()**, which initialises the data elements; **increment()**, which calculates the next number in the sequence; and **display()**, which outputs the current number. The code for each of the member functions is very short, and so has been implemented inline. The whole structure bears a very close resemblance to the function **fibon()** which we met in Program 5.2.

A simple test program to generate the first 40 numbers in the Fibonacci sequence might look like this:

```
main()
{
   fibonacci first_num; // declare an object of type fibonacci
   for (int counter=0; counter<40; counter++) {
      first_num.display(); // display a value
      first_num.increment(); // and move on to the next
      cout << "\n";
   }
}
```

The **for** loop will cause the current value of the Fibonacci object **first_num** to be displayed, and the next value calculated. Type the program and the structure into your computer and test them out to be sure that you understand how they work.

Incidentally, if you try to derive Fibonacci values which are much higher than those generated by this program, you will find that the results suffer from overflow error. The Zortech C++ Tools package (included with the C++ Developer's Edition) includes a BCD (Binary Coded Decimal) data type which can handle very large integers, and this could be used if you want to explore larger numbers.

Although the structure **fibonacci** works very well, it suffers from the disadvantage that it can very easily be subverted from its true course. For instance, there is nothing to prevent you (or someone else) from inserting this line in the **for** loop in **main()**:

```
first_num.result=first_num.result+2;
```

Because the reliable operation of **fibonacci** depends on the integrity of all its data elements, such tinkering with any one of them would have a catastrophic effect on the accuracy of the program. Unfortunately, structures provide you with no way of preventing this kind of unauthorised 'breaking and entering'. It is for this reason that some form of data hiding is essential if abstract data types are to be created which aren't susceptible to some form of forced entry.

Data hiding with classes

The answer is to use a different kind of abstract data type, the **class**. C++ classes are very similar to structures – indeed, they are best considered as structures which have special additional features – and all the trappings of structures, such as data elements, member functions, constructors, destructors and so on can be used in classes.

One significant difference between classes and structures is that classes permit data hiding. This is done by placing the reserved word **public** before those member functions and data elements which you wish to be accessible outside the class, and the reserved word **private** before any data or member functions which are to be treated as private to the class. These latter can only be accessed or modified by the member functions. By default any section which is not identified as **public** or **private** is treated as **private**; the sections can be placed in any order, but it is recommended that the **public** section should come first.

Program 8.1 shows how **fibonacci** could be organised as a class rather than as a structure; it includes a simple **main()** to call the public functions **increment()** and **display()**.

Program 8.1

```
#include <stream.hpp>
class fibonacci
{
   public: // accessible outside the class:-
   fibonacci() {var1=0;var2=1;result=var1+var2; }
   void increment() {var1=var2;var2=result;
      result=var1+var2; }
   void display() {cout << result; }
   private: // not accessible from outside
   unsigned long int var1,var2,result;
};

main()
{
   fibonacci first_num;
   for (int counter=0;counter<40;counter++) {
      first_num.display();
      first_num.increment();
      cout << "\n";
   }
}
```

As you can see, this class really does look very much like an ordinary structure. The two most important differences are that it is declared by the reserved word **class** rather than **struct**, and that nothing which is in the **private** section can be altered, or even displayed, except by means of the **public** member functions. Incidentally, note that the reserved words **public** and **private** must be followed by colons : as if they were labels.

Should you now try to place a command such as **first_num.result = first_num.result+2** in **main()**, compilation will fail; data hiding has resulted in objects of type **fibonacci** retaining their integrity despite any attempts that might be made to compromise them.

The copy constructor

One of the aims of object oriented programming is to allow user-created abstract data types to be handled, as far as possible, in the same way as the language's predefined types, such as char and int. We have clearly not yet reached this point with the **fibonacci** class.

For instance, variables of type int, float or char can be set equal to some other variable of the same type, using an assignment statement like this:

```
int a=b;
```

To do this with objects of classes of our own devising it is good practice to include a special kind of constructor called a **copy constructor** or **copy initialiser**; class **fibonacci** already has a constructor, so we are actually overloading that function.

Simplifying slightly, for reasons which will become apparent later, the purpose of a copy constructor is to set all the data elements of the object on the left-hand side of the = operator in an assignment statement to the same value as the object to the right of the = operator.

Coding a copy constructor A copy constructor for class **fibonacci** would look like this if coded inline:

```
fibonacci (fibonacci & p)
   {var1=p.var1;var2=p.var2;result=p.result;}
```

As you can see, **p** is declared as a reference variable of type **fibonacci**; it actually points to the object which occurs to the right of the = operator.

Because copy constructors are usually very short, they can almost always be coded inline. If not, they must be declared (in the **public** section of the class definition) using this idiom:

```
fibonacci (fibonacci &);
```

The code in the action part (after the closing brace of the class) would then look like this:

```
fibonacci::fibonacci (fibonacci & p)
{
   var1=p.var1;
   var2=p.var2;
   result=p.result;
}
```

An example with a copy constructor

Program 8.2 shows how our Fibonacci program would look with a copy constructor. Two objects of type **fibonacci** are declared: **first_num** is declared first, and is used to display the first 20 numbers in the Fibonacci series; then **second_num** is set equal to **first_num** and is used to display the next 20 numbers.

Program 8.2

```cpp
#include <stream.hpp>
class fibonacci
{
   public:
   // ordinary constructor
   fibonacci(){var1=0;var2=1;result=var1+var2;}
   // copy constructor
   fibonacci (fibonacci & p)
   {var1=p.var1;var2=p.var2;result=p.result;}
   void increment()
   {var1=var2;var2=result;result=var1+var2;}
   void display(){cout << result;}
   private:
   unsigned long int var1,var2,result;
};

main()
{
   fibonacci first_num; // this calls the ordinary constructor
   for (int counter=0;counter<20;counter++){
   first_num.display();
   first_num.increment();
   cout << "\n";
   }
   fibonacci second_num=first_num;
          // this calls the copy constructor
   for (counter=0;counter<20;counter++){
      second_num.display();
      second_num.increment();
      cout << "\n";
   }
}
```

A copy constructor may be required even if you don't intend to declare and initialise objects in the same statement; if an object is ever returned from a function, or passed to a function as an argument, then a copy constructor will required, because in both cases a new object is created by reference to an existing one.

It is therefore good practice to include a copy constructor if there is any possibility of the object you have created ever being used in any of the ways described. Remember when you are creating a new class that in years to come, you – or someone else – may decide to use it in ways that go far beyond your present intentions, so it makes sense to incorporate as many possibilities as you can think of in the new class.

The default copy constructor

If you don't include your own copy constructor, then the compiler will create a default copy constructor for you. This will work perfectly satisfactorily in most cases – indeed, Program 8.2 will work if no copy constructor is included – but it can cause problems.

To see why, you need to understand something of how the default copy constructor works. Basically, it sets every data element of the object on the left of the = operator equal to the value of the equivalent data element of the object on the right of the = operator.

Where no pointers are involved, this will work quite satisfactorily. However, where pointers are used, the default copy constructor will set the value of a pointer element on the left of the = operator equal to the equivalent element on the right of the = operator; that is, both pointers will point at the same address.

If this is not what you want, then you will have to write your own copy constructor specifying exactly what value you wish the pointer variables (and the others as well) to take. For instance, you may want to use the library function **strcpy()** to copy a string from one array to another rather than merely point both arrays at the same location in memory as the default copy constructor would do.

Introducing friends

The whole purpose of the **class** construct is to ensure that the private portions of a data structure are immune from unwarranted interference from outside the class. Those data elements of a class which are in the **private** section can only be manipulated (and accessed) by the member functions of the class, thus guaranteeing their integrity. The result of this is that once you get a class to work properly, you can be quite certain that it will *always* work, even in some completely different programming situation. It functions just as a 'black box' ought to function.

There are, however, some disadvantages which result from locking portions of a class away where they can't be reached. For instance, you may at some future date want to modify an existing class to perform some task which wasn't part of your original specification, only to find that you can't achieve this without 'burgling' the private data. This may have serious effects on the integrity of the class.

There is, however, a way around this problem: this is to declare some other class to be a **friend** to the one which you have created. Once this is done, the friend class – but nothing else – can access the private section of the class to which it is a friend. (It is also possible to have friend functions; we shall meet these later in this chapter).

If you think of the private data elements of a C++ class as being surrounded by a wall, a friend class can be thought of as a way of boring a hole through that wall.

It goes without saying that you should exercise a good deal of restraint when creating friends; if you create too many, then once again the integrity of the whole class will be threatened. Indeed, some C++ programmers are unhappy about the whole idea of friends, considering that it imposes unacceptable compromises on the whole concept of data hiding.

Despite this, friends can be very helpful if they are sensibly used, and there are certain circumstances in which they provide a very natural way of solving programming problems. A good general principle is that you should not use friends unless you have a good reason for doing so.

Using friends

It is very easy to make one class a friend of another. For instance, if we wanted to have a class **counter** which was a friend of class **fibonacci** described earlier, this would be done by placing the following statement within the **fibonacci** class definition, like this:

```
friend class counter;
```

It makes no difference where this statement is placed; it can be in either the private or the public part of the class definition. In either case the effect will be the same: member functions of the class **counter** will be able to use the arrow operator -> to manipulate the private data elements of class **fibonacci** without let or hindrance.

Singly linked lists – a worked example of a friend

One situation in which the friend construction can be especially useful is the setting up of the dynamic data structure known as a **singly linked list**. In the next few pages, we shall explore this structure in some detail, and see how useful the friend construct can be.

If you already know how a singly linked list works, you may wish to skip the next section.

Nodes and data

The basic structure of a singly linked list is shown in the following diagram:

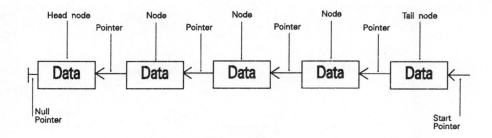

As you can see, the list is made up of a number of **nodes**, each one of which contains both 'ordinary' data – such as a name, a telephone number, or whatever – and a pointer to the address of the next node. The first node to be placed in the list is referred to as the **head**, and the most recent node at any given moment is the **tail**.

It is obviously necessary to mark the head node in such a way as to make it plain that it stands at one end of the list. One conventional way of doing this is to set the pointer of the head node to zero; this is known as a **null pointer**.

When a singly linked list contains more than one node, only the address of the current tail node is directly 'known' to the program; the other nodes (and the data that they contain) can only be reached by 'daisy-chaining' forwards along the list in the direction of the head. Backwards movements – from the head towards the tail – are not possible.

Several variations are possible on this basic theme. One rather elegant scheme requires the head node to have a pointer back to the tail rather than the null pointer outlined above. This creates a **circular list**, in which it is possible to reach every node from every other by moving forwards:

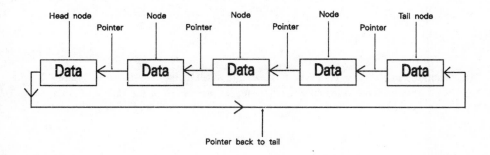

A singly linked list is particularly useful when new nodes will be added only at the tail end of the list, and when deletions also take place from the tail. Such a structure is perfectly adequate for a very large number of applications.

This diagram shows the situation when the list comprises a single node; that is, when the head and the tail are the same:

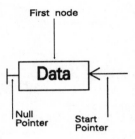

As you can see, the first node contains a null pointer (to show that there are no nodes beyond it in the list), and is itself pointed to by the special pointer **start**.

Adding a new node at the tail end has the effect of 'pushing' the head node further up the list, like this:

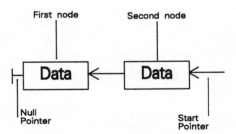

The pointer **start** now points to the new tail, which itself contains a pointer to the head. This process continues as more new nodes are added at the tail of the list:

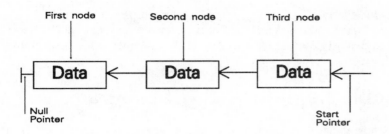

Removing nodes from the tail end is a very simple process; the pointer **start** is reset to point to the next node, and then the memory space which the deleted node occupied is reclaimed using **delete**:

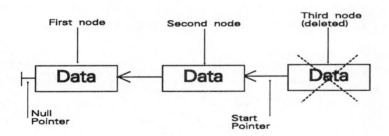

As you can see, because nodes are both added and removed at the tail end of the list, the head node is both the first to be placed in the list and the last node to be removed from it.

Such a list functions, therefore, in exactly the same way as a stack (sometimes known as a Last In, First Out structure, or LIFO for short). Adding a new node at the tail end of the list is the same as Pushing an item onto a data stack, while removing a node from the tail of the list is the same as Popping it off the stack.

About stacks: Stacks provide a very convenient way of storing information when it is necessary to retrieve it in the reverse order from the order in which it was placed on the stack: we shall look at a specific example of this feature later in this chapter.

The traditional way of explaining a stack is to compare it to a pile of plates in a cafeteria, with the additional limitation that plates can only be added or removed one at a time; obviously the last plate to be added to the pile will be the first one to be removed.

A simple singly-linked list program

We shall now create a program which uses a very elementary singly linked list in order to maintain a simple telephone directory. Only the most basic operations are supported; these include adding and removing nodes at the tail end of the list, as well as outputting the contents of the entire list. When you have studied this example, you should find it very simple to modify it to provide a circular list or to add a new node at the head of the list rather than at the tail, or even to create a doubly-linked list, where each node has pointers to the nodes on each side of it.

The node class

Our implementation of the singly linked list requires two classes: **node** and **list**; the first of these looks like this:

```
class node
{
    friend class list;
    node *next;
    char name[20];
    int tel_number;
};
```

As you can see, this class consists of just three data elements: a node pointer **next**, which will contain the address of the next node in the list; and the familiar character array and integer variable to hold a name and telephone number.

The class **node** has no public elements; consequently by default the entire class is private. However, the line **friend class list;** allows an important exception to this rule: objects of class **node** will be accessible to the member functions of class **list**, but not to any other portion of the program.

The list class

The **list** class contains all the member functions which we shall use to manipulate the **node** class. It looks like this:

```
class list
{
   public:
   list(){start=0;}
   ~list();
   void insert();
   void display_all();
   void extract();
   private:
   node *start;
};
```

In contrast to the listing for class **node** which has no public section, class **list** is very much more like a structure than a list, with only one private data element, the pointer to **start**. The rest of the class consists entirely of member functions.

We shall now look at the member functions in detail. As you can see, they comprise a constructor **list()**, and its corresponding destructor **~list()**; and functions to insert, display, and extract single nodes.

The constructor is very simple, and is accordingly defined inline; it merely initialises the pointer **start** to zero when a new object of class **list** is created.

insert(): The **insert()** function is called when a new node is to be added to the list.

The code looks like this:

```
void list::insert()
{
   node *temp;
   temp=new node;
   if (!temp) { // no more room on the heap, so quit
      cout << "Out of space\n";
      return;
   }
   if (!start) { // first node in the list (head node)
      start=temp;
      temp->next=0;
   }
   else{ // not the head node
      temp->next=start;
      start=temp;
   }
```

```
cout << "Name : "; // get the data
cin >> temp->name;
cout << "Phone number : ";
cin >> temp->tel_number;
}
```

insert() begins by checking that there is enough room in the heap to hold **temp**, which is an object of type **node**; if there is not sufficient room, then a suitable message is displayed and the operation is abandoned.

Assuming that sufficient space is available, the function then checks whether the new node will be the first node in the list – that is, whether it will be the head node – by checking whether the pointer **start** is equal to zero; if it is, then this will be the first node.

If this is indeed the first node, then **start** is set to the address of **temp**; then the pointer **next** from class **node** is set to zero.

Note the way in which the arrow operator **->** is used inside class **list** to identify the data elements of class **node**. We have just created a new node on the heap, and have pointed the pointer **temp** at it; we can now access all the data elements of **temp** from inside the friend class **list**.

If the new node is not the first one in the list, then the pointer **next** is set equal to the pointer **start** – which is pointing at the previous tail node; then **start** is reset to point to the node which we have just added. In this way, **start** points to the new tail, and the new tail's **next** pointer is pointed at the address of the previous tail.

The final job of the member function **insert()** is to prompt for and input values for the data elements **name** and **tel_number**. These are both data elements of class **node**, and are consequently accessed by means of the arrow operator **->**.

extract(): The **extract()** function removes the current tail node from the list, resets the pointers, reclaims the heap space, and displays the contents of the node which has been extracted.

The code for **extract()** looks like this:

```
void list::extract()
{
   node *p1,*p2;
   if (!start) { // check that the list isn't already empty
      cout << "\nEmpty list\n";
      return;
   }
```

```
p1=start; // if not, reset the pointer to next node
p2=p1->next;
        // display the values
cout << p1->name << "\n" << p1->tel_number << "\n";
delete p1; // and reclaim the space
start=p2; // then reset pointer start
}
```

The function **extract()** has two pointers to nodes, **p1** and **p2**. Although the nodes themselves are created on the heap, these pointers are automatic variables, created when the function **extract()** is called and going out of scope when it exits.

The first task of function **extract()** is to check whether the list is empty or not. It does this by checking whether the pointer **start** is set to zero; if it is, then the list must be empty and there is nothing for it to do.

If the list is not empty, then pointer **p1** is set to the address of the current tail. Then pointer **p2** is set to the address contained in that node's **next** pointer. This is done by the expression **p2=p1->next;** We need to know the address contained in this pointer – that is, the address of the next node – so that when the current tail node has been removed, we can set the pointer **start** to the address of the next node, which will form the new tail.

With pointers **p1** and **p2** duly set, we can display the values contained in the data elements **name** and **tel_number** of the node which we are extracting.

Finally, the heap space allocated to this node is recovered, using **delete**, and the pointer **start** is set to the address of the next node, which now becomes the tail.

display_all(): The next function is **display_all()**. The purpose of this is to output to the screen all the data contained in all the nodes in the list.

The code for this function looks like this:

```
void list::display_all()
{
   node *cursor=start;
   while(cursor){
      cout << cursor->name << "\n";
      cout << cursor->tel_number << "\n";
      cursor=cursor->next;
   }
}
```

Like **extract()**, **display_all()** makes use of an automatic (local) pointer; we have called it **cursor**. When **display_all()** is called, **cursor** is set to the address of the tail node.

Then the contents of the data elements of that node are displayed, **cursor** is reset to the address contained in the tail node's **next** pointer, and the operation is repeated until the **next** pointer contains a null; this marks the head node, and the function exits.

The destructor: The last of the member functions is the destructor **~list()**; this is automatically called when the list goes out of scope, and its purpose is to reclaim the heap space occupied by the list.

The code for **~list()** looks like this:

```
list::~list()
{
   node *p1,*p2;
   p1=start;
   if (!start) return; // list already empty
   p1=start;
   while(p1){
      p2=p1->next; // daisy-chain along the list
      delete p1; // destroying one node at a time
      p1=p2; // and resetting the pointers
   }
}
```

Just as when we were displaying the contents of all the nodes in the list, we had to begin with the tail node and then 'daisy-chain' along the list, so we must do the same thing when we need to destroy the complete list.

When extracting a node from the list, we needed two automatic (local) pointers in order to keep track of the relevant addresses. Exactly the same situation occurs when we are destroying the complete list, so the function begins by declaring the two pointers **p1** and **p2**.

If the list is already empty – checked in the usual way by seeing whether **start** contains a null value – then we can return without any more ado. Otherwise we shall have to daisy-chain along the list, setting **p1** to the address of the current node and **p2** to the address contained in that node's **next** pointer, then removing the current node from the heap and moving on to the next node. This continues until **next** contains a null value, at which point we must have reached the head of the list.

The complete program

The complete code for classes **node** and **list** is printed as Program 8.3. A simple test program has been added in **main()** to show that everything works properly.

Program 8.3

```
#include <stream.hpp>
class node
{
   friend class list;
   node *next;
   char name[20];
   int tel_number;
};

class list
{
   public:
   list(){start=0;}
   ~list();
   void insert();
   void display_all();
   void extract();
   private:
   node *start;
};

list::~list()
{
   node *p1,*p2;
   if (!start) return;
   p1=start;
   while(p1){
      p2=p1->next;
      delete p1;
      p1=p2;
   }
}

void list::insert()
{
   node *temp;
   temp=new node;
```

```
      if (!temp){
         cout << "Out of space\n";
         return;
      }
      if (!start){
         start=temp;
         temp->next=0;
      }
      else{
         temp->next=start;
         start=temp;
      }
      cout << "Name : ";
      cin >> temp->name;
      cout << "Phone number : ";
      cin >> temp->tel_number;
   }

void list::display_all()
{
   node *cursor=start;
   while(cursor){
      cout << cursor->name << "\n";
      cout << cursor->tel_number << "\n";
      cursor=cursor->next;
   }
}

void list::extract()
{
   node *p1,*p2;
   if (!start){
      cout << "\nEmpty list\n";
      return;
   }
   p1=start;
   p2=p1->next;
   cout << p1->name << "\n" << p1->tel_number << "\n";
   delete p1;
   start=p2;
}

main()
{
```

```
    list mylist;
    mylist.extract();
    mylist.insert();
    mylist.insert();
    mylist.insert();
    mylist.insert();
    mylist.display_all();
    mylist.extract();
    mylist.extract();
    cout << "Two nodes extracted
       - here's the rest of the list:\n";
    mylist.display_all();
}
```

If you are interested in seeing how closely a singly linked list approximates to a stack, you might like to work through Program 8.4, which sets up two classes, **node** and **stack**. As in Program 8.3, the second class is implemented as a friend of the first.

Program 8.4 differs from Program 8.3 chiefly in its greater simplicity, as the only member functions required (apart from the constructor and destructor) are **push()** and **pop()**.

Note that both **push()** and **pop()** return a value. If there is insufficient space for a new node to be added, then **push()** returns a zero; otherwise it returns 1. This makes it very easy for **main()** to check whether or not the stack is full.

pop() returns the value of the item being popped off the stack, or zero if the stack is empty.

main() consists of a simple routine to input a word and then push it onto the stack one character at a time, beginning at the first letter. Then the characters are popped off the stack and displayed on the screen; they are thus output in reverse sequence from that in which they were input, so that typing in *Catastrophe* would result in the output *ehportsataC*.

Program 8.4

```
#include <stream.hpp>
class node
{
    friend class stack;
    node *next;
    char data_item;
};
```

```
class stack
{
   node *start;
   public:
   stack(){start=0;}
   ~stack();
   int push(char a);
   char pop();
};

stack::~stack()
{
   node *p1,*p2;
   if (!start) return;
   p1=start;
   while(p1){
      p2=p1->next;
      delete p1;
      p1=p2;
   }
}

int stack::push(char a)
{
   node *temp;
   temp=new node;
   if (!temp) return 0;
   if (!start){
      start=temp;
      temp->next=0;
   }
   else{
      temp->next=start;
      start=temp;
   }
   temp->data_item=a;
   return 1;
}

char stack::pop()
{
   node *p1,*p2;
   if (!start) return 0;
```

```
    p1=start;
    p2=p1->next;
    delete p1;
    start=p2;
    return p1->data_item;
}

main()
{
    stack mystack;
    char return_value;
    char word[20], *pt;
    cout << "Type in a word\n";
    cin >> word;
    pt=word;
    while (*pt) mystack.push(*pt++);
    cout << "Now backwards ... ";
    for (;;) {
        return_value=mystack.pop();
        if (!return_value) break;
        cout << return_value;
    }
}
```

Friend functions

So far, we have seen how a complete class can become a friend of another class. It is also possible for one or more functions to be declared as a friend of a class. You might want to do this for just the same reason that you might want to create a complete friend class, namely to give limited access to the private data elements of a class without actually adding a member function to the class.

Remember that friend functions, like friend classes, tend to weaken the security of a class; they should therefore only be used where they provide a real benefit in terms of program maintenance or performance.

A simple example

To show how a friend function might be used, we shall first consider a simple class which does not use a friend function, and then rewrite the code to show how a friend function could be applied.

To keep matters simple, we shall create a class **percent**. Objects of this class may contain any positive integer between 0 and 100, and the only operations (functions) which we shall permit are **increment()**, **decrement()** and **display()**; the names of these operations should be self-explanatory.

Class percent: The code for class **percent** looks like this:

```
class percent
{
   public:
   void display () {cout << value; }
   void increment () ;
   void decrement () ;
   percent () {value=0; }
   percent (int a) {value=a; if (value>100 || value<0) value=0; }
   percent (percent &a) {value=a.value; }
   private:
   int value;
};
```

As you can see, the class has only one data element, **value**, and this is private.

There are three constructors. The first allows an object of the class to be declared with the line:

```
percent var_name;
```

which gives the object **var_name** the initial value zero.

The second constructor allows an object to be declared with an initial value, like this:

```
percent var_name(20);
```

In this case, the object **var_name** has the value 20. This constructor contains some simple inline code to make sure that illegal initial values (those above 100 or below 0) are set to zero.

The final constructor is a copy constructor, to allow for declarations such as

```
percent var_name1;
percent var_name2=var_name1;
```

The public section of the class declaration also declares the three member functions which we have already mentioned, **display()**, **increment()** and **decrement()**. The first of these is implemented inline; its only purpose is to output on the screen the value of the private data element **value**.

The other member functions: The code for the other member functions should contain no surprises. Here is **increment()**:

```
void percent::increment()
{
   value++;
   if(value==100)value=0;
}
```

If **value** equals 100, then it is automatically reset to zero.

decrement() looks like this:

```
void percent::decrement()
{
   value--;
   if(value==-1)value=100;
}
```

As you might expect, this is simply the complement of **increment()**. If **value** falls below zero, it is automatically reset to 100.

The complete code: Program 8.5 contains the complete code for class **percent**, together with a simple driver program which you can use to test it.

Program 8.5

```
#include <stream.hpp>
class percent
{
   public:
   percent(){value=0;}
   percent(int a){value=a;if (value>100 || value<0) value=0;}
   percent(percent &a){value=a.value;}
   void display(){cout << value;}
   void increment();
   void decrement();
   private:
   int value;
};

void percent::increment()
{
   value++;
```

```
    if(value==100)value=0;
}

void percent::decrement()
{
    value--;
    if(value==-1)value=100;
}

main()
{
    percent myvalue(90);
    for(int counter=0;counter<20;counter++){
        myvalue.increment();
        myvalue.display();
        cout << "\n";
    }
    percent myvalue2=myvalue;
    for(counter=0;counter<20;counter++){
        myvalue2.decrement();
        myvalue2.display();
        cout << "\n";
    }
}
```

Using a friend function

We shall now approach the same problem in a slightly different way: instead of incorporating the function **display()** into the class as a full member function, we shall instead declare it as a friend function.

It should be explained right away that in this particular case this is an eccentric thing to do, because the code which results is neither more compact nor much easier to understand. We have done it only so that you can see how a friend function works. Later in this chapter, and again in the next, you will see that there are some cases in which friend functions can actually be easier to handle than member functions; but for the moment, please take this on trust.

The class code: As before, we begin with the code for the class **percent**. It now looks like this:

```
class percent
{
    public:
```

```
   int value;
   percent () {value=0;}
   percent (int a) {value=a; if (value>100 || value<0) value=0;}
   percent (percent &a) {value=a.value;}
   friend void display (percent); // this is a friend function
   void increment (); // but the next two are class members
   void decrement (); // in the usual way
   private:
   int value;
};
```

As you can see, there are two important differences in the way in which **display()** is declared: the reserved word **friend** is placed at the beginning of the line; and the argument list is no longer empty, but instead shows that an object of class **percent** will be passed to the function.

This is necessary because a function which is a friend of a class does not 'belong' to that class in the same way as a member function does. Consequently, it does not have automatic access to the data elements of the class in the same way as a member function does.

Instead, the complete class must be passed to the function; its individual data elements can then be accessed using the dot operator.

Apart from the fact that **display()** is treated as a friend function, the implementation of the class is identical to that printed in Program 8.5.

Declaring the friend function: The next step is to declare the friend function; this looks much like any other function declaration:

```
void display (percent);
```

The function definition: The friend function **display()** is then defined. It looks like this:

```
void display (percent a)
{
   cout << a.value;
}
```

The class which is passed to the friend function is identified as **a**, and its data element **value** is therefore accessed by means of the idiom **a.value**.

Remember that because **display()** is now a friend of class **percent** rather than a member of that class, it cannot be called from **main()** with the line

```
myvalue.display(); // this won't work
```

Instead, you must pass the complete class to the function like this:

```
display(object_name);
```

where *object_name* is the name of the object you are passing to the function. This is much more like an ordinary function call than we have so far seen when using classes.

Program 8.6 shows how the new implementation of the class **percent** would look; the driver **main()** produces the same output as it does in Program 8.5.

Program 8.6

```
#include <stream.hpp>
class percent
{
   public:
   percent() {value=0;}
   percent (int a) {value=a; if (value>100 || value<0) value=0;}
   percent(percent &a) {value=a.value;}
   friend void display(percent);
   void increment();
   void decrement();
   private:
   int value;
};

void percent::increment()
{
   value++;
   if(value>100) value=0;
}
```

```
void percent::decrement()
{
   value--;
   if(value<0)value=100;
}

void display(percent a)
{
   cout << a.value;
}

main()
{
   percent myvalue(90);
   for(int counter=0;counter<20;counter++){
      myvalue.increment();
      display(myvalue);
      cout << "\n";
   }
   percent myvalue2=myvalue;
   for(counter=0;counter<20;counter++){
      myvalue2.decrement();
      display(myvalue2);
      cout << "\n";
   }

}
```

Other uses for friend functions

As we have already suggested, implementing **display()** as a friend function rather than as a member of class **percent** is probably not a very sensible thing to do. However, there are some cases where using a friend function can actually simplify your code.

Friends as bridges between classes

We have already seen that it is possible to nest one structure within another; this is how we nested a complete **name** structure inside the **phone_directory** structure in Chapter Seven. It is possible to nest classes in just the same way.

An alternative is to leave the two classes 'un-nested', but to use a function which is a friend of both classes – and which therefore has privileged access to the private data elements of both classes – to function as a bridge from one class to the other.

A simple example of a bridge

Meaningful examples of using friend functions as bridges tend to be rather lengthy, and their length can obscure the way in which they work. The following (admittedly artificial) example is about as brief as it is possible to be.

The two classes: We shall begin by creating two classes, **first** and **second**. Each of these consists of a single private data element – **first_element** in class **first** and **second_element** in **second**. There is also a function **bridge()** which is a friend to both classes, and by which we can display the private elements of both classes on the screen.

Defining the classes: The code for **first** looks like this:

```
class first
{
   int first_value; // only one data element
   first(int i){first_value=i;} // a simple inline constructor
   // declaring the bridge function
   friend void bridge(first,second);
};
```

second is almost exactly the same:

```
class second
{
   int second_value;
   second(int i){second_value=i;}
   friend void bridge(first,second);
};
```

Both classes have a simple constructor, allowing a value for the private data elements to be passed from **main()** when objects are declared.

The bridge() function: Because **bridge()** is to be a friend of both classes, the names of both classes must appear in the argument list in the function declaration.

The code for **bridge()** looks like this:

```
void bridge(first one,second two)
{
   cout << "Private elements of both classes are accessible
     from here\n";
   cout << one.first_value << " " << two.second_value << "\n";
}
```

This function has direct access to the private data elements of both the classes which have been passed to it as arguments. When it is called, it makes its own local copy of each class object, and the elements of those copies are freely accessible to it. Remember, however, that any modifications which the function might make to those local elements will not be reflected in the original classes.

Advance declaration: So far, there is nothing very surprising or startling about any of the code. However, there is one important point which needs to be borne in mind: when the compiler first looks at class **first**, it will see that it includes a reference – in the **bridge()** function argument list – to something called **second**. However, at this stage the compiler has not yet encountered **second**, which will be declared *after* **first**.

To prevent an error, we must make sure that the compiler already has some information about class **second** before it meets it in the function argument list. Obviously it would not be helpful to put class **second** before **first** in our code, because this would not resolve the ambiguity: the compiler would then encounter the name **first** in the argument list before that class had been declared, and we would be no further ahead.

The solution is to make an advance declaration (only) of the class **second** *before* any mention of it is made in the function argument list. This will ensure that the compiler already knows about it – and knows, specifically, that it is a class rather than an ordinary variable, for instance – before it encounters it as an argument.

To do this, it is only necessary to place the following class declaration above the declaration of class **first**:

```
class second;
```

The complete code for our program, including a simple **main()** to drive it, now looks like Program 8.7.

Program 8.7

```
#include <stream.hpp>
class second; // advance declaration

class first
{
   int first_value;
   public:
   first(int i){first_value=i;} // constructor
   friend void bridge(first,second); // friend function
};
```

```
class second
{
   int second_value;
   public:
   second(int i){second_value=i;}
   friend void bridge(first,second);
};

void bridge(first one,second two)
{
   cout << "Private elements of both classes are
      accessible from here\n";
   cout << one.first_value << " " << two.second_value << "\n";
}

main()
{
   first example1(5); // an object of class first
   second example2(20); // and of class second
   bridge(example1,example2); // then call bridge()
}
```

Modifying private data with a friend function

Although in the last example the friend function **bridge()** was shared by both classes, and could accordingly display private data elements from both, it was not capable of modifying these private elements for the simple reason that modifications made locally in a function are not carried back to the classes when the function ends.

It is, however, possible to get around this by using reference variables. You will remember that when this is done, local copies of variables (and classes) are not made; instead, a pointer to the address of the original variable (or class) is passed, so that any changes made in the course of the function are 'remembered' even after the function has ended.

Accordingly, it is possible – though rather naughty – to alter the value of the private data elements of a class by means of a friend function and a call by reference. You should not do this unless you know why you are doing it, because it flies in the face of all the principles of data hiding: for the contents of a private data element to be accessed by a member function is one thing; for it to be not only accessed but deliberately changed by a mere friend function is quite a different kettle of fish.

Despite these warnings, this is probably the best way to pass values from the private elements of one class to the private elements of a different class, using a function which is a friend of both classes.

Program 8.8 takes the joint-friend concept illustrated in Program 8.7 and extends it. Once again there are two classes, **first** and **second**, and a function **bridge()** which is a friend to both classes. However, this time the purpose of **bridge()** is to take the contents of the data element **first_value** from class **first** and to transfer it to **second_value** in class **second**.

Program 8.8

```
#include <stream.hpp>

class second;

class first
{
   int first_value;
   friend void bridge(first&,second&);
   public:
   first(int i){first_value=i;}
};

class second
{
   int second_value;
   friend void bridge(first&,second&);
   public:
   void display(){cout << second_value << "\n";}
};

void bridge(first &one,second &two)
{
   two.second_value=one.first_value;
}

main()
{
   first example1(10);
   second example2;
   bridge(example1,example2);
   example2.display();
}
```

Remember that the technique described here is not intended to become a regular part of your repertoire! Indeed, the reason why it has not been described in more detail is that you should only use it if you completely understand it; the advantages of data hiding offered by C++ classes are so great that you should think long and carefully before subverting them as drastically as we have shown here.

Postscript to Chapter Eight

In this chapter, we have seen how to overcome the chief disadvantage of structures, namely the fact that all the data elements are freely available outside the structures themselves; this makes them vulnerable to accidental alteration resulting from careless programming.

C++ offers a system of data hiding based on classes rather than structures. The private elements of a class cannot be accessed from outside the class; however, they can be manipulated by member functions of the class. This ensures that the only operations which can be performed on the data elements of a class are those which are designed into that class.

Some relaxation of this rule is permitted by the use of friends. Friends can either be classes or functions. In both cases, they have access to the private section of the class of which they are friends.

Friend classes provide the simplest way of manipulating various kinds of dynamic data structures such as linked lists and stacks. Friend functions make it possible to access private data elements from more than one class, or even to interchange the values of private elements between classes.

It is never absolutely necessary to use friends; the same effects can always be achieved by other means. However, there is no reason not to use friends when they make your code easier to debug and maintain, or when they result in shorter or faster-operating code.

Exercises to Chapter Eight

1. If you haven't yet entered and run the programs in Chapter Eight, do so now.

2. Rewrite the **books** structure from the exercises at the end of Chapter Seven using a class instead of a structure and incorporate an array of 100 **books** in a simple program.

3. Rewrite the **books** program to use a singly-linked list instead of an array.

4. Create a doubly-linked list instead of a singly-linked list.

9

Overloading Operators

We have already seen that one of the major advantages of an object oriented programming language such as C++ is the ability it gives the user to create new abstract data types, and then to handle these in similar ways to the types which are already built in to the language. One of the mechanisms by which this is performed is data hiding, which we met in Chapter Eight. In this chapter we shall meet another mechanism which goes even further than data hiding in enabling us to handle our new abstract data types just as if they were built in to the language in the same way as native types such as long, char and int.

Introducing operator overloading

The mechanism by which this is done is called **operator overloading**. A brief example will show what is meant by this term, and how useful it can be.

In Chapter Eight we created a class **fibonacci**, which could be used to display numbers in the Fibonacci sequence. The class had three private data elements, **var1**, **var2** and **result**, and public functions **display()** – to output the current value of **result** – and **increment ()** – to calculate the next value in the Fibonacci sequence. The code of the class is reproduced here for convenience:

```
class fibonacci
{
   public:
   fibonacci(){var1=0;var2=1;result=var1+var2;}
   fibonacci (fibonacci & p)
      {var1=p.var1;var2=p.var2;result=p.result;}
```

```
increment(){var1=var2;var2=result;result=var1+var2;}
void display(){cout << result;}
private:
unsigned long int var1,var2,result;
};
```

To calculate the next value in the sequence, **main()** had to operate through the public member function **increment()**; another way of expressing this would be to say that the 'message' **increment()** is sent to an object of class **fibonacci**.

Although this works perfectly well, it is certainly different from the way in which instances of such built in classes as int would be incremented; there, the operator ++ would be used instead of a function.

The purpose of operator overloading is to allow the meaning of ++ and the other operators which already exist in C++ to be extended so that they can be applied to types which we have created as well as to those which already exist in the language.

For instance, imagine that we have created a class of binary coded decimal (BCD) numbers which can contain an integer of perhaps 50 or more digits without suffering from any rounding error. (Such a class in fact forms part of the Zortech C++ Tools package which is supplied with the Developer's Edition). With operator overloading it would be possible to write code like this:

```
bcd first_big_num,second_big_num; // create two bcds
// initialise them
first_big_num=123456789;second_big_num=987654321;
bcd third_big_num; // another bcd
// do some arithmetic
third_big_num=first_big_num+second_big_num;
```

In other words, we would be able to extend the use of the + operator to work on the new **bcd** class in addition to its inbuilt use with ints, floats and the like. The whole thing would look so natural that a newcomer to C++ might well assume that binary coded decimals were a regular part of the language.

Why overloading?

We have already seen that it is possible for C++ functions to be overloaded: that is, for several functions to share the same name, but to expect different types or numbers of arguments to be passed to them. This facility is most frequently used with constructors, so that an object can be initialised in any of a variety of different ways. Operator overloading merely takes this concept and applies it to the arithmetic and logic operators, so operators such as −, + or * can be used with both the native and the new abstract data types.

Some form of operator overloading is actually built in to every high level computer language. For instance, in Basic the operator + can be used to carry out three quite different operations: adding integers; adding real numbers; and concatenating (joining) strings.

Most Basic programmers would concede that there is a significant difference between 'adding' real numbers and 'adding' (concatenating) strings. They would probably not realise that there is also a significant difference between adding real numbers and adding integers: to add together two integers requires just one machine code instruction; to add together two real numbers can require 70 or more machine code instructions. Clearly the two operations are really radically different; they merely appear similar to the programmer because the same operator + is used in both cases. In other words, it is overloaded.

Where C++ differs from other languages is that it opens the way for the programmer to overload operators for abstract data types. The result can be to create code which is much easier to read and debug; unfortunately, if due care is not taken, it can also create confusion and annoyance.

A simple example

Before examining the rules of operator overloading in any detail, we shall first look at a simple example, using the class **fibonacci** described above. We want to replace the function **increment()** with an overloaded operator ++.

Operator overloading is accomplished by means of a special kind of function; this can either be a member function of the appropriate class or a friend of that class. (We shall see later that there are rules about when it is best to use one of these forms rather than the other, but we can ignore these for the moment.)

The first step is to declare an appropriate function as a member of class **fibonacci**. The declaration should look like this:

```
void operator++();
```

Note the use of the reserved word **operator**, immediately followed (no spaces) by the operator which is being overloaded – in this case ++. Because we are creating a member function which has privileged access to the private data elements of the class, the argument list is empty, and no value is returned.

We can now define the function in the action section of the code as usual. It should look like this:

```
void fibonacci::operator++()
{
    var1=var2;var2=result;result=var1+var2;
}
```

If you look back to the beginning of this chapter, you will see that the code between the braces is exactly the same as that which was used in the **increment()** function. However, if an object of the class called **first_num** were created, it would now be possible to calculate the next value in the sequence for that object by using the command

```
first_num++;
```

Program 9.1 presents the program as amended, using the overloaded ++ operator. It is identical to the program outlined above, except that the overloaded operator function **operator++()** has been coded inline to save space and time. Type it in and verify for yourself that it does work.

Program 9.1

```
#include <stream.hpp>
class fibonacci
{
    public:
    fibonacci(){var1=0;var2=1;result=var1+var2;}
    fibonacci (fibonacci & p)
        {var1=p.var1;var2=p.var2;result=p.result;}
    void operator++()
        {var1=var2;var2=result;result=var1+var2;}
    void display(){cout << result;}
    private:
    unsigned long int var1,var2,result;
};

main()
{
    fibonacci first_num;
    for (int counter=0;counter<20;counter++){
        first_num.display();
        first_num++;
        cout << "\n";
    }
```

```
fibonacci second_num=first_num;
for (counter=0;counter<20;counter++){
   second_num.display();
   second_num++;
   cout << "\n";
}
}
```

Using a friend function

It would also be possible to code the **operator++()** function as a friend of class **fibonacci**. Remember that friend functions do not have the same automatic access to class data elements as do member functions, and that arguments therefore must be explicitly passed to them.

Because the whole purpose of an overloaded operator function is to modify one or more values in the class to which it is a friend, it also follows that some way must be found of modifying those values in the original class, rather than in the local copy of that class which the friend function will otherwise create.

This is similar to the problem we faced at the end of Chapter Eight when we allowed a friend function to pass values from the private portion of one class to the private portion of another. There we used the pass by reference technique to pass the address of the class object rather than to make a local copy of it, and we can use the same method here; the data elements will then be manipulated by means of the dot operator . in the usual way.

The declaration of the friend function inside class **fibonacci** should look like this:

```
friend void operator++(fibonacci&);
```

The action portion of the code will look like this:

```
void operator++(fibonacci &a)
{
   a.var1=a.var2;
   a.var2=a.result;
   a.result=a.var1+a.var2;
}
```

As you can see, the code is very similar to that used in the member function, except for the need to pass an explicit reference to the class and then modify the data elements by means of the . dot operator. The complete code for this version of the program would look like the listing overleaf:

Program 9.2

```
#include <stream.hpp>
class fibonacci
{
   public:
   fibonacci(){var1=0;var2=1;result=var1+var2;}
   fibonacci (fibonacci &p)
      {var1=p.var1;var2=p.var2;result=p.result;}
   friend void operator++(fibonacci&);
   void display(){cout << result;}
   private:
   unsigned long int var1,var2,result;
};

void operator++(fibonacci &a)
{
   a.var1=a.var2;
   a.var2=a.result;
   a.result=a.var1+a.var2;
}

main()
{
   fibonacci first_num;
   for (int counter=0;counter<20;counter++){
      first_num.display();
      first_num++;
      cout << "\n";
   }
   fibonacci second_num=first_num;
   for (counter=0;counter<20;counter++){
      second_num.display();
      second_num++;
      cout << "\n";
   }
}
```

If you compare the versions of **main**() in programs 9.1 and 9.2, you will see that they are identical. As far as the user is concerned, it makes no difference whether you use a friend function or a member function when an overloaded operator is used.

Some rules for overloaded operators

When you have read as far as this, you may be thinking to yourself that overloaded operators are pretty simple. Although this is essentially true, the basic simplicity is overlaid by a series of rules which you need to know before you can use overloaded operators with impunity. Like some other things in C++, they are not quite as easy to use as they appear to be at first sight!

Rule 1 – Only operators that already exist can be used.

C++ offers a very wide range of operators, including several that you might not think of as operators at all such as () and **new**. Almost all of these operators can be overloaded, but you can't create brand new operators of your own such as **$** or **@**.

Rule 2 – You can't change an operator's 'template'.

Every C++ operator comes with its own 'template' which defines certain aspects of its use, such as whether it is a binary or a unary operator, its place in order of precedence, and the like. This template is fixed and can't be altered by overloading. Thus ++ and -- can never be other than unary operators.

The unary operators which can be overloaded are these:

        ++   --   !   ~

The following operators can be overloaded in either a binary or a unary sense (or both):

        +   -   &   *

Incidentally, you should note that one useful feature of the ++ and -- operators is lost during overloading: the distinction between suffixed and affixed operators (as in **abc++** and **++abc**) does not carry through to their overloaded use. Thus in **main()** in Programs 9.1 and 9.2, there is no difference between writing **fibonacci++** and **++fibonacci**.

Rule 3 – Operators can only be overloaded when used with abstract data classes.

It isn't possible to redefine an operator in a situation where no user defined classes are involved. For instance, although you can extend the use of the ++ operator to cover objects of new classes such as **fibonacci**, you can't change the way in which ++ works with integers.

This is obviously a sensible restriction, as otherwise it would be all too easy to reduce any code to total incomprehensibility by forcing such common operators as + and – to behave in new and unnatural ways.

From this rule follows something else which isn't an actual rule but which you should always remember: *never give an overloaded operator a meaning which is radically different from its natural meaning.* For instance, although it would be quite possible to overload the – operator so that it could be used to perform addition on objects of your own classes instead of subtraction, this would obviously be a very foolish thing to do because it would render the resulting code unreadable.

Where no specific operator exists in C++ to cover the operation which you envisage, try to use an operator which makes 'metaphorical' sense; for instance, if you want to overload an operator to concatenate two strings, you might reasonably choose the + operator, as there is a conceptual similarity between adding two numbers and 'adding' two strings. This is, indeed, exactly the basis on which Basic uses the + operator to concatenate strings, as mentioned earlier.

Rule 4 – Unary operators overloaded by means of a member function take no explicit arguments and return no explicit values; unary operators overloaded by means of a friend function take one reference argument, namely the name of the relevant class.

Actually, when a unary operator is overloaded by means of a member function, an implicit value is passed to it; it is **this**, which is a pointer to the current object.

If you look back at the code of Programs 9.1 and 9.2 you should be able to gain a clear picture of how unary operators can be overloaded.

Overloading binary operators

The rules outlined above are the only ones you need to bother about when overloading unary operators. Although overloading binary operators involves essentially the same process, there are some subtle and important differences. To see what these are, we shall begin by developing some simple overloaded binary operators for class **percent** which we created in Chapter Eight (Program 8.5); then we shall develop some more rules to cover overloading binary operators.

For convenience we shall reprint Program 8.5 here as Program 9.3:

Program 9.3

```
#include <stream.hpp>
class percent
{
   public:
   percent(){value=0;}
   percent(int a){value=a;if (value>100 || value<0) value=0;}
   percent(percent &a){value=a.value;}
```

```
  void display(){cout << value;}
  void increment();
  void decrement();
  private:
  int value;
};

void percent::increment()
{
  value++;
  if(value==100)value=0;
}

void percent::decrement()
{
  value--;
  if(value==-1)value=100;
}

main()
{
  percent myvalue(90);
  for(int counter=0;counter<20;counter++){
    myvalue.increment();
    myvalue.display();
    cout << "\n";
  }
  percent myvalue2=myvalue;
  for(counter=0;counter<20;counter++){
    myvalue2.decrement();
    myvalue2.display();
    cout << "\n";
  }
}
```

The reason for working with class **percent** is that it will be possible to develop a very large number of overloaded operators for it, involving both operations with other members of the same class and integers. Such diversity is neither possible nor desirable with some classes, and you should certainly not assume that such a full set of operators should be provided for every user-defined class which you create; but in the context of showing how overloaded operators work, the **percent** class should demonstrate something of what is possible.

We shall assume that we wish to add two overloaded binary operators to the **percent** class: += and –=; the purpose of these will be to make it possible to add ordinary integers to objects of class **percent** or to subtract integers from such objects.

For the moment we shan't bother to overload the ++ and -- operators to replace the existing **increment()** and **decrement()** functions; this is straightforward, and if you have followed the discussion above on overloading unary operators you should be able to do this on your own.

Overloading a binary operator as a member function

We shall begin by overloading the += operator as a member function of class **percent**. (Remember that += is a single operator, and not an amalgam of two operators.)

The declaration of the function to overload this operator should look like this:

```
void operator+=(int);
```

Note that although we are dealing with a binary operator, we only pass one argument to it, and that this is the value which comes to the *right* of the operator. The value to the left of the operator is supplied implicitly; it is **this** – that is, the current object.

The action part of the code The action part of the code is very simple; here it is:

```
void percent::operator+=(int a)
{
   value+=a;
}
```

When the function **operator+=()** is called, the integer value which is to be added to the data element **value** in the class object is copied into the local variable **a**. (It would also be possible to pass the value by reference, and this would save a little memory space while the program is running.)

Then the value contained in **a** is added to the data element **value** and the function ends.

The code for **operator–=()** is very similar:

```
void percent::operator-=(int a)
{
   value-=a;
}
```

The code for the entire class, together with a simple driver program, is printed as Program 9.4.

Program 9.4

```
#include <stream.hpp>
class percent
{
   public:
   percent(){value=0;}
   percent(int a){value=a;if (value>100 || value<0) value=0;}
   percent(percent &a){value=a.value;}
   void display(){cout << value;}
   void increment();
   void decrement();
   void operator+=(int);
   void operator-=(int);
   private:
   int value;
};

void percent::increment()
{
   value++;
   if(value==100)value=0;
}

void percent::decrement()
{
   value--;
   if(value==-1)value=100;
}

void percent::operator+=(int a)
{
   value+=a;
}

void percent::operator-=(int a)
{
   value-=a;
}

main()
```

```
{
   percent myvalue(40);
   myvalue+=20;
   myvalue.display();
   cout << "\n";
   myvalue-=15;
   myvalue.display();
}
```

A source of confusion Something which newcomers to operator overloading frequently find confusing is that the operator which they are overloading may be used in its 'original' sense in the course of the very function which serves to overload it.

A typical example of this occurs in the += and −= examples given above. In the function header, the line

```
void percent::operator+=(int a)
```

uses the operator in what will be its overloaded sense: that is, to allow an integer value to be added to an object of class **percent**.

In the body of the function, the line

```
value+=a;
```

uses the same operator, but in its original sense: to add the value of integer variable **a** to the integer element **value**.

You may find that it helps to avoid confusion if you remember that the overloaded operator still carries its original meaning in every situation except the one for which it has been overloaded, and that this includes the body of the function in which the overloading is carried out.

Overloading the += and −= operators using friend functions

The += and −= operators can also be overloaded using friend functions rather than member functions.

Friend functions used in overloading binary operators must be explicitly passed two arguments instead of one: both the argument to the right and to the left of the operator must be passed. It's not possible with a friend function to let **this** refer to the argument to the left of the operator.

The declaration of the friend function **operator+=()** would look like this:

```
friend void operator+=(percent &, int);
```

and the actual function code would be like this:

```
void operator+=(percent &a,int b)
{
   a.value+=b;
}
```

Note that the first argument – the class **percent** itself – *must* be passed by reference. This is because we want to modify the original value stored in the member variable **value** rather than just the local copy of that variable.

Which technique is best? When overloading most operators, it makes little difference whether you choose to use member functions or friend functions. Member functions are perhaps a little easier to use – since it is only necessary to pass a single argument rather than the two needed with friend functions – but basically the choice is almost always a matter of personal preference.

However, there are certain cases when the use of friend functions is essential; we shall meet these later in this chapter.

Whichever technique you use, the code in **main()** which actually makes use of the overloaded operators will be exactly the same in both cases.

We can now state what we have learned as another formal Rule:

Rule 5 – Binary operators overloaded by means of a member function take one explicit argument; binary operators overloaded by means of a friend function take two explicit reference arguments.

Other binary operators

So far, we have concentrated on the += and –= operators because they are actually a little easier to handle than most of the other binary operators. The reason for this is that it is permissible – indeed, it is obligatory – for the argument on the left of these operators to be modified by the arithmetic which they perform. This is emphatically not the case with other binary operators such as +, – and =.

Consider the expression **num1+=num2**, where **num1** and **num2** are either integer variables or some other type for which this is a permissible operation. The command has the effect of taking the original value contained in **num1**, adding the value of **num2** to it, and then storing the new value back in **num1**.

This is completely different from the expression **num1+num2**, where the contents of neither **num1** nor **num2** are changed by the addition. Be sure that you understand this point, or you will not see why the code for overloading the + operator must be quite different from the code for overloading +=.

Rule 6 – Binary arithmetic operators such as +, –, * and / must explicitly return a value; they must not change their own arguments.

Overloading + and – as member functions

We shall begin by overloading the + and – operators as member functions of class **percent**.

The declaration of the **operator** +() function would look like this:

```
percent operator+(int);
```

and the action part of the class would read like this:

```
percent percent::operator+(int a)
{
   percent b;
   b.value=value+a;
   return b;
}
```

You will see that – as in the member function version of overloading the += operator – only a single argument has to be explicitly passed to the function, and that this is the argument which is placed on the right of the overloaded + operator. The implicit argument to the left of the operator is once more the pointer **this**.

The data element **value** of the argument to the left of the function – the current object – can be directly accessed by the member function.

An important distinction between the previous **operator+=()** function and the present **operator+()** function is that the latter must explicitly return a value – that is, a class member – and that this value must be different from either of the two arguments (implicit or explicit) which were passed to the function. This is because, as mentioned earlier, the arguments of the + operator should not themselves be altered by the addition operation.

The solution is to create an automatic member of class percent within the **operator+()** function, and then to return this at the end of the function.

The operator–() function: The member function to overload the – operator is substantially the same as that used to overload the + operator. The declaration looks like this:

```
percent operator-(int);
```

Here is the action part of the code:

```
percent percent::operator-(int a)
{
   percent b;
   b.value=value-a;
   return b;
}
```

Note that both the **operator+()** and **operator-()** functions as we have specified them so far expect that the implicit argument (to the left of the operator) will be a member of class **percent**, and that the explicit argument (to the right of the operator) will be an integer.

In other words, we can at present use expressions of the form **score+12** or **score-54**, where **score** is an object of class **percent**; but we cannot yet use an expression of the form **score1+score2** – where both arguments are objects of class **percent** – nor one of the form **12+score**, where the order of the arguments is different from that stated in the function declaration.

When both arguments are in the same class

Where the arguments on both the left side (implicit) and the right side (explicit) of the binary operator which is being overloaded are members of the same class, it is a trivial matter to devise a new member function to cope with the situation. The declaration for a suitable function for the – operator would look like this:

```
percent operator-(percent &);
```

and the action part of the code would look like this:

```
percent percent::operator-(percent &a)
{
   percent b;
   b.value=value-a.value;
   return b;
}
```

The function to overload the + operator would obviously work in the same general way.

Because we are creating several different **operator+()** and **operator–()** functions to accept different types of argument, we are in effect overloading the functions by which the operator overloading is performed. Note that when overloaded functions are used to overload operators, it is not necessary to use the reserved word **overload**.

Overloading the = operator

Before we can use the newly overloaded + and – operators in complex expressions such as **score1=score2+score3–score4+13** (where **score1**, **score2**, **score3** and **score4** are all members of class percent) we must overload the = operator. This is a little more complicated than the code for overloading the + and – operators, but not much.

The declaration for the function **operator=()** looks like this:

```
percent operator=(percent &);
```

and the action part of the code looks like this:

```
percent percent::operator=(percent &a)
{
   value=a.value;
   return *this;
}
```

As with the other binary operators where the overloading is implemented by means of member functions, only one value is passed explicitly to the function: this is the value to the right of the operator which is being overloaded. The value to the left of the operator is the implicit pointer **this**.

We want the = operator to have the effect of making the value of the argument on its left equal to the value of the argument on its right, and we can do this by returning the amended value of the current object, which is pointed to by **this**. However, because **this** is a pointer rather than a value, we must dereference it by means of the * operator; hence the final line of the **operator=()** function reads **return *this;**.

Using friend functions to overload the +, – and = operators

Just as it was possible to overload the += and –= operators with friend functions rather than member functions, so also the –, + and = operators can be overloaded by means of friend functions.

The rules for doing this are very similar to those we have already met. Remember that friend functions do not have automatic access to the class data elements, and so both arguments need to be passed explicitly to them.

Coding **operator+()** as a friend function would require the following declaration:

```
friend percent operator+(percent &,int);
```

and the action part of the code would look like this:

```
percent operator+(percent &a,int b)
{
   percent c;
   c.value=a.value+b;
   return c;
}
```

Apart from the fact that two arguments have been explicitly passed instead of one, this is virtually identical to the code which we have already seen when writing this as a member function.

When a friend function is compulsory

There is one important situation when it is compulsory to use a friend function instead of a member function: this is when the argument on the left of the binary operator is a native type such as an int or a float.

You will recall that when a member function is used, the implicit left argument is **this**, a pointer to a member of the appropriate class. From this follows our next Rule:

Rule 7 – If the left argument is not a member of the class but a native type, then a member function cannot be used; instead, a friend function is required.

Overloading the = operator as a friend function

It is quite straightforward to overload the = operator using a friend rather than a member function. Here is the declaration:

```
friend void operator=(percent &, percent &)
```

and here is the action part of the code:

```
void operator=(percent &a,percent &b)
{
   a.value=b.value;
}
```

A newcomer to operator overloading might perhaps find this a little easier to understand than the member function version printed earlier.

Overloading the () operator

C++, like its predecessor language C, has a very wide range of operators. So far in this chapter we have looked at ways in which a number of these can be overloaded for use with your own user defined types. However, it is often forgotten that even the () operator can be overloaded. In this section, we shall see how to overload this operator.

Before we do so, a word of caution: there are few situations under which there is any real value in overloading the () operator, and you may well find that you never need to do anything even remotely similar to what we are doing here.

We have seen that when operators are being overloaded for use with user-defined types, it is important to preserve both their original 'template' and their meaning. The intrinsic meaning of the () operator is 'function call', and in C++ this is extended to allow conversions from one data type to another.

Such type conversions can be very useful, and so we shall now overload the () operator so as to make it possible to convert data from class **percent** to the inbuilt class int. This will enable us to use expressions such as **num1=int(score1)**, where **num1** is an integer and **score1** is an object of class percent.

First of all, the declaration section of the code to overload the () operator (as a member function) must look like this:

```
operator int();
```

The action part of the code is very straightforward; here it is:

```
percent::operator int()
{
   return value;
}
```

Because this is implemented as a member function, it has automatic access to the data elements in the current class object. All that is therefore necessary is for it to return the contents of the data element **value**.

Putting it all together

So that you can see how all the various elements described in this chapter might come together, we now print as Program 9.5 the complete code needed to implement all the overloaded operators described in this chapter. Work through the code carefully to be sure that you understand it.

Most of the operator overloading has been done by means of member functions rather than friend functions, and friends have been used only where necessary. This is simply a question of personal preference; every function could be implemented as a friend if you wished.

Program 9.5

```
#include <stream.hpp>
class percent
{
   public:
   percent(){value=0;}
   percent(int a){value=a;if (value>100 || value<0) value=0;}
   percent(percent &a){value=a.value;}
   void display(){cout << value;}
   void operator++(); // usage: score++;
   void operator--(); // usage: score--;
   percent operator+(int); // usage: score+20;
   percent operator-(int); // usage: score-20
   percent operator=(percent &); // usage: score=score+20 etc;
   percent operator+(percent &); // usage: score1+score2;
   percent operator-(percent &); // usage: score1-score2;
   operator int(); //: usage int i=int(score);
   friend percent operator+(int,percent &);
      // usage: 20+score;
   friend percent operator-(int,percent &);
      // usage: 20-score;
   private:
   int value;
};

void percent::operator++()
{
   value++;
   if(value==100)value=0;
}

void percent::operator--()
{
   value--;
   if(value==-1)value=100;
}
```

```
percent percent::operator+(int a)
{
   percent b;
   b.value=value+a;
   return b;
}

percent percent::operator-(int a)
{
   percent b;
   b.value=value-a;
   return b;
}

percent percent::operator=(percent &a)
{
   value=a.value;
   return *this;
}

percent percent::operator+(percent &a)
{
   percent b;
   b.value=value+a.value;
   return b;
}

percent percent::operator-(percent &a)
{
   percent b;
   b.value=value-a.value;
   return b;
}

percent::operator int()
{
   return value;
}

percent operator+(int a,percent &b)
{
   percent c;
```

```
      c.value=a+b.value;
      return c;
}

percent operator-(int a,percent &b)
{
   percent c;
   c.value=a-b.value;
   return c;
}

main()
{
   int num;
   // declare some objects
   percent myvalue1(40),myvalue2(20),myvalue3;
   myvalue1--; // test the -- operator
   myvalue2++; // and the ++ operator as well
   // try a complex expression
   myvalue3=5+myvalue1+10+myvalue2-21;
   myvalue3.display();// output the result
   cout << "\n";
   num=int(myvalue3); // test the overloaded ()
   cout << num << "\n";
}
```

Overloading the input and output operators

The great advantage of using overloaded operators to manipulate user defined types is that it is much easier and more natural to be able to write something like **own_class1 + own_class2** than to have to resort to a member function to accomplish the same result.

However, even in Program 9.5 we were still obliged to use the member function **display()** in order to output the values contained in our user defined **percent** class. It would obviously be much better if we could write something like **cout << myvalue3** instead of **myvalue3.display()**.

So that you can understand how to do this, you should first know that in C++ (as in plain C) all input and output procedures are implemented as file operations; **cin** and **cout** are actually files which are automatically opened when a C++ program is run.

Both input and output are treated as 'streams' of characters, even when binary rather than Ascii values are being handled. C++ makes use of two pre-defined C++ classes,

istream and **ostream**. As you may guess from their names, these classes handle input and output respectively. Part of the definition of these classes allows them to overload the >> and << operators, which were originally intended for right and left shift operations respectively.

We shall look at the input and output streams in much more detail in Chapter Eleven. For the moment, we shall merely look at the mechanics of further overloading the >> and << operators so that they can be used with user defined classes.

Overloading the << operator with a function

If you are already using a member function to output the values held in a class, then the simplest way of proceeding is to use that function to return the value which you wish to output to a member of class **ostream**.

To do this with our **percent** class, the **display()** function should be rewritten to look like this:

```
int display(){return value;}
```

You next need to add a new operator overloading function to the predefined class **ostream**; the effect of this will simply be to call the new **display()** function which is a member of class **percent**.

This is very straightforward; the code for the new function looks like this:

```
ostream& operator<<(ostream& a, percent b)
{
   return a << b.display();
}
```

Because **value** is a private data element of the class **percent**, it can't be accessed directly; however, it *can* be accessed by means of the **display()** function, as here.

You can now output the contents of any object of class **percent** by using this simple command:

```
cout << myvalue;
```

instead of the much clumsier

```
myvalue.display();
```

Program 9.6 consists of a shortened version of Program 9.5, and is included to clarify the implementation of the overloaded << operator.

Program 9.6

```
#include <stream.hpp>
class percent
{
   public:
   int display(){return value;}
   percent(){value=0;}
   percent(int a){value=a;if(value>100 || value<0) value=0;}
   percent(percent &a){value=a.value;}
   void operator++(); // usage: score++;
   void operator--(); // usage: score--;
   private:
   int value;
};

void percent::operator++()
{
   value++;
   if(value==100)value=0;
}

void percent::operator--()
{
   value--;
   if(value==-1)value=100;
}

ostream& operator<<(ostream& a, percent b)
{
   return a << b.display();
}

main()
{
   percent myvalue1(40);
   myvalue1--;
   cout << myvalue1;
   cout << "\n";

}
```

Overloading the << operator with a friend function

An alternative method of overloading the << operator exists which is in some ways easier to use, though perhaps it is more difficult to understand.

Remember that it isn't possible simply to overload the << and >> operators as members of the class **percent**, because they are already members of the predefined **istream** and **ostream** classes respectively. However, it is possible to overload them by using friend functions of the **percent** class.

To do this, the public section of the class definition must include the appropriate friend function definitions. In the case of the << operator, this might look like this:

```
friend ostream& operator<<(ostream&,percent);
```

The action part of the code would look like this:

```
ostream& operator<<(ostream& a,percent b)
{
   return a << b.value;
}
```

Overloading the >> operator

The >> operator can be overloaded in much the same way; however, because we are passing a value in to an object of a user defined class, that class has to be passed as a reference. Remember too that we are working with the predefined class **istream** rather than **ostream**.

The definition of the friend function looks like this:

```
friend istream& operator>>(istream&, percent&);
```

and the action part of the code looks like this:

```
istream& operator>>(istream& a,percent& b)
{
   int c;
   a >> c;
   b.value=c;
   return a;
}
```

Program 9.7 shows how both the >> and << operator can be overloaded as friend functions.

Program 9.7

```
#include <stream.hpp>
class percent
{
   public:
   percent(){value=0;}
   percent(int a){value=a;if (value>100 || value<0) value=0;}
   percent(percent &a){value=a.value;}
   friend istream& operator>>(istream&, percent&);
   friend ostream& operator<<(ostream&, percent);
   void operator++(); // usage: score++;
   void operator--(); // usage: score--;
   private:
   int value;
};

void percent::operator++()
{
   value++;
   if(value==100)value=0;
}

void percent::operator--()
{
   value--;
   if(value==-1)value=100;
}

ostream& operator<<(ostream& a,percent b)
{
   a << b.value;
   return a;
}

istream& operator>>(istream& a,percent& b)
{
   int c;
   a >> c;
   b.value=c;
   return a;
}

main()
{
```

```
    percent myvalue1;
    cout << "Type in a value\n";
    cin >> myvalue1;
    myvalue1--;
    cout << myvalue1;
    cout << "\n";
}
```

Postscript to Chapter Nine

By the time that you reach this point, you should have a good understanding of how to overload the C++ operators so that you can manipulate your own user-defined classes in just the same way as you can handle those which are already built-in to the C++ language. The result of this is that your code becomes much easier to read, since addition, subtraction and other operations are seen to be carried out using the 'natural' operators rather than by means of functions.

When overloading functions, it is very important that you should consider all the possibilities which another user may try; for instance, if you overload the + operator to allow an integer value to be added to objects of your user-defined class, you should cater both for those circumstances when the integer precedes the + operator as well as for those when it follows it.

The most important points to bear in mind when overloading operators are that only those operators which already exist in the language can be overloaded, and that overloading cannot alter either the basic 'template' of an operator, nor its place in the order of precedence. It isn't possible to overload operators when neither of their arguments is a user-defined class, so that you can't overload the + operator in an expression like **3+5**.

Generally speaking, operator overloading can be carried out by means of either member functions or friend functions. Unary operators overloaded by member functions take no formal arguments; unary operators overloaded by friend functions take a single argument.

Binary operators overloaded by means of member functions take one formal argument, which is the value to the right of the operator; binary operators overloaded by means of friend functions take two arguments.

Finally, remember that although operator overloading is very powerful, there is no point in using it just 'because it's there'. There is no point in complicating simple code just in order to use operator overloading, or where a particular implementation doesn't make your code easier to read and debug.

Exercises to Chapter Nine

1. If you haven't yet entered and run the programs in Chapter Nine, do so now.

2. Rewrite Program 9.5 using friend functions throughout for operator overloading.

10

Data Type Derivation

At the beginning of Chapter Eight, we mentioned briefly that one of the characteristics of a true object oriented language is that it permits **data type derivation**. This chapter is devoted to this topic; we will begin with a brief discussion of just what data type derivation means and why it provides the programmer with a useful tool for development and maintenance, and then proceed to demonstrate some specific examples.

What is Data Type Derivation?

Data type derivation is a technique by which an existing user-defined class is used by a programmer to serve as the basis for a new user-derived class. The existing user-defined class is called the **base class**; the new class derived from it is called the **derived class**. The base class and any classes which are derived from it are said to be **cognate** with each other.

The terms **base class** and **user defined class** are both relative rather than absolute, so that a class which has been derived from an original base class can itself serve as a base class for another derived class. There are in theory no limits as to how far this derivation can extend, although most programmers will probably find that practical limits exist beyond which further class derivation will not be helpful.

The advantages of data type derivation

Because data type derivation allows a programmer to make use of base classes which may have been created by someone else, and to adapt them to his specific requirements without compromising the integrity of the base classes, a great deal of development and debugging time can be saved. It is not even necessary to have the source code of the original base class; as long as you have access to an object (.OBJ) file for a given base class, you can derive new classes from it quite freely.

This ability to derive new classes from old ones helps to strengthen the modular approach which is one of the greatest advantages of C++; new classes can be 'plugged in' to old ones, thus encouraging the programmer to perceive classes as 'black boxes', the precise internal workings of which are not directly relevant.

A second advantage of using derived classes is that they provide a more flexible method of allowing one class to be 'contained' inside another than is possible using the class nesting technique described in Chapter Seven.

Because the code for each base class is automatically 'contained' in the classes which are derived from it, all the time and effort which would otherwise be necessary to enter the same code several times is saved, and the possibility of errors is largely eliminated. Program development is therefore much easier and faster, and the resulting code is easier to read and debug.

Some examples may be useful here. Imagine that you are developing a program which will keep track of the maintenance requirements of a fleet of buses. It would be perfectly possible to create a new **bus** class, complete with its own data elements and member functions; however, if you or someone else have already written the code for a class **truck**, which is nearly but not quite the same as your intended **bus** class, it would be possible to derive your new class from **truck**, taking over those features of **truck** which you need and adding others, while bypassing any features of the base class which you do not need. At a later time, you could even create a **minibus** class derived from your **bus** class.

Or you might be creating a graphics program which provides special tools for drawing shapes on the screen. You could begin with a simple base class – a square, perhaps – and then derive a series of other classes, such as rectangles, parallelograms and the like from that simple base class.

At least potentially, a great deal of C++ programming can be accomplished by merely using libraries of ready-defined base classes, and deriving new classes from these as necessary. The provision of such ready-made base classes in the form of programmers' toolkits will no doubt be a major aim of software houses over the next few years.

Preserving the integrity of base classes

In our discussion of data hiding, we have already seen that one of the most important advantages of C++ is that it allows certain parts of a class – the public section – to be freely available from outside the class, while entry to other (private) areas is completely forbidden. Both data elements and member functions can be hidden in this way.

Something of the same sort is necessary when new classes are derived from old ones. It would clearly be dangerous if a derived class were able to subvert the whole operation of the base class by tampering with private elements or functions in such a way as to make the whole base class insecure.

However, situations may exist in which it is quite proper for a derived class to gain access to the private section of the base class from which it is derived, although it is essential that that section should not be accessed by other portions of the program. The answer to this is provided by the reserved word **protected**; a protected portion of a base class is treated as if it were private as far as every portion of the code is concerned *except* that it is accessible to classes derived from that base class; a derived class will have access to the protected section of its base class in the same way as if it were a private section of the derived class itself. We shall see how this works later in this chapter.

A simple example

We shall now develop a simple example to show how easy it is to derive one or more new classes from an existing base class. We shall begin by considering how to write a very simple program to keep track of material on deposit in a library.

All library materials have certain things in common, so it makes sense to create a base class with room for these common elements. In this case, we shall assume that all materials in the library have a shelf mark and a value, and so we can create a base class with just these two data elements, **shelf_mark** and **value**. Later on we shall come back to create the other classes which will be derived from this.

(Actually, most programmers would prefer to be able to work out the fine details of the base class and all its derived classes before sitting down to write code; and in an ideal world, this would certainly be the simplest course of action. However, real-world programming often involves working with base classes that have been created by someone else, and adapting them for purposes that the original programmer may never even have considered.)

Creating a simple base class

We shall begin by creating, in Program 10.1, the code for the class **library_material**, together with a very short **main()** driver program to show how it works. We especially recommend that you test Program 10.1 (and the other programs which derive from it in the remainder of this chapter) by entering them into your own computer.

Program 10.1

```
#include <stream.hpp>
#include <string.h>

class library_material
{
   public:
   make_item(char *a,float &b);
   void display_item();
   private:
   char *shelf_mark;
   float *value;
};

library_material::make_item(char *a,float &b)
{
   shelf_mark=new char[strlen(a)+1];
   strcpy(shelf_mark,a);
   value=new float;
   value=&b;
}

void library_material::display_item()
{
   cout << shelf_mark << "\n";
   cout << form("%3.2f%s",*value,"\n");
}

main()
{
   library_material first;
   first.make_item("SK1356",13.20);
   first.display_item();
}
```

There are only a few points which need to be made about the code for the new **library_material** class.

First, in the interests of simplicity we have omitted many of the data elements which would be needed in a 'real' program; for instance, no provision has been made to record the date of acquisition, which would certainly be needed in the real world.

Second, no constructors or destructors have been used. This is because there are special rules governing the use of constructors and destructors in derived classes;

these rules are actually quite straightforward, but it will be simpler if we return to them later. Instead, there is a simple 'pseudo constructor' which has to be explicitly called, but which otherwise functions in much the same way as a standard constructor by passing values into the class **library_material** and reserving space on the heap for both **value** and **shelf_mark**. No destructor has been provided; this is because destructors, like constructors, have to be handled in a special way when derived classes are involved.

Third, although we are going to use this class as the base class for several derived classes, there is actually nothing unusual or new about the way in which the class has been coded.

This is an important point to grasp: a base class is a perfectly ordinary C++ class, and so any C++ class can be used as a base class from which another class or classes an be derived. It is worth emphasising the point again that even a class which is itself derived can be used as a base class for further derivations; indeed, we shall be doing just that later in this chapter.

Adding a derived class to the base class

We shall now add a new derived class to the **library_material** class which we have just created. However, rather than just jumping in and making a **book** or **periodical** class, we will consider that most real library systems deal with two basically different categories of materials, namely reference works and others. There are several differences between these two categories: for instance, reference materials are not available for loan, while non-reference works can be borrowed freely; again, reference works include periodicals which are published on a regular basis, but this does not apply to non-reference works.

It makes a good deal of sense to recognise this basic division in the classes which we are creating. We shall therefore derive two classes **reference_work** and **non_reference** from the base class **library_material**. .

The derived class **non_reference** has an additional data element, **borrowers_number**, as well as new **add_work()** and **display_work()** functions to handle this new element; class **reference_work** has the new element **frequency**, together with appropriate pseudo-constructor and output functions. (The **borrowers_number** field is intended to contain the borrower's ticket number which will identify the borrower of a non-reference work; **frequency** will contain a string stating the frequency of publication.)

Program 10.2 shows how the program will appear with just the **non_reference** class added; as you can see, the code for the base class **library_material** has not been affected in any way by the addition of the new class.

Program 10.2

```
#include <stream.hpp>
#include <string.h>

class library_material
{
   public:
   make_item(char *a, float &b);
   void display_item();
   private:
   char *shelf_mark;
   float *value;
};

library_material::make_item(char *a, float &b)
{
   shelf_mark=new char [strlen(a)+1];
   strcpy(shelf_mark,a);
   value=new float;
   value=&b;
}

void library_material::display_item()
{
   cout << shelf_mark << "\n";
   cout << form("%3.2f%s", *value, "\n");
}

class non_reference : library_material
{
   public:
   add_work(char *a, float &b, int &c);
   void display_work();
   private:
   int *borrowers_number;
};

non_reference::add_work(char *a, float &b, int &c)
{
   make_item(a,b);
   borrowers_number=new int;
   borrowers_number=&c;
}
```

```
void non_reference::display_work()
{
   display_item();
   cout << *borrowers_number << "\n";
}

main()
{
   non_reference first;
   first.add_work("SK1356",13.20,512);
   first.display_work();
}
```

The most interesting parts of this code are the declaration of the new **non_reference** class and the action sections of its two member functions. We shall now look at these separately.

Declaring a derived class

Declaring a derived class is exactly the same as declaring any other kind of class, except that it is necessary to add the name of the base class after the name of the derived class; the two names are separated by a colon, thus:

```
class non_reference : public library_material
```

When in due course we derive further classes from **non_reference** – a **books** class, for instance – we shall do so by using code which is identical in structure:

```
class book : public non_reference
```

In other words, we only specify the name of the class from which the new class is immediately derived; it is not necessary (or correct) to give the name of the 'original ancestor' from which the immediate base class is finally derived. (It is, however, possible to derive a new class from more than one base class; this is called **multiple inheritance**, and we shall see how to do this later.)

Note, incidentally, the use of the reserved word **public** before the name of the base class. The purpose of this is to make the base class **library_material** accessible to the derived class; the public section of the base class is thus available not only to the derived class but also to any further classes which may be derived from that.

If we had not specified that the base class was to be public to the derived class, then all the elements and member functions of the base class would have been treated as private members of the derived class, and would then not have been directly available to any further derived classes.

It is also possible to explicitly state that a base class is to be private to a derived class by using the access specifier **private** instead of **public**; this is a feature of C++ Version 2. In the interests of clarity and easy debugging, it is probably a good idea to include the specifier **private** rather than to rely on the fact that if **public** is omitted, the base class is private by default.

Data elements and member functions of a derived class

Because the derived class 'contains' its base class, all the data elements of the base class become data elements of the derived class. If they are public elements (or protected elements) in the base class, then they can be manipulated by the derived class. However, if (as here) we wish to access private elements of the base class, then this cannot be done directly; instead, they must be manipulated by means of the public member functions of the base class.

Passing values to the base class and the derived class: To see how this works in practice, consider a pseudo-constructor for the derived class **non_reference**. This will have to pass three arguments to the newly created instance of the **non_reference** class: **shelf_mark**, **value**, and **borrowers_number**. The first two of these arguments 'belong' to the private data elements of the base class **library_material**; the last one 'belongs' only to the derived class **non_reference**.

The technique to do this is actually very simple. Here is the code for the pseudo-constructor for class **non_reference**:

```
non_reference::add_work(char *a,float &b,int &c)
{
   make_item(a,b);
   borrowers_number=new int;
   borrowers_number=&c;
}
```

As you would expect, the parentheses in the header line contain the three formal arguments which are being passed to the new class.

The first two arguments, which 'belong' to the base class, are passed to it by simply calling the pseudo-constructor of the base class **make_item**(). Since this is in the public section of the code of the base class, it is directly available to the derived class, just as if it were a member function of the derived class.

The last argument is the one which 'belongs' to the derived class; the last two lines of the code reserve space for the int variable **borrowers_number** on the heap and pass this value to that variable.

Another example: Displaying the data items of class **non_reference** is performed in a very similar manner by the function **display_work()**:

```
void non_reference::display_work()
{
  display_item();
  cout << *borrowers_number << "\n";
}
```

Once again, the data elements which are private to the base class are accessed by invoking a base class member function – in this case **display_item()**. **borrowers_number** belongs to the derived class, and can thus be displayed directly.

Adding another derived class

The code for the derived class reference_work is very similar to that for **non_reference**. First, here is the class definition:

```
class reference_work : library_material
{
  char *frequency_of_issue;
  public:
  add_work(char *a,float &b,char *a);
  void display_work();
};
```

As you can see, the member functions **add_work()** and **display_work()** have the same names as the equivalent functions for the **non_reference** class. This isn't necessary, of course, but it does help to make the resulting code a little easier to read.

The code for the action part of this version of **add_work()** looks like this:

```
reference_work::add_work(char *a,float &b,char *c)
{
  make_item(a,b);
  frequency_of_issue=new char[strlen(c)+1];
  strcpy(frequency_of_issue,c);
}
```

and the code for **display_work** () is like this:

```
void reference_work::display_work()
{
   display_item();
   cout << frequency_of_issue << "\n";
}
```

Program 10.3 shows how the program will look when the new derived class has been added. As before, **main()** is a simple driver to test that everything is working properly.

Program 10.3

```
#include <stream.hpp>
#include <string.h>

class library_material
{
   public:
   make_item(char *a,float &b);
   void display_item();
   private:
   char *shelf_mark;
   float *value;
};

library_material::make_item(char *a,float &b)
{
   shelf_mark=new char[strlen(a)+1];
   strcpy(shelf_mark,a);
   value=new float;
   value=&b;
}

void library_material::display_item()
{
   cout << shelf_mark << "\n";
   cout << form("%3.2f%s",*value,"\n");
}

class non_reference : library_material
{
   public:
```

```
   add_work(char *a,float &b,int &c);
   void display_work();
   private:
   int *borrowers_number;
};

non_reference::add_work(char *a,float &b,int &c)
{
   make_item(a,b);
   borrowers_number=new int;
   borrowers_number=&c;
}

void non_reference::display_work()
{
   display_item();
   cout << *borrowers_number << "\n";
}

class reference_work : library_material
{
   public:
   add_work(char *a,float &b,char *a);
   void display_work();
   private:
   char *frequency_of_issue;
};

reference_work::add_work(char *a,float &b,char *c)
{
   make_item(a,b);
   frequency_of_issue=new char[strlen(c)+1];
   strcpy(frequency_of_issue,c);
}

void reference_work::display_work()
{
   display_item();
   cout << frequency_of_issue << "\n";
}

main()
{
```

```
non_reference first;
first.add_work("SK1356",13.20,512);
first.display_work();
reference_work second;
second.add_work("OP53",20.50,"Quarterly");
second.display_work();
}
```

The private and protected reserved words

So far, we have considered the situation which applies when the derived class has no privileged access to the private section of the base class, and all manipulation of the private elements has to be carried out by means of member functions which form part of the public section of the base class. Functions which are created for this purpose are sometimes referred to as **access functions**.

For instance, the **add_work()** and **display_work()** functions in both our derived classes can only access the private data elements of the base class **library_material** by calling the base class public access functions **make_item()** and **display_item()**. This is clearly a rather clumsy way of proceeding.

If the base class data elements were in the public rather than the private section of the class definition, this difficulty would not arise; however, the whole integrity of the base class might then be compromised, because the private elements would be freely available throughout any program in which that class was used, and all the advantages gained by data hiding would be lost.

Fortunately, a simple solution to this difficulty is provided by the access specifier **protected**. A section of the base class which is preceded by **protected** is freely available to any class derived from that base class, but not elsewhere in the program. Specifically, those elements of the base class which are **protected** are treated as if they were ordinary private members of the derived class.

Using the reserved word protected: Returning to our sample program, it should be clear that if the data elements **shelf_mark** and **value** had been protected members of the base class **library_material** rather than being private members, it would have been possible for the derived classes **reference_work** and **non_reference** to access these elements directly, rather than *via* the base class member functions **display_item()** and **make_item()**.

Program 10.4 is a revised version of Program 10.3, showing how the derived classes can directly access the data elements in the protected section of the base class **library_material**.

Program 10.4

```cpp
#include <stream.hpp>
#include <string.h>

class library_material
{
   public:
   make_item(char *a,float &b);
   void display_item();
   protected:
   char *shelf_mark;
   float *value;
};

library_material::make_item(char *a,float &b)
{
   shelf_mark=new char[strlen(a)+1];
   strcpy(shelf_mark,a);
   value=new float;
   value=&b;
}

void library_material::display_item()
{
   cout << shelf_mark << "\n";
   cout << form("%3.2f%s",*value,"\n");
}

class non_reference : public library_material
{
   public:
   add_work(char *a,float &b,int &c);
   void display_work();
   protected:
   int *borrowers_number;
};

non_reference::add_work(char *a,float &b,int &c)
{
   shelf_mark=new char[strlen(a)+1];
   strcpy(shelf_mark,a);
   value=new float;
   value=&b;
   borrowers_number=new int;
```

```
      borrowers_number=&c;
}

void non_reference::display_work()
{
   cout << shelf_mark << "\n";
   cout << form("%3.2f%s",*value,"\n");
   cout << *borrowers_number << "\n";
}

class reference_work : public library_material
{
   public:
   add_work(char *a,float &b,char *a);
   void display_work();
   protected:
   char *frequency_of_issue;
};

reference_work::add_work(char *a,float &b,char *c)
{
   shelf_mark=new char[strlen(a)+1];
   strcpy(shelf_mark,a);
   value=new float;
   value=&b;
   frequency_of_issue=new char[strlen(c)+1];
   strcpy(frequency_of_issue,c);
}

void reference_work::display_work()
{
   cout << shelf_mark << "\n";
   cout << form("%3.2f%s",*value,"\n");
   cout << frequency_of_issue << "\n";
}

main()
{
   non_reference first;
   first.add_work("SK1356",13.20,512);
   first.display_work();
   reference_work second;
   second.add_work("OP53",20.50,"Quarterly");
   second.display_work();
}
```

As you can see, it is no longer necessary for the derived class functions **display_work()** and **add_work()** to invoke the base class functions **make_item()** and **display_item()** to access the base class data elements; these elements are as accessible as if they were private members of the derived class.

Using constructors and destructors with derived classes

So far in our discussion of class derivation we have carefully avoided the use of constructors and destructors; the latter have simply been omitted altogether, while proper constructors were simulated by means of pseudo-constructors which had to be explicitly called when class instances were created.

Base class constructors and destructors

Base class constructors and destructors are really no different from the constructors and destructors that you have already met. It is, after all, fundamental to the philosophy of C++ type derivation that a base class is perfectly ordinary, and has no special distinguishing characteristics.

A simple constructor for the base class **library_material** designed to carry out the same tasks as the pseudo-constructor **make_item()** we have been using so far would therefore look like this:

```
library_material::library_material(char *a,float &b)
{
   shelf_mark=new char[strlen(a)+1];
   strcpy(shelf_mark,a);
   value=new float;
   value=&b;
}
```

A simple base class destructor would look like this:

```
library_material::~library_material();
{
   delete shelf_mark;
   delete value;
}
```

Constructors in derived classes

Before you can understand how constructors work in derived classes, there is one important point which should be understood: where a base class and a derived class both have constructors, then the constructor for the base class is called first; only when it has completed its tasks is the constructor for the derived class called.

Where no arguments are to be passed to the base class constructor, this point is purely academic. However, where both the derived class and the base class have constructors which expect arguments to be passed to them, it is essential to devise some method by which the appropriate arguments can be passed to the base class constructor *before* the derived class constructor has been called.

The method of doing this is actually quite simple. Imagine that **base_class()** is a constructor to a base class, and that **derived_class()** is a constructor to a derived class. Two integer arguments have to be passed to **base_class()**, while **derived_class()** expects a single argument of type float.

The header of the constructor **derived_class()** might look like this:

```
derived_class::derived_class(int a,int b,float c)  :  (a,b)
```

while the header of the constructor **base_class()** could look like this:

```
base_class::base_class(int a,int b)
```

As you can see, the header of the derived class ends in the code : **(a,b)** where the notation **(a,b)** represents the arguments of type int which are to be passed to the base class constructor. This is done before the derived class constructor is called.

The only rule to remember when creating a constructor for a derived class can therefore be summed up as follows: the argument list in the declaration or prototype for a derived class constructor should include the arguments and argument-types for both the base class and the derived class; in addition, the arguments (but not the argument-types) for the base class should be enclosed in parentheses and appended to the end of the statement, preceded by a semi-colon.

Program 10.5 shows how our sample program would look with constructors in both of the derived classes and also in the base class.

Program 10.5

```
#include <stream.hpp>
#include <string.h>

class library_material
{
   public:
   library_material(char *a,float &b);
   void display_item();
   protected:
   char *shelf_mark;
   float *value;
};

library_material::library_material(char *a,float &b)
{
   shelf_mark=new char[strlen(a)+1];
   strcpy(shelf_mark,a);
   value=new float;
   value=&b;
}

void library_material::display_item()
{
   cout << shelf_mark << "\n";
   cout << form("%3.2f%s",*value,"\n");
}

class non_reference : public library_material
{
   public:
   non_reference(char *a,float &b,int &c);
   void display_work();
   protected:
   int *borrowers_number;
};

non_reference::non_reference(char *a,float &b,int &c) :
   (a,b)
{
   shelf_mark=new char[strlen(a)+1];
   strcpy(shelf_mark,a);
   value=new float;
   value=&b;
```

```
    borrowers_number=new int;
    borrowers_number=&c;
}

void non_reference::display_work()
{
    cout << shelf_mark << "\n";
    cout << form("%3.2f%s",*value,"\n");
    cout << *borrowers_number << "\n";
}

class reference_work : public library_material
{
    public:
    reference_work(char *a,float &b,char *a);
    void display_work();
    protected:
    char *frequency_of_issue;
};

reference_work::reference_work(char *a,float &b,char *c) :
    (a,b)
{
    shelf_mark=new char[strlen(a)+1];
    strcpy(shelf_mark,a);
    value=new float;
    value=&b;
    frequency_of_issue=new char[strlen(c)+1];
    strcpy(frequency_of_issue,c);
}

void reference_work::display_work()
{
    cout << shelf_mark << "\n";
    cout << form("%3.2f%s",*value,"\n");
    cout << frequency_of_issue << "\n";
}

main()
{
    non_reference first("SK1356",13.20,512);
    first.display_work();
    reference_work second("OP53",20.50,"Quarterly");
    second.display_work();
}
```

Destructors in derived classes

The rule regarding the relationship between destructors in derived classes and base classes is the converse of the rule applying to constructors: the destructor for the derived class is called first, followed by the destructor for the base class. Because destructors do not pass arguments, the destructor of a derived class does not require any special syntax.

In reality, the situation is often not quite as simple as this rather straightforward rule would indicate.

This is because it is very easy to make the error of trying to reclaim the same heap space more than once. Imagine, for instance, the situation in which a dynamic variable **base_var**, which is a protected element of the class **base_class**, is accessed from within the derived class **derived_class**. You might incorrectly try to reclaim the space occupied by **base_var** twice, once using the **derived_class** destructor and once using the **base_class** destructor.

This problem can be avoided by careful programming; study the way in which the destructors have been arranged in the next version of our library program (Program 10.6) in order to avoid trying to delete any dynamic variable more than once.

Program 10.6

```
#include <stream.hpp>
#include <string.h>

class library_material
{
   public:
   library_material(char *a,float b);
   ~library_material(){delete shelf_mark;delete value;}
   void display_item();
   protected:
   char *shelf_mark;
   float *value;
};

library_material::library_material(char *a,float b)
{
   shelf_mark=new char[strlen(a)+1];
   value=new float;
   strcpy(shelf_mark,a);
   *value=b;
```

```
      }

      void library_material::display_item()
      {
         cout << shelf_mark << "\n";
         cout << form("%3.2f%s",*value,"\n");
      }

      class non_reference : public library_material
      {
         public:
         non_reference(char *a,float b,int c);
         ~non_reference(){delete borrowers_number;}
         void display_work();
         protected:
         int *borrowers_number;
      };

      non_reference::non_reference(char *a,float b,int c) :
         (a,b)
      {
         borrowers_number=new int;
         *borrowers_number=c;
      }

      void non_reference::display_work()
      {
         cout << shelf_mark << "\n";
         cout << form("%3.2f%s",*value,"\n");
         cout << *borrowers_number << "\n";
      }

      class reference_work : public library_material
      {
         public:
         reference_work(char *a,float b,char *c);
         ~reference_work(){delete frequency_of_issue;}
         void display_work();
         protected:
         char *frequency_of_issue;
      };

      reference_work::reference_work(char *a,float b,char *c) :
         (a,b)
```

```
{
   frequency_of_issue=new char[strlen(a)+1];
   strcpy(frequency_of_issue,c);
}

void reference_work::display_work()
{
   cout << shelf_mark << "\n";
   cout << form("%3.2f%s",*value,"\n");
   cout << frequency_of_issue << "\n";
}

main()
{
   non_reference first("SK1356",13.20,512);
   first.display_work();
   reference_work second("OP53",20.50,"Quarterly");
   second.display_work();
}
```

Creating a new level of derived classes

Now that we have the basic framework set up, we can create yet another level of derived classes. We shall derive the classes **fiction_book** and **compact_disc** from class **non_reference** and derive **periodical** from class **reference_work**.

The new derived classes: In addition to the variables **shelf_mark**, **value** and **borrowers_number** which have been derived from the lower level classes, the **fiction_book** and **compact_disc** classes will need some variables of their own. For **fiction_book** we shall assume that we need strings to store the name of the author and the book's title; for **compact_disc**, we shall need strings for the composer and the title of the work. (Remember that we are only creating a simple example here; a 'real' program would have to be much more flexible than this.)

Here is the code for **fiction_book**:

```
class fiction_book : public non_reference
{
   public:
   fiction_book(char *a,float b,int c,char *d,char *e);
   ~fiction_book(){delete author;delete title;}
   void display_work();
```

```
  protected:
  char *author;
  char *title;
};

fiction_book::fiction_book
   (char *a,float b,int c,char *d,char *e) : (a,b,c)
{
  author=new char[strlen(d)+1];
  title=new char[strlen(e)+1];
  strcpy(author,d);
  strcpy(title,e);
}

void fiction_book::display_work()
{
  cout << shelf_mark << "\n";
  cout << form("%3.2f%s",*value,"\n");
  cout << *borrowers_number << "\n";
  cout << author << "\n";
  cout << title << "\n";
}
```

As you can see, this derived class is handled in exactly the same way as the class **non_reference** from which it is immediately derived; its ultimate derivation from the base class **library_material** is completely invisible. As far as the programmer is concerned, **non_reference** *is* the base class. Even in the constructor, the programmer doesn't need to know how many of the arguments are being passed all the way to **library_material**, and how many go only as far as the 'immediate' base class **non_reference**.

The situation is exactly the same as far as the code for the class **compact_disc** is concerned:

```
class compact_disc : public non_reference
{
  public:
  compact_disc(char *a,float b,int c,char *d,char *e);
  ~compact_disc(){delete composer;delete music_title;}
  void display_work();
  protected:
  char *composer;
  char *music_title;
};
```

```
compact_disc::compact_disc
   (char *a,float b,int c,char *d,char *e) : (a,b,c)
{
   composer=new char[strlen(d)+1];
   music_title=new char[strlen(e)+1];
   strcpy(composer,d);
   strcpy(music_title,e);
}

void compact_disc::display_work()
{
   cout << shelf_mark << "\n";
   cout << form("%3.2f%s",*value,"\n");
   cout << *borrowers_number << "\n";
   cout << composer << "\n";
   cout << music_title << "\n";
}
```

Finally, we can create a **periodical** class which will be derived from class **reference_work**. Once again, the code is quite straightforward:

```
class periodical : public reference_work
{
   public:
   periodical(char *a,float b,char *c,char *d);
   ~periodical(){delete title;}
   void display_work();
   protected:
   char *title;
};

periodical::periodical
   (char *a,float b,char *c,char *d) : (a,b,c)
{
   title=new char[strlen(d)+1];
   strcpy(title,d);
}

void periodical::display_work()
{
   cout << shelf_mark << "\n";
   cout << form("%3.2f%s",*value,"\n");
   cout << frequency_of_issue << "\n";
   cout << title << "\n";
}
```

Putting it together

It is now possible to add our three latest derived classes to the existing program. Program 10.7 shows this, together with a simple **main**() driver to demonstrate that it really works.

Program 10.7

```
#include <stream.hpp>
#include <string.h>

class library_material
{
   public:
   library_material(char *a,float b);
   ~library_material(){delete shelf_mark;delete value;}
   void display_item();
   protected:
   char *shelf_mark;
   float *value;
};

library_material::library_material(char *a,float b)
{
   shelf_mark=new char[strlen(a)+1];
   value=new float;
   strcpy(shelf_mark,a);
   *value=b;
}

void library_material::display_item()
{
   cout << shelf_mark << "\n";
   cout << form("%3.2f%s",*value,"\n");
}

class non_reference : public library_material
{
   public:
   non_reference(char *a,float b,int c);
   ~non_reference(){delete borrowers_number;}
   void display_work();
   protected:
```

```
      int *borrowers_number;
};

non_reference::non_reference(char *a,float b,int c)  :
   (a,b)
{
   borrowers_number=new int;
   *borrowers_number=c;
}

void non_reference::display_work()
{
   cout << shelf_mark << "\n";
   cout << form("%3.2f%s",*value,"\n");
   cout << *borrowers_number << "\n";
}

class reference_work : public library_material
{
   public:
   reference_work(char *a,float b,char *c);
   ~reference_work(){delete frequency_of_issue;}
   void display_work();
   protected:
   char *frequency_of_issue;
};

reference_work::reference_work(char *a,float b,char *c)  :
   (a,b)
{
   frequency_of_issue=new char[strlen(c)+1];
   strcpy(frequency_of_issue,c);
}

void reference_work::display_work()
{
   cout << shelf_mark << "\n";
   cout << form("%3.2f%s",*value,"\n");
   cout << frequency_of_issue << "\n";
}

class fiction_book : public non_reference
{
```

```
     public:
     fiction_book(char *a,float b,int c,char *d,char *e);
     ~fiction_book(){delete author;delete title;}
     void display_work();
     protected:
     char *author;
     char *title;
};

fiction_book::fiction_book
     (char *a,float b,int c,char *d,char *e) : (a,b,c)
{
     author=new char[strlen(d)+1];
     title=new char[strlen(e)+1];
     strcpy(author,d);
     strcpy(title,e);
}

void fiction_book::display_work()
{
     cout << shelf_mark << "\n";
     cout << form("%3.2f%s",*value,"\n");
     cout << *borrowers_number << "\n";
     cout << author << "\n";
     cout << title << "\n";
}

class compact_disc : public non_reference
{
     public:
     compact_disc(char *a,float b,int c,char *d,char *e);
     ~compact_disc(){delete composer;delete music_title;}
     void display_work();
     protected:
     char *composer;
     char *music_title;
};

compact_disc::compact_disc
     (char *a,float b,int c,char *d,char *e) : (a,b,c)
{
     composer=new char[strlen(d)+1];
     music_title=new char[strlen(e)+1];
```

```
   strcpy(composer,d);
   strcpy(music_title,e);
}

void compact_disc::display_work()
{
   cout << shelf_mark << "\n";
   cout << form("%3.2f%s",*value,"\n");
   cout << *borrowers_number << "\n";
   cout << composer << "\n";
   cout << music_title << "\n";
}

class periodical : public reference_work
{
   public:
   periodical(char *a,float b,char *c,char *d);
   ~periodical(){delete title;}
   void display_work();
   protected:
   char *title;
};

periodical::periodical(char *a,float b,char *c,char *d) :
   (a,b,c)
{
   title=new char[strlen(d)+1];
   strcpy(title,d);
}

void periodical::display_work()
{
   cout << shelf_mark << "\n";
   cout << form("%3.2f%s",*value,"\n");
   cout << frequency_of_issue << "\n";
   cout << title << "\n";
}

main()
{
   fiction_book novel("SK1110",
      12.20,444,"Mark Twain","Tom Sawyer");
   novel.display_work();
```

```
compact_disc classical("RE123",
    9.00,000,"Edward Elgar","First Symphony");
classical.display_work();
periodical magazine("PA334",10.10,"Monthly",
    "Recording Guide");
magazine.display_work();
}
```

Member functions and the scope resolution operator

If you look carefully through Program 10.7, you will notice that all the derived classes use their own version of the function **display_work()** in order to output their contents. It would also have been quite possible to have given the same name to the output function in the ultimate base class **library_material**; the only reason this was not done was to avoid introducing an extra level of difficulty towards the beginning of the chapter.

As you can see, if several cognate classes have identically-named functions, each one will automatically call its own version of the function. This is obviously much simpler to handle than the alternative of giving each class a function with a slightly different name from its close relative in another class; it is also much easier to debug. It also allows you full freedom to choose the most suitable names for your derived class functions regardless of the names of functions in the base class.

Calling a base class function

There is, however, a price to be paid for this freedom: when a derived class function has the same name as a base class function, it is not possible for the derived class to directly access the base class function should this be necessary.

For instance, in Program 10.7 the code of the function **display_work()** in the derived class **periodical** has perforce to incorporate code to output all the data elements of the base class **reference_work** as well as its own data element **title**. This is rather wasteful of space, as the code to display the base class data elements **shelf_mark**, **value** and **frequency_of_issue** is repeated in the derived class function. It would clearly be more efficient if we could omit all this duplicated code and let the derived class call the base class **display_work()** function. However, this isn't directly possible because any attempt inside the derived class **periodical** to call the function **display_work()** will end up calling the derived class version of that function rather than the base class version.

The simplest way of handling this problem is by means of the scope resolution operator ::, which we have already met in rather simpler circumstances in earlier chapters. The idiom to do this is as follows:

```
base_class::base_class_function();
```

It would thus be possible to rewrite the **display_work**() function in the derived class **periodical** to look like this:

```
void periodical::display_work()
{
    reference_work::display_work();
    cout << title << "\n";
}
```

Here, the single line **reference_work::display_work();** replaces the three lines of code which we used in Program 10.7 in order to output the contents of the variables **shelf_mark**, **value** and **frequency_of_issue**.

Multiple inheritance

It is perfectly legitimate to derive a class from two or more base classes at the same time; this is known as **multiple inheritance**. When this is done, the new derived class will inherit all the data elements and member functions of both its base classes.

The command to derive a class from more than one base class is quite straightforward:

```
class derived_class : base_class1, base_class2, ...
    base_classn
```

Each of the base classes may be given the identifier **public** or **private**; if no identifier is given, then that base class is private to the derived class by default.

Calling constructors for classes with more than one base

Where a class has been derived from more than one base class, it may be necessary to call constructors for several base classes. This requires a special idiom in the constructor for the derived class.

For instance, if a class **derived_class** has been derived from two base classes **base1** and **base2**, the prototype for the constructor of the derived class might look like this:

```
derived_class::derived class
    (int a, int b, float c) :base1(a), base2(b)
```

Here, the **base1** class constructor is passed the argument **a** and the **base2** class constructor is passed the argument **b**; argument **c** is used within the constructor of the derived class.

Incidentally, it is quite acceptable to name the base class in the derived class constructor even where multiple inheritance is not used. Thus in our library program, the header for the constructor for class **periodical** could quite properly have been written like this:

```
periodical::periodical(char *a,float b,char *c,char *d) :
   reference_work (a,b,c)
```

Problems with multiple inheritance

Certain problems may occur with multiple inheritance which do not occur where a class is derived from only a single base class. A particular problem to watch out for occurs when a data element or member function in one of the base classes happens to have the same name as an element or function in another base class.

Resolving ambiguities of data identifiers: For instance, if **base1** and **base2** both happen to have member elements called **length**, then any attempt in **derived_class**, which is derived from both **base1** and **base2**, to access **length** will result in a compiler error.

The solution to this problem is shown in Program 10.8:

Program 10.8

```
#include <stream.hpp>
class base1
{
   public:
   base1(){length=6;}
   protected:
   int length;
};

class base2
{
   public:
   base2(){length=6;}
   protected:
   int length;
};
```

```
class derived_class : public base1,public base2
{
  public:
  void check(){if (base1::length==base2::length)
    cout << "The same!\n";}
};

main()
{
  derived_class sample;
  sample.check();
}
```

Here, we have used the scope resolution operator :: to specify which base class data element is being referred to at any given moment. Thus the code

```
if (base1::length==base2::length) cout << "The same!\n";}
```

is able to refer to identically-named data elements in each of the two base classes.

The ability to use the scope reference operator to specify exactly which data element you are referring to can be especially useful in situations where you are obliged to use ready-compiled code which you have not written yourself, and where you have no choice but to accept the variable names already assigned.

Resolving ambiguities of function identifiers: The best way of resolving ambiguities between function names which happen to be shared between more than one base class is by creating new functions in the derived class, each of which invokes the appropriate base class function using the scope reference operator.

This situation is shown in Program 10.9, where classes **base1** and **base2** both have functions called **display()**. The derived class **derived_class** has two functions **display1()** and **display2()**, the sole purpose of which in each case is to call the **display()** function from the relevant base class, specifying which one is to be used by means of the scope resolution operator.

Program 10.9

```
#include <stream.hpp>
class base1
{
  public:
  void display(){cout << "This is base1\n";}
};
```

```
class base2
{
  public:
  void display(){cout << "This is base2\n";}
};

class derived_class : public base1,public base2
{
  public:
  void display1(){base1::display();}
  void display2(){base2::display();}
};

main()
{
  derived_class sample;
  sample.display1();
  sample.display2();
}
```

Introducing virtual classes

Another problem which can arise when multiple inheritance is used concerns the possible derivation of the same base class member functions and data elements by more than one route.

Inheriting the same elements by different routes

This is best illustrated by means of a simple example. Imagine a base class **ultimate_base**, which has its own member functions and data elements. From this class are derived two other classes **derived_1** and **derived_2**, which again each have member functions and appropriate data elements.

Another class **top_level** is derived by multiple inheritance from both **derived_1** and **derived_2**. This means that the possibility exists of **top_level** having two sets of data elements derived from **ultimate_base**: one set is derived through **derived_1** and the other through **derived_2**.

To avoid the problems that this would cause, the base classes should be declared to be **virtual** at the point at which the clash might occur. This is done by placing the reserved word **virtual** before the name of each base class. This means that only a single copy of the ambiguous data elements and member functions will be passed into the derived class.

How this works is demonstrated by Program 10.10.

Program 10.10

```cpp
#include <stream.hpp>

class ultimate_base
{
  public:
  void display_base(){cout << "This is from
    class ultimate_base\n";}
};

class derived_1 : public ultimate_base
{
  public:
  void display_1(){cout << "This is from class derived_1\n";}
};

class derived_2 : public ultimate_base
{
  public:
  void display_2(){cout << "This is from class derived_2\n";}
};

class top_level : virtual public derived_1,
  virtual public derived_2
{
  public:
  void top_display(){cout << "This is from class
    top_level\n";}
};

main()
{
  top_level instance;
  instance.top_display(); // top_level message;
  instance.display_1(); // message from derived_1
  instance.display_2(); // message from derived_2
  instance.display_base(); // message from ultimate_base
        // route determined by compiler
}
```

By describing classes **derived_1** and **derived_2** as **virtual**, we ensure that the compiler only passes a single copy of the base class **ultimate_base** into class

top_level. Consequently, the reference in **main()** to the **ultimate_base** class function **display_base()** is quite unambiguous, and the compiler will determine which of the intermediate classes **derived_1** and **derived_2** provides the route by which this function is made available to class **top_level**.

The order of keywords: Where the reserved word **virtual** occurs together with either **public** or **private**, the order in which they are placed is immaterial. Thus in Program 10.10, we used the code

```
class top_level : virtual public derived_1,
   virtual public derived_2
```

but we could just as easily have written

```
class top_level : public virtual derived_1,
   public virtual derived_2
```

Consistency of description: Where a base class is being inherited into a derived class by more than one route, it is important that all the routes should be consistently marked as **virtual**. If this is not done, then although only a single copy of the base class will be inherited through all the instances which are marked as **virtual**, further copies will be inherited through all the instances which are not so marked, thus making ambiguities possible.

Virtual functions

We have already seen that in C++, a function in derived classes may use the same name as a function in a base class; the decision as to which function it is appropriate to use is made when the program is compiled. This is called **early binding**.

C++ also makes it possible to force the appropriate function to be selected at run time; this is called **late binding**, and it is accomplished by applying the keyword **virtual** to the appropriate function *in the base class*. Once a function has been declared to be **virtual** in the base class, all redefinitions of that function in derived classes are also treated as **virtual** provided that they match the base class function *precisely* in terms of the numbers and types of arguments passed to them, and in the type of value which they return (if any). Should they not match exactly, then they are treated as ordinary overloaded functions.

The great advantage of using virtual functions is that if you choose not to redefine a particular function in any derived class, then the (virtual) function in the base class will automatically be used as a default; if no such function is available in the immediate base class, then the hierarchy of classes will be searched towards the ultimate root until an appropriate function is found.

This is so obviously useful that you might wonder why this is not done automatically in any case. The answer is that there is a slight penalty to be paid for this flexibility: using virtual functions can slow down the running of the program a little. Because of this, the choice of whether or not to specify a virtual function is left up to the programmer.

Program 10.11 shows a simple illustration of the use of a virtual function.

Program 10.11

```
#include <stream.hpp>

class ultimate_base
{
  public:
  virtual void display() {cout << "This is the ultimate_base
    function\n";}
};

class level_1 : public ultimate_base
{
  public:
  void display() {cout << "This is the level_1 function\n";}
};

class level_2 : public level_1
{
  public:
  void level_2_display() {cout << "This is the level_2
    function\n";}
};

main()
{
  ultimate_base first; // create instances of each class
  level_1 second;
  level_2 third;
  first.display(); // calls ultimate_base class display()
  second.display(); // calls level_1 display()
  third.display(); // no such level_2 function, so
         // calls the function from level_1
  third.level_2_display(); // calls the special level_2
    //function
}
```

Notice that when the function **display()** is declared (in class **ultimate_base**), the reserved word **virtual** must precede everything else.

If you 'walk through' the code for Program 10.11, you will see that the line **third.display()** in **main()** cannot invoke the **display()** function in class **level_2** – since there is no such function – and so it reverts to the default **display()** function in class **level_1**, which is at the next level of the hierarchy. If no such function were available in class **level_1** either, then the **display()** function in class **ultimate_base** would be invoked instead.

Postscript to Chapter Ten

The ability to derive classes from other classes is a very important feature of C++. With it, you can create object-oriented databases – like the simple library database which we developed at the beginning of the chapter – or create hierarchies of screen windows, drawing tools and the like.

The most important advantage of inheritance is that it enables you to reuse code which already exists, adapting it to meet your needs where necessary.

The **private, protected** and **public** reserved words enable the programmer to gain all the advantages of inheritance without compromising the security of code which has already been written.

When constructors are used, the base class constructor is called first, any necessary arguments being passed to it by the derived class. Destructors, on the other hand, are called in the reverse order, with the destructor for the derived class being invoked first.

It is possible for a class to be derived from more than one base class. The possibility of ambiguity which this can give rise to can be avoided by the use of the scope resolution operator **::** and the use of virtual classes.

Virtual functions are the way in which C++ allows for late binding. Virtual functions can be freely redefined in derived classes; where a derived class does not redefine a virtual function, the default version in the base class will be used instead.

Exercises to Chapter Ten

1. If you haven't yet entered and run the programs in Chapter Ten, do so now.

2. Using Program 10.7 as a starting point, write a simple object-oriented database for any application with which you are familiar.

11

File operations in C++

Almost all the input and output operations that we have carried out in this book have involved the use of the special C++ idioms **cout <<** and **cin >>** instead of the C functions **printf()**, **scanf()** and others which are their near-equivalents. The reason for this is simple: the C++ forms are easier and more flexible to use. For instance, it is possible in C++ to use a line like

```
cin >> variable_1;
```

without worrying about whether **variable_1** is of type int, char, float, a character string or whatever; indeed, we have already seen in Chapter Nine that it is even possible to use this form with user-defined classes.

In the original C language, however, the form of the command to display the value of a variable on the screen would vary depending on the type of the variable being displayed. For instance, you would use this:

```
printf("%d",variable_1);
```

if **variable_1** is a decimal number,

```
printf("%s",variable_1);
```

if **variable_1** is a pointer to a character string, and so on.

It is obvious that the C++ syntax is much easier to use; indeed, it is probably fair to say that many would-be learners of the original C language have been very much put off by the difficulties offered by simple input and output; the fact that these difficulties have been eliminated at a stroke is one of the most obvious advantages for anyone beginning to learn C++.

However, it is important to realise that the new C++ commands do not completely replace the old C input/output functions; indeed, it is perfectly possible to mix the old and new styles if you wish to do so. The reason for this is that **cin >>** and **cout <<** do not provide completely new ways of handling input and output; rather, they use the C++ ability to overload the << and >> operators to form a protective shell – that is, one that protects the programmer – over the less friendly **printf()** and **scanf()** functions.

Looking in detail at C++ output

Although it is perfectly permissible for a newcomer to C++ to think of **cout <<** as merely the equivalent of the PRINT statement in Basic or the WRITE function in Pascal, this is actually a considerable oversimplification. It is better to understand that **cout** is a member of the predefined class **ostream**, just as **cin** is a member of the predefined class **istream**.

Bearing this in mind, consider the following, which is a portion of the code for the predefined class **ostream** which defines how the << operator is overloaded:

```
ostream& operator<<(const streambuf&);
ostream& operator<<(const char*);
ostream& operator<<(int a);
. . . . .
```

As you can see, the << operator has been overloaded to enable it to cope with a variety of different types of variable; that is why it is possible to write

```
cout << variable_1
```

without needing to worry about whether **variable_1** is an integer, a character, or whatever.

Of course, **cout** is not the only member of class **ostream**; in the Zortech implementation of C++ Version 2, there are no fewer than 4 different **ostreams** available. These are

```
stdout – standard output – reached through cout
stdprn – parallel printer port PRN (or LPT1) – reached through cprn
stdaux – serial port COM1 – reached through caux
stderr – standard error – reached through cerr
```

Just as you can direct output to the screen with **cout** <<, you can also direct output to the printer with **cprn** << or to the serial port with **caux** <<.

cerr is in some ways a special case. Its purpose is to allow error messages to continue to be displayed on the screen even if **cout** has been redirected to some other device; you can also redirect **cerr** so that certain messages are sent to some different device, such as a disc file. (It is for this reason that most DOS messages are directed to stderr rather than stdout.) This can be particularly useful if you are working on a program and do not want your error messages to interfere with screen output while it is being debugged and tested. We describe how to redirect **cerr** later in the chapter.

The ostream functions

As well as defining the various overloaded meanings for the << operator, the **ostream** class also defines two member functions: **flush()** and **put()**.

flush(): The purpose of **flush()** is to make sure that the buffer in which data is stored before being sent to a disc file has been properly emptied before the file is closed. Accordingly, it is always invoked by the destructor **~ostream()**, which is automatically called whenever the object goes out of scope, or when a program ends.

The elegance of this arrangement is that it is not normally necessary for the programmer to need to worry about flushing the buffer or closing a file, as this will be done automatically by means of the destructor mechanism. (Actually, closing the file is done by means of the **close()** function which is a member function of the predefined class **filebuf** which we shall meet later.)

put(): The **put()** function exists in order to send a single character to an output (typically a file). Although there are several other ways in which it is possible to handle file input and output, the ability to output just one character at a time can be extremely useful, as we shall see later.

Sending output to a disc file

We shall now learn how to send simple output to a disc file. The process is not a difficult one; indeed, C++ carefully shields the programmer from most of the awkward aspects of the operation.

Opening a file

Before it is possible to carry out any input or output operations on a disc file, that file must first be opened. In C++, this is done by assigning a buffer to the file and invoking the member function **open()**. The buffer is an object of the predefined type **filebuf** which we mentioned briefly above.

Because there are circumstances under which it may not be possible for a file to be opened – for instance, attempting to open a file for writing on a disc which is write-protected or already full – it is customary to check whether or not the operation has succeeded; this is very easy because the function **open**() returns 1 if the operation was successful and 0 if it was not.

The form of the command to open a file is thus as follows:

```
filebuf myfile; // declare an instance of class filebuf
if(myfile.open("FILENAME.EXT",output)==0) exit(1);
        // open file, abandon if not possible
```

In this example, *FILENAME.EXT* represents any legal DOS filename and extension, or a character string containing such a filename. It's also possible to include a DOS path, so that the following would also be perfectly proper:

```
if(myfile.open("A:\DIRNAME\FILENAME.EXT",output)==0)
   exit(1);
```

where *A:\DIRNAME\FILENAME.EXT* represents a legal path on your system. If no path specification is given, then the default drive and path will be used.

Incidentally, there's no need to enter the filename in upper case characters, as DOS doesn't distinguish between upper and lower case characters in file names and path specifiers.

Different file modes

In the example given above, we opened the file for output; hence the specifier **output** as the final argument in the list for the function **open**(). When a command is issued to open a file for output, the directory is checked to see whether or not a file with that name already exists. If it does not, then it is created and opened for writing; if it already exists, the existing file is given the extension .BAK (and any other file with the same name which already has the .BAK extension is deleted from the directory) and a new file is then opened for writing.

open () is actually one of the members of the enumerated type **open_mode**. The full list is as follows:

```
enum open_mode(input=0,output=1,append=2);
```

Opening a file in input mode means that it will be possible to read data from that file; we shall see examples of this later. Opening a file in append mode means that if the file already exists, it will not be deleted; instead, any new data which is sent to it will be added at the end of the existing file.

It isn't possible to designate a file as being simultaneously open for input (or append) and for output.

Attaching the file to ostream

Once the file has been successfully opened, the next step is to attach that file to class **ostream**. The command to do this is

```
ostream output_file(&myfile);
```

This calls the constructor for class **ostream** and attaches the buffer **myfile** to it.

Sending data to the file

It is now possible to send data to the newly-opened file. The command to do this is

```
output_file << "Hello there\n";
```

This will write the string **Hello there** on the disc file FILENAME.EXT; exiting from the program will then cause the file to be closed.

A complete example

Putting everything together, Program 11.1 incorporates all the code necessary to create a disc file on the default drive and directory:

Program 11.1

```
#include <stream.hpp>
#include <stdlib.h>

main()
{
   filebuf myfile; // declare an object of type filebuf
      // open the file, or exit if not possible
   if (myfile.open("FILENAME.EXT",output)==0) exit(1);
      // declare an object of type ostream and
      // attach it to the buffer
   ostream output_file(&myfile);
      // use the << operator to output the data
   output_file << "Hello there\n";
}
```

A simple key-to-disc program

We shall now use the techniques described in the previous section to create a simple key-to-disc program. This will take input from the keyboard a line at a time and save it in a disc file. The complete program is printed as Program 11.2

Program 11.2

```
#include <stream.hpp>
#include <stdio.h>
#include <stdlib.h>

main(int argc,char *argv[])
{
   char string[80];
   if(argc!=2)
   {
      cout << "No file-name - aborting ...\n";
      exit(1);
   }
   filebuf myfile;
   if(myfile.open(argv[1],output)==0)exit(1);
   ostream output_file(&myfile);
   cout << "Key in text; enter dot in Column 1 to quit\n\n";
   for(;;){
      gets(string);
      if (string[0]=='.') break;
      output_file << string << "\r\n";
   }
}
```

To run program 11.2, the name of the disc file on which the keyboard input is to be stored must be entered as the command tail; for instance, if the program is compiled as KEYDISC.EXE and you want to save the data in a file called TEXT.DAT on Drive A, you would enter the command

```
KEYDISC A:TEXT.DAT
```

at the DOS prompt. If you fail to enter a filename, the program will abort after displaying a suitable message; it will also abort if for any reason it can't open a file on the specified drive.

Once the file has been opened, the user is prompted to enter data one line at a time, pressing RETURN at the end of each line. Note that we have used the **gets()** function to input the data rather than **cin >>** as we need to input the complete string in one go, rather than as a succession of shorter strings separated by spaces.

Each line is then written to the named disc file – or, more exactly, it is sent to the disc buffer, from which it will be transferred to the file itself when the buffer is full or when the file is closed. Because the **gets()** function doesn't include the carriage return as a part of the string, this has to be separately written to the disc file at the end of each line; hence the command

```
output_file << string << "\r\n";
```

This sends both a carriage return \r and a newline \n to the file.

The program is terminated by entering a single dot at the beginning of a line and pressing RETURN. The dot is not treated as part of the file, and is thus not saved to disc. (The dot was chosen to mark the end of the file because this is a convention of some email systems; there is nothing to prevent you from replacing it with some other character if you prefer.)

Test the program to see that it works. You can display the text which has been saved to disc by using the DOS TYPE command; later on in this chapter we shall develop a simple program to read the file off the disc and display it on the screen.

Writing to a file with the put() function

It's also possible to send data to a file by means of the **put()** function, which is a public member function of class **ostream**, and which can thus be invoked by means of the dot operator. This function differs from the << operator in that it only transmits a single character at a time to the disc.

Program 11.3 shows how **put()** could be used in the key-to-disc program.

Program 11.3

```
#include <stream.hpp>
#include <stdio.h>
#include <stdlib.h>

main(int argc,char *argv[])
{
   char string[80],*c;
   if(argc!=2)
   {
     cout << "No file-name - aborting ...\n";
```

```
        exit(1);
    }
    filebuf myfile;
    if(myfile.open(argv[1],output)==0)exit(1);
    ostream output_file(&myfile);
    cout << "Key in text; enter dot in Column 1 to quit\n\n";
    for(;;){
        gets(string);
        if (string[0]=='.') break;
        for(c=string;*c;c++)output_file.put(*c);
        output_file.put(10);output_file.put(13);
    }
}
```

As you can see, this program is almost identical to Program 11.2; the only significant difference resulting from the use of the **put**() function lies in the use of the char pointer ***c** which is pointed in turn at every character in **string** and then written to the disc buffer. Note also how we have written the newline and carriage return values to the file at the end of each line using their Ascii values 13 and 10.

File input with C++

In general, C++ handles input from a file in ways which are very similar to those which we have already described for file output. It is necessary to declare an object of type **filebuf**, and then to open the file for input; then an object of type **istream** must be declared, and attached to the buffer; finally, the input can be carried out using either the >> operator or the function **get**(), which is a public member function of class **istream**, and is thus the equivalent of the public **ostream put**() function. It reads one character at a time from the file buffer.

Opening a file for input

The code to open a file for input is as follows:

```
filebuf myfile; // declare an object of type filebuf;
if(myfile.open("FILENAME.EXT",input)==0);
```

It is normal to check that the file has been successfully opened for input, and the second line of the code printed here shows how this ought to be done. This parallels the procedure used when opening a file for output. If the file is not found on the disc or path given, then the attempt to open the file will be abandoned.

Associating an istream with the buffer

The next step is to associate an object of type **istream** with the buffer which we have opened. The code to do this looks like this:

```
istream input_file(&myfile);
```

As you can see, this too is very similar to the code used when a file is being prepared for output.

Reading data from a file

With the file open for input, we are now ready to begin reading data from it. The procedure is rather similar to that used when outputting data to a file; however, there are some major differences which you need to know about.

Consider the situation which arises when you need to read a text file, for example, from a disc. Since you usually have no idea of how many characters the program will need to read, the simplest way of proceeding is simply to keep on reading characters until the End Of File (EOF) character is read.

In DOS systems, the CTRL-Z character is conventionally used to mark the end of a text file; it would therefore be possible to explicitly examine each character as it is input in order to see if it is the EOF character, and to finish reading data as soon as it has been found. However, C++ provides a simpler solution and this will be described in the next section.

Stream states

Associated with the **istream** and **ostream** classes are a series of flags which are stored in the private data element **state_value**. These describe the condition of an input or output stream – the **stream state**. Four possible conditions are defined:

_good means that the last i/o operation was successful.

_eof means that the last operation reached the end of the file.

_fail means that an error occurred, but that no characters have been lost.

_bad means that an error occurred during the last i/o operation, and that characters may have been lost.

Each condition is associated with a numeric value: **_good=0**, **_eof=1**, **_fail=2** and **_bad=3**.

Each of these stream states can be tested by an appropriate public **istream** member function; these are **eof()**, **good()**, **bad()** and **fail()**. Each of these returns True when its associated flag is set – that is, when the condition for which it tests has been met – and False otherwise.

For example, the function **eof()** returns True when the EOF character is found and False otherwise. Thus we can keep reading a file as long as **eof()** returns False; or, more simply, we can continue to read as long as **!eof()** returns True.

Reducing this to practical code, we could read one character at a time from a file, stopping when the end of the file has been met, using the following code:

```
while(!input_file.eof()) input_file.get(c);
```

where **c** is a variable of type char.

A problem with the >> operator

You will be aware (from the behaviour of **cin** when taking data from the keyboard) that an important feature of the >> input operator is that it 'stops' when it encounters spaces. For instance, the line

```
cin >> char-string;
```

will input characters into **char_string** only as far as the first space.

Similarly,

```
cin >> char_string1 >> char-string2;
```

expects two strings separated by a space to be typed in at the keyboard; the characters which precede the space will be input into **char_string1**, and the characters which come after the space are placed into **char_string2**. The spaces themselves are simply discarded. It is precisely because the C++ input command **cin >>** behaves in this way that we used the function **gets()** in Program 11.2 to read a complete string including spaces from the keyboard.

Much the same problem will occur if we use the >> operator when reading data from a file: each set of non-space characters will be read and stored as a variable, but the intervening spaces will be discarded. This is unlikely to be what we require; when reading data from a file, we generally want all of it, spaces included.

There are two possible solutions to the problem. The first is to use the **istream** public member function **get()** to read one character at a time from the file; we shall show how this is done later. The second solution is to use the public member function

skip() to change temporarily the way in which the >> operator behaves. Incidentally, don't get **get()** and **put()**, which are member functions of **istream** and **ostream** respectively, confused with **gets()** and **puts()**, which are found in the stdio.h library.

The skip() function

The purpose of the **skip()** function is to force the >> operator to treat spaces and other **whitespace** characters as valid strings, rather than discarding them. (**White space** characters are tabs, vertical tabs, carriage returns, newlines, formfeeds, and spaces.)

By default, whitespace skipping is enabled. To turn whitespace skipping off for **cin**, you would use the command

```
cin.skip(0);
```

and to turn it on again, you would enter

```
cin.skip(1);
```

To see how this works, look at the following fragment:

```
cin.skip(0);
cin >> char_string1 >> char_string2 >> char-string3;
```

If two words are typed in separated by a space, the first word will be stored in **char_string1**, the space will be stored in **char_string2**, and the second word will be stored in **char_string3**. In other words, the space will no longer be discarded as it would have been when whitespace skipping was enabled.

In general, this is not a terribly useful trick to use with the C++ command **cin** >>, because we normally either want to input complete lines – in which case we would use the **gets()** function – or we want to input individual items or items separated by a space – in which case **cin** >> with whitespace skipping enabled will suit us fine.

However, when we want to use the >> operator to read data from a file, it makes a great deal of sense to turn off the whitespace skipping, thus ensuring that the spaces and other whitespace characters won't be discarded.

Reading data from a file with the >> operator The following code will read data from a file using the >> operator and display it on the screen:

```
char string[80];
input_file.skip(0); // disable whitespace skipping
for(;;){ // start of infinite loop to read file
```

```
    input_file >> string; // read a string
    if (input_file.eof()) break; // quit if EOF
    cout << string; // otherwise display the string
}
```

Notice that although the char array variable **string** is long enough to allow for a string of 80 characters, this doesn't correspond to a normal screen line; instead, it corresponds to what would normally either be a single word, or the space(s) separating one word from the next.

Program 11.4 puts everything together. It is the converse of our first key-to-disc Program 11.2.

The program expects the name of the file to be read to be placed in the command tail. If no name is given, or if the file named cannot be opened, the program aborts; otherwise, the file is opened for input.

Each word or set of spaces between words is then read and displayed on the screen; when the end of file marker is reached, the program ends.

Program 11.4

```
#include <stream.hpp>
#include <stdio.h>
#include <stdlib.h>

main(int argc, char *argv[])
{
    char string[80];
    if(argc!=2){
        cout << "No file-name - aborting ...\n";
        exit(1);
    }
    filebuf myfile;
    if(myfile.open(argv[1],input)==0)exit(1);
    istream input_file(&myfile);
    input_file.skip(0);
    for(;;){
        input_file >> string;
        if (input_file.eof()) break;
        cout << string;
    }
}
```

If you use the key-to-disc program to save data to a file, you can use this program to recover that data and display it.

Using the get() function

An alternative way of reading data from a file is to do so one character at a time, using the **istream** public member function **get()**. Program 11.5 shows what changes would need to be made to Program 11.4 if this function were used.

Program 11.5

```
#include <stream.hpp>
#include <stdio.h>
#include <stdlib.h>

main(int argc,char *argv[])
{
   char c;
   if(argc!=2){
      cout << "No file-name - aborting ...\n";
      exit(1);
   }
   filebuf myfile;
   if(myfile.open(argv[1],input)==0)exit(1);
   istream input_file(&myfile);
   while(!input_file.eof()){
      input_file.get(c);
      cout << c;
   }
}
```

A program to convert Wordstar files to Ascii

In Chapter Two we noted that WordStar and some other word processing programs mark the last character of every word by setting the high order bit. The result of this is that when such a file is displayed on the screen using the DOS TYPE command, or sent directly to the printer with the DOS PRINT command, or perhaps imported into another word processing program which doesn't expect the high order bit to be set, garbage graphics characters appear instead of ordinary letters.

We shall now create a simple program to convert WordStar files into ordinary Ascii files. The technique is simple: the WordStar file will be opened for reading, and a new file will be opened for writing; then the contents of the WordStar file will be read, one character at a time, and each character will be ANDed with the value 127 in order to reset the high level bit. As we remarked earlier, the ability to read or write one character at a time can be very advantageous in some cases.

(The method used here to convert a WordStar file into Ascii was first described in Chapter Two; refer back to that chapter if you wish to refresh your memory of how the technique works.)

Program 11.6

```
#include <stream.hpp>
#include <stdio.h>
#include <stdlib.h>

main(int argc,char *argv[])
{
   char c;
   if(argc!=3) { // check that we have input and output files
      cout << "You must specify both the input and output
         files\n";
      exit(1); // and abort if not
   }
   filebuf myfile1,myfile2;
   if(myfile1.open(argv[1],input)==0
      || myfile2.open(argv[2],output)==0)exit(1);
         // abort if either file can't be opened
   istream input_file(&myfile1); // input file
   ostream output_file(&myfile2); // output file
   cout << "Converting ....\n"; // display a message and
   while(!input_file.eof()) { // continue to end of input file
      input_file.get(c); // read a character
      c&=127; // AND it with 127
      output_file.put(c); // and write it to output file
   }
   cout << "Job completed\n"; // display a message
} // and quit
```

As in the previous examples in this chapter, the names of the input and output files must be included in the command tail. If the filenames are forgotten, or if it isn't possible to open either file, then the program will abort; otherwise, the message **Converting ....** will be displayed, and the conversion will begin. Incidentally, the program runs quickly, and is quite usable as a 'real' program. If you wish to use it as such, you might like to add some more 'bells and whistles'; for instance, it would be very simple to display on-screen a running count of the number of characters that have been converted.

Returning characters to the buffer

It is occasionally necessary to 'taste' a character which is in the buffer without actually removing it from the buffer. For instance, you may set up a text file in such a way that the first character is either a special flag character – say # – in which case the rest of the file ought to be directed to the screen – or it is any other character, in which case the entire file will be sent to the printer. The contents of the file itself would thus determine the device to which it ought to be sent.

Although you would probably be quite happy to discard the # flag character if output was to be sent to the screen, if the first character was anything other than the flag you would not wish to lose it, but rather send it to the printer along with the rest of the file.

The simplest way of accomplishing this is by using the **istream** public member function **putback()**. This enables a single character which has been read to be pushed back onto the buffer; only the most recent character to be read can be pushed back, and it can only be pushed back once. If the last character to be read is the EOF marker, then it cannot in any case be pushed back.

The following fragment of code shows how a single character **c** can be read from the buffer **input_file**, displayed on the screen, and then pushed back onto the buffer:

```
char c;
input_file.get(c);
cout << c;
input_file.putback(c);
```

Resetting the stream states

One rather surprising feature of the C++ stream states **_good, _eof, _fail** and **_bad** is that although they are normally set by the condition found during a file access – by encountering the end of a file, for example – it is also possible to force them to a particular value under program control.

This is done by means of the two **clear()** functions, one of which is a public member of **istream** and one of which is a public member of **ostream**.

For instance, if you are reading a file and the **_fail** condition occurs, it may be possible to recover from the error. (Remember that **_fail**, unlike **_bad**, presumes that no characters have been lost.) To make the program try to continue reading the file after a **_fail** condition, you could force the stream state to **_good** as in the example overleaf:

```
char c;
cout << "File read failure - R to Retry, other key to
   abort\n";
c=getch();
if(c=='R'||c='r') input_file.clear(0);
else exit(1);
```

The effect of this code is to display the message **File read failure – R to Retry, other key to abort** on the screen and then to wait until a key is pressed. If either **R** or **r** is pressed, the stream state will be forced to **_good**; otherwise, the program will end.

(Remember that the **getch()** function waits for a key to be pressed; the program continues as soon as any key has been touched – without waiting for [RETURN] – and nothing is echoed to the screen. Before you can use **getch()**, you must use the line

```
#include <conio.h>
```

at the beginning of your code.

Redirecting output

We have already mentioned that it is quite possible to redirect output, so that – for instance – **cout** and **cerr** can be used to send data to other destinations that the screen.

The occasions on which it is wise to redirect output are likely to be few and far between. In particular, it is unlikely that you will ever gain much advantage from redirecting **cout** – although we do so below in order to show how the trick can be done. The most likely candidate for redirection is **cerr**. This normally outputs to the screen, but screen displays may change so rapidly that you are left with no record of which messages have appeared; redirecting **cerr** to the printer or to a disc file will enable you to gain a more lasting record.

Redirecting output to a disc file: Imagine, for instance, that you wish to use **cerr** to send data to a disc file. The code for this would look like this:

```
filebuf file1;
if(file1.open("SAMPLE.DAT",output)==0)exit(1);
ostream cerr(&file1);
cerr << "Hello world\n";
```

Here, we have declared that **cerr** is a member of class **ostream**, and have then directed it to **file1**, which we have already declared to be a member of class **filebuf**.

The result of this is that the last line of the program will send the message **Hello world** to the file SAMPLE.DAT on the default drive rather than to the standard error output – that is, the screen.

Redirection to a printer: Redirecting standard error output to a printer is equally simple. The code to redirect **cerr** to a parallel printer would look like this:

```
filebuf file1(stdprn);
ostream cerr(&file1);
cerr << "Hello world\n";
```

Note how when declaring **file1** to be a member of class **filebuf**, we have passed the argument **stdprn**. **stdprn** is the 'standard printer' – that is, the device known to DOS as LPT1 or PRN.

As well as **stdprn**, C++ recognises the following device names: **stderr**, **stdout** and **stdaux**; the first two of these refer to the screen, the last-named refers to the serial port COM1. Thus the following code will redirect **cout** to the serial port:

```
filebuf file1(stdaux);
ostream cout(&file1);
cout << "Hello world\n";
```

Other file functions

As well as the methods described above, which are peculiar to C++, all the functions developed for the original C language are also available, and these can be mixed freely with the C++ commands. Although the original commands are, in general, not quite so friendly to use as those provided in C++, they can on occasion provide a useful alternative way of inputting and outputting disc file data.

High and low level file functions

In the original C language it is usual to distinguish between the so-called **high level** and **low level** functions which the language provides. The former are easier to use because they allow a great deal of the file housekeeping – such as the management of the file pointer – to be carried out automatically; the low level functions – sometimes referred to as **Unix-like functions** – are trickier to use, but often create faster-running code than their high-level counterparts.

In this book, we concern ourselves only with the high level functions. This is because the others are apt to cause difficulties to newcomers to the language; the high level functions are in any case quite capable of handling any programming situation that you are likely to meet, and it is an error to attempt to mix the high level and low level functions.

Opening a file

As with the C++ commands that we have already looked at, it is necessary to open a file for either reading, writing or appending before it is possible to send data to it or to receive data from it. This is done by means of the **fopen()** function. The form of this is as follows:

```
FILE file_pointer;
if ((file_pointer=fopen("FILENAME.EXT","w"))==0)exit(1)
```

In the first line of this code, **file_pointer** is defined as a pointer variable of type FILE; the result of the code

```
file_pointer=fopen("FILENAME.EXT","w")
```

in the next line is that the computer will attempt to open a file FILENAME.EXT for writing (hence the **"w"**), and if it is possible to open that file successfully, it will assign a value other than zero to **file_pointer**. If it is not possible to create the file (perhaps because the disc is write-protected or full) then **file_pointer** will be given the value zero, and the program will stop.

File-type output to other devices Incidentally, it is also possible to use **fopen()** to open hardware devices such as printers or the monitor for the output of data. For instance, the following code will set up output to the printer *via* the parallel port:

```
FILE file_pointer; file_pointer=fopen("PRN","w");
```

It is also possible to use **fopen()** to send output to the console – that is, the monitor screen; the code to do so would look like this:

```
FILE file_pointer; fp=fopen("CON","wb");
```

Here, the form **"wb"** indicates that the 'file' is to be opened for writing in binary mode, as opposed to the normal text mode.

Sending data to an opened file

Once a disc file has been opened, you can choose from a variety of functions to send data to it. The most important are **putc()**, which writes a single character to the stream pointed to by the file pointer, and **fprintf()**, which sends a number of characters whose format depends on the **format string**.

Writing data with putc(): The **putc()** function provides a very simple way of storing a string of characters in a disc file, one character at a time. The command to write the character string **string** to the disc file pointed at by **file_pointer** looks like this:

```
char *c; for(c=string;*c;c++) {putc(c,file_pointer);
if(*c==EOF)break;}
```

The reason for the last line **if(*c==EOF)break;** is that **putc()** returns an EOF if any error occurs – such as a full disc – and consequently it is wise to check for this condition after every invocation of **putc()**.

Storing data with fprintf(): The **fprintf()** function is a much more complex one than **putc()**. It allows variables of every type to be written to disc according to a format chosen by the programmer. This is incorporated in the **format string** which contains a series of **conversion commands**. These are the same as those which are available for **printf()**, which we have already referred to in Chapter One.

Using the C file commands

To see how the C file commands would work, we shall now rewrite our key-to-disc program in the C manner.

Program 11.7

```
#include <stream.hpp>
#include <stdio.h>
#include <stdlib.h>

main(int argc,char *argv[])
{
   char string[80];
   FILE *fp; // declare pointer to FILE
   if(argc!=2){
      cout << "No file-name - aborting ...\n";
      exit(1);
   }
   // open file to write
   if((fp=fopen(argv[1],"w"))==NULL)exit(1);
   cout << "Key in text; enter dot in Column 1 to quit\n\n";
   for(;;){
      gets(string);
      if (string[0]=='.') break;
      fprintf(fp,"%s\r\n",string); // write string + CRLF
   }
   fclose(fp); // close the file
}
```

You may find it instructive to compare this program with Program 11.2, which is the exact equivalent using the C++ **ostream** and **filebuf** classes instead of the high level file functions of the original C language. Both programs work in exactly the same way, and the output from both is identical.

Closing the file: One point about using the original C file-handling techniques is that it is necessary to use the function **fclose()** to close the open file before the program comes to an end. This makes sure that all the buffers are flushed and that the files are properly closed.

The only reason that it is not necessary to explicitly close any open files when using the C++ commands described earlier is that when the final brace of the program is reached, destructors are called for the classes **ostream** and **istream**, and one of the jobs performed by these destructors is to close any open files.

Reading a disc file with the C functions

Program 11.8 is the equivalent using the original C functions of Program 11.5; like the **istream** public function **get()**, the function **gets()** reads and displays a file one character at a time.

Program 11.8

```
#include <stream.hpp>
#include <stdio.h>
#include <stdlib.h>

main(int argc,char *argv[])
{
   char c;
   FILE *fp;
   if(argc!=2){
      cout << "No file-name - aborting ...\n";
      exit(1);
   }
   // open for reading
   if((fp=fopen(argv[1],"r"))==NULL)exit(1);
   for(;;){ // start the read/output loop
      c=getc(fp); // fetch a character
      if(c==EOF) break; // break if EOF
      cout << c; // otherwise output the char
   }
   fclose(fp); // close the file
}
```

Random file access

So far we have only considered the situation in which we have been reading or writing a complete file. However, it is also possible to read or write individual bytes without affecting the remainder of the file in any way.

This is accomplished by means of the **fseek()** function, which moves a pointer to the byte at which reading or writing will take place.

The formal definition of the **fseek()** function looks like this:

```
fseek(FILE *fp, long offset, int origin)
```

More simply, the first argument is the pointer to the file being accessed; the second is the number of the byte you wish to access, expressed as the offset from the 'origin'; and the third argument is the 'origin', which must be either the beginning of the file (0), the current position (1), or the end of the file (2). The beginning of the file is also known as **SEEK_SET**; the current position is **SEEK_CUR**; and the EOF position is **SEEK_END**.

fseek() returns zero if the pointer has been successfully moved to the required position; if a pointer error occurs, a non-zero value will be returned.

When the **fseek()** function is used with a text file, either the origin must be at the physical beginning of the file or the offset must be zero.

For instance, to access the first byte of a text file, the function call would look like this:

```
fseek(fp,0,0);
```

Here, the first argument is the pointer to the file being accessed; the second argument **0** is the number of bytes which it is required to move beyond the origin; and the final argument declares that the origin is the beginning of the file.

A reverse file-display program: Program 11.9 is a 'backward' version of our file-display program; it uses the function **filesize()** (which needs the **#include io.h** directive) to determine the size of the target file, and assigns this value to the variable **size**. It also displays the filesize in bytes.

Then, setting the origin to the beginning of the file and making the offset equal to the size of the file in bytes – and thus pointing to the final byte – it works through the file decrementing the file pointer and outputting one character at a time until the complete file has been displayed on the screen backwards. When the file pointer indicates that the offset is zero, and that the first character has therefore been reached and output, the program ends.

Program 11.9

```
#include <stream.hpp>
#include <stdio.h>
#include <stdlib.h>
#include <io.h>

main(int argc,char *argv[])
{
   char c;
   FILE *fp;
   long file_counter,size;
   if(argc!=2){
      cout << "No file-name - aborting ...\n";
      exit(1);
   }
   size=filesize(argv[1]);
   cout << "The size of the file is " << size << " bytes\n";
   if((fp=fopen(argv[1],"r"))==NULL)exit(1);
   if (fseek(fp,size,SEEK_SET)){
      cout << "File error - aborting ...\n";
      exit(1);
   }
   for(;size>=0;){
      if(c=='\n')size--; // avoid double spacing
      fseek(fp,size--,SEEK_SET);
      c=getc(fp);
      cout << c;
   }
   fclose(fp);
}
```

The line **if(c=='\n')size--;** is necessary to prevent a blank line being printed between each line of the file.

Reading and writing to the same file

Normally, both **fopen()** and the **filebuf** function **open()** allow a file to be opened for reading, writing or for data to be appended to an existing file. It is also possible to use **fopen()** to open a file for both reading and writing.

The way in which the **fopen()** function would be used to enable this looks like this:

```
if((fp=fopen"FILENAME.EXT","r+"))==NULL)exit(1);
```

You will see that the file has been opened in **r+** mode; this means that it can be both written to and read at the current position of the file pointer (as located by the **fseek()** function); indeed, an **fseek()** must be performed on the file between the reading and writing operations, except that you can change to a write operation without **fseek()** if the last read operation found EOF.

A safe-erase program: Program 11.10 shows how it is possible to overwrite an existing file.

Normally, when a file is deleted it remains on disc and can be recovered – and the contents read – as long as the disc space has not been used for some other file. This can have important security implications, as anyone armed with one of the commercially-available 'unerase' programs may be able to resurrect a file which you had erased.

The only solution to this is to overwrite every character in the file with some other character; Program 11.10 writes a sequence of '@' characters over the file contents.

Program 11.10

```
#include <stream.hpp>
#include <stdio.h>
#include <stdlib.h>
#include <io.h>

main(int argc,char *argv[])
{
    char c, answer;
    FILE *fp;
    long file_counter=0,size;
    if(argc!=2){
        cout << "No file-name - aborting ...\n";
        exit(1);
    }
    size=filesize(argv[1]);
    cout << "Are you sure you want to safe-delete " << argv[1]
        << " Y/N ?\n";
    answer=getch();
    if(answer!='y' && answer!='Y')exit(1);
    cout << "Overwriting file ...\n";
    if((fp=fopen(argv[1],"w"))==NULL)exit(1);
    for(;file_counter!=size;){
        fputc('@',fp);
        fseek(fp,file_counter++,SEEK_SET);
    }
    fclose(fp);
    cout << "Deleting file ...\n";
    remove(argv[1]);
}
```

Other read-write modes: As well as the **r+** mode, there are two other modes which allow for both reading and writing. These are **w+** and **a+**.

w+ causes the file to be created if it does not exist; if it already exists, then it is truncated at the current position of the file pointer, and new material is then added after the point at which truncation occurred.

a+ also creates the file if it does not exist; however, in this case the pointer is moved to EOF, and new material is appended after this point.

Writing in text or binary mode

So far, all our file handling has been carried out in text mode; that is, all material has been written to the disc file as a string of characters, in exactly the same way as it would be output to the screen or the printer.

Text mode is the default mode for writing and reading material to disc; it has the great advantage of being easy to understand, and it can be used with variables of all types.

For instance, consider the following fragment of code:

```
float a=123.45;int b=46;char c='d';
output_file << a << b << c;
```

This will send the following sequence of characters to **output_file**:

```
123.4546d
```

As you can see, all the values have been sent to the file just as they are, without even spaces being added between them.

Although there is nothing to prevent you from using text mode for writing values, it is faster, and takes up less file-space, to specify binary mode when opening a file to write numeric values. Numbers are then written to the file in the same format as is used for RAM storage. An integer number which might take five bytes to express as text will only take up two bytes of the file if written in binary mode, so the saving in space can be considerable.

To open a file to write binary values, use the **fopen()** function like this:

```
if((fp=fopen("FILENAME.EXT","wb"))==NULL)exit(1);
```

Similarly, use this form to open a file to read binary values:

```
if((fp=fopen("FILENAME.EXT","rb"))==NULL)exit(1);
```

Postscript to Chapter Eleven

C++ offers two different ways of manipulating data files: files can be attached to **istream** or **ostream** and then read or written with the << and >> operators, as well as the public member functions such as **put**() and **get**(); and they can also be handled with the original C functions.

Regardless of which system you use, a file must be opened before it can be accessed. If you use the original C functions, the file must also be explicitly closed before the program ends; in C++, the **ostream** and **istream** destructors handle file-closing automatically.

The standard streams **stderr**, **stdin**, **stdaux**, **stdout** and **stdprn** can all be redirected, enabling output to **stderr** to be sent to the screen or printer, for example.

The **fseek**() function allows a file to be accessed non-sequentially, by moving a file pointer relative to a stated point of origin, which may be either the beginning or end of a file, or the current position.

Exercises to Chapter Eleven

1. If you haven't yet entered and run the programs in Chapter Eleven, do so now.

2. Modify the WordStar to Ascii Program 11.6 to maintain an on-screen counter of the number of bytes converted while the program is running.

3. Write a program to accept the names of two disc files from the command line and to compare the files; if the two files are identical, output a suitable message; if they are different, output the offset from the beginning of the file of the first difference between the files.

4. Write a program that will copy one disc file to another using command line arguments.

Index

C++ Operators and Directives

!, 58, 229
!=, 56

#define, 14, 46
#include, 14, 16, 19, 121, 123

%, 34, 37
%=, 45

&, 41, 82, 83, 96, 131, 147, 160, 167, 229
&&, 57, 58
&=, 45

( ), 37, 100, 240

*, 32 – 37, 82, 83, 96, 130, 148, 151, 167,
    175, 224, 229
*=, 45

+, 32, 34, 224, 225, 229, 235, 236
++, 34, 36, 93, 224, 225, 229
+=, 45, 232

– , 32, 34, 36, 224, 229, 235 – 237
– – , 34, 36, 229
– =, 45, 232
–> arrow operator, 167, 173, 175
– w compiler flag, 57

., 158, 171, 227
..., 118

.OBJ files, 122

/, 32, 34, 36, 37
/=, 45

:, 192, 257
::, 170, 286

<conio.h>, 302

=, 33, 34, 193, 195, 235, 238
==, 56

<, 45, 244, 246, 293
>, 45, 56, 58, 244, 246, 296, 297
>= , 58
<, 58
<=, 56, 58

? :., 45

^, 41, 43
^=, 45

_bad, 295, 301
_eof, 295, 301
_fail, 295, 301
_good, 295, 301

{ }, 53, 156

|, 41, 42
|=, 45
||, 57, 58

~, 41, 43, 181, 229

HAMPSHIRE RAILWAYS
The History of Steam

Colin Maggs

COUNTRYSIDE BOOKS
NEWBURY BERKSHIRE

CONTENTS

ABBREVIATIONS

■

BR	British Railways
DNSR	Didcot, Newbury & Southampton Railway
GWR	Great Western Railway
LBSCR	London, Brighton & South Coast Railway
LMR	Longmoor Military Railway
LMS	London, Midland & Scottish Railway
LNER	London & North Eastern Railway
LSWR	London & South Western Railway
MR	Midland Railway
MSWJR	Midland & South Western Junction Railway
SDJR	Somerset & Dorset Joint Railway
SR	Southern Railway

STEAMING INTO THE COUNTY

·

ALTHOUGH, AT FIRST, Hampshire's rail routes might seem complicated, basically they are simple. They consist of lines to and from London, a line to and from the Midlands and a line from South Wales to Portsmouth. From these main lines, branches were developed to reach other areas of the county.

Hampshire was served principally by the London & South Western Railway (LSWR), with the London, Brighton & South Coast Railway (LBSCR) making inroads from the east, and the Great Western Railway (GWR) from the north. Of the LSWR's two competitors for traffic, the GWR was considered the greatest.

Hampshire had three areas of rail traffic: Portsmouth for its docks and being the main gateway to the Isle of Wight; Southampton, one of the country's major ports; and Bournemouth, a principal seaside resort. The latter, of course, since the local government reorganisation of 1974 is now in the county of Dorset.

LONDON TO SOUTHAMPTON AND PORTSMOUTH

What became the LSWR's London to Southampton line started as an idea for constructing a canal from Spithead to London. The scheme proved impracticable as it was realised that a railway would offer better communication.

On 26 February 1831, a year after the Liverpool & Manchester Railway opened, a meeting was held at the home of Abel Rous Dottin, MP for Southampton. This was followed by a public meeting on 6 April at which the scheme was cumbersomely entitled the Southampton, London & Branch Railway & Dock Company, the branch being Basingstoke to Bristol. In order to obtain powers to secure land for building the line, an Act of Parliament had to be sought. By the time the Bill came before the House in 1834, the line's title had been curtailed to the London & Southampton Railway.

The Southampton line was not built by one major contractor, but divided into segments and carried out by relatively small contractors. Work was started on the first at Shapley Heath, near Winchfield, on 6 October 1834 by Messrs Treadwell. The initial turf was turned by Mr Bainbridge, a local landowner who had actually given, not sold, part of his estate to the railway.

The policy of Francis Giles, the company's engineer, of employing small contractors who had little capital, was poor, because these builders completed the easy part of their length and then stopped work and demanded more money. These demands of the small contractors meant that the company had to choose whether to yield to them, or delay the works. By 31 August 1835 only four miles of the seventy-eight had been completed. This cost Francis his job. He was forced to resign and was replaced in 1837 by Joseph Locke who had assisted George Stephenson in building the Liverpool & Manchester

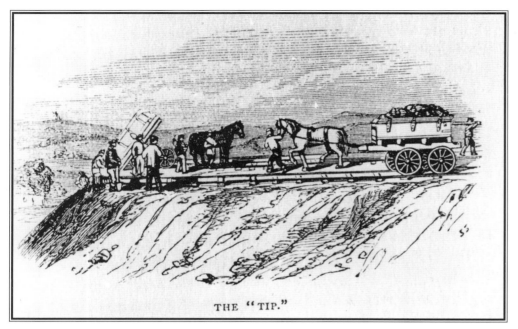

THE "TIP."

■ *Making an embankment. A horse draws a wagon of spoil dug from a cutting and it is tipped to form an embankment.* (Author's collection) ■

idle life. They were in one of two shifts: 3 am till noon, or noon till 9 pm, a 40-minute break being allowed for meals. However, Thomas Brassey showed great care for the navvies he employed by creating a benefit society for them. As many workmen received treatment at the Winchester County Hospital, he proposed that the London & Southampton should donate a sum and also provide for 'the cost of a frame used in conveying men injured on the works to hospital'.

Initially, horse-drawn wagons carried spoil from a cutting to an embankment but as soon as sufficient track had been laid, locomotives were used. To reduce labour, the surveyor usually arranged that a cutting would be followed by an embankment.

Opening a railway always caused some stagecoaches to become redundant. William James Chaplin, principal partner in the coaching firm of Chaplin & Horne, which owned 64 coaches, 1,500 horses and some hotels, foresaw the danger and in 1837 wisely sold most of the coaching business and invested in the London & Southampton Railway. The board elected him director in 1843.

The line opened from Nine Elms, London to Winchfield on 24 September 1838, and to Basingstoke on 10 June 1839; this

Railway. Locke dismissed many of the small contractors, replacing them with Thomas Brassey on the Basingstoke to Winchester contract and David McIntosh for that between Winchester and Southampton.

The navvies were well-paid and earned three to four shillings a day, compared with an agricultural labourer's wage of ten shillings a week, but the navvies certainly did not live an

■ *Adams T3 class 4-4-0 No 574 heads a Down train at Basingstoke. Built in October 1893, it was withdrawn in July 1933.*
Notice the shine on the buffers. The different forms of gas lamps are worth a second glance, too. (Author's collection) ■

latter date also saw the opening of the Winchester to Southampton line. The terminus there was a temporary one at Northam Road as William Tite's Southampton Terminus was not ready until the opening of the entire line on 11 May 1840.

Unfortunately, the winter of 1839/40 brought more rain than any other within living memory, so the line with its unusually high embankments and cuttings suffered slips involving costly repairs.

At 4.30 am on 11 May, 21 empty coaches reached Southampton from London and at 6.30 am the first Up train departed. Near Micheldever, Brassey entertained the directors in marquees, while navvies feasted on roast ox and beer. The Southampton press was unable to report a terrible disaster, the only accidents being 'the decapitation of a dog who had got in front of a train and the smashing of a pair of gates at Northam in the middle of the night by an engine making a passage through them'.

Initially, a passenger booked at a counter and was given a paper ticket torn from books with five to a page and stamped with the destination and date. The Edmondson system of card tickets was not used by the company until 1845 when alterations were made to entrance halls to allow only one passenger at a time to book before each clerk.

The first passengers hardly received a warm welcome. They were presented with a leaflet listing regulations that forbade them opening a coach door, or alighting without assistance from the staff. Having booked, they were generously allowed to board a train if there was room, but passengers travelling the longest distance took preference. If a ticket was lost, one was required to pay the fare from the station where the train originated, while smoking was punished by removal from the premises and forfeiture of the fare.

First class passengers did not enjoy lights until December 1841, while second class passengers were exposed, above shoulder height, to the elements. Third class passengers were even less fortunate; they travelled in open coaches attached to goods trains. In 1882 Sam Fay, later Superintendent of the LSWR, in his book *A Royal Road*, a history of the company, revealed that the first class coaches had compartments so narrow that:

> *… travellers' knees were pressed uncomfortably hard against those of their opposite neighbour. Much as a first class passenger might grumble at the small space allotted him, his fellow traveller in a second class had far greater discomfort to complain of; his seat was a bare board, his knees in as close proximity to his vis a vis as in the superior carriage, and unless provided with a good umbrella, the chances argued in favour of a wet skin, for all second class carriages were open to the weather on either side. First class luggage was loaded on the roof, while all belongings of second class passengers were deposited in two boots placed across their carriage, underneath the seats, and opening from the outside.*

Third class passengers were people who hitherto had been accustomed to travelling on the outside of a mail coach, so no covering for them was thought necessary. Fay wrote:

> *A frame work with seats, fitted on the bed of a carriage truck, constituted the vehicle in which third class passengers travelled in those days; the frame work was removed upon the truck being required for its ordinary purpose … On a wet day the condition of the poor wretches condemned by poverty to travel in such conveyances may be more easily imagined than described; if they turned their backs to the storm the rain ran down their necks, if they faced it their eyes became blinded and their pockets filled with water; an umbrella was a useless impediment, and their truck really resolved itself into a species of horizontal shower bath from whose searching power there was no escape.*

These open coaches were attached to goods trains which, at first, were in the charge of three boys aged about fifteen and took upwards of six hours to travel from London to Southampton. It was soon found that the boys devoted more attention to playing games than to the company's goods traffic and they were superseded by guards. Initially there was no guard's van, the guard riding in 'Noah's Ark', which conveyed small packages for stations. The wagons had dumb buffers and springless drawgear. When a train was ready to start, the guard scotched the last wagon and the engine backed to slacken the couplings to enable it to take the weight of the train a wagon at a time.

Fay continued:

> *An Act was passed by Parliament in 1845, compelling railway companies to run one cheap train daily, charging at the rate of one penny per mile, and travelling at an average speed of twelve miles an hour for the whole journey; passengers to be provided with seats and protected from the weather. Only the latter clause affected the arrangements then in force on the South Western, and to remedy this, carriages were built with two glass lights in each roof, but no glass windows at the sides or to the doors; there were spaces all along the sides at the top for air, closed by curtains. Third class travelling on the South Western was then described as the best in England, few companies favouring their customers with glass in any part of the vehicle; in the majority of instances too, their seats were very narrow, and, apparently with a design to afford a maximum of discomfort, were ranged round the carriage sides.*

At first the London & Southampton refused to accept responsibility for mails, so the bags were placed in a stout waterproof box on a coach roof, a Post Office guard riding outside to keep an eye on them. When mails were eventually accepted, mail train guards sat inside until on 11 November 1843, three vehicles were damaged by thrown stones, so the authorities ruled: '… in future the guards sit outside the carriages instead of in the closed box, and that they be provided with coffee at the Woking and Basingstoke station.'

At this period an ordinary passenger guard sat on the roof of a first class coach where he worked a brake to assist the engine drivers – continuous brakes being very much in the future.

The first porters wore fustian jackets with arm badges and chocolate-coloured caps. Guards wore chocolate-coloured frock coats with dark trousers. Ticket collectors, watchmen and policemen (the latter also acted as signalmen) wore swallow-tailed chocolate-coloured coats, dark trousers and tall hats with leather crowns. Discipline was severe and carelessness punished by fines, dismissal or even prosecution. Sir John Easthope, LSWR chairman, was alleged to have recruited all staff from Leicester where he was MP.

■ *Ex-LBSCR No B626 stands in the train shed at Gosport in the 1920s. The station chimney is of an unusual design.* (Lens of Sutton) ■

Eyes to Portsmouth

Almost as soon as the London & Southampton Act was passed, the company turned its eyes towards Portsmouth, intending to build a branch from Southampton, but the proud citizens of Portsmouth were unhappy with this, wanting their own direct railway, not one via Southampton. Eventually, in 1839, the extension was authorised from Southampton to Gosport, but in deference to the fortifications, the railway was required to build Gosport station no higher than the local commanding Royal Engineer permitted. The company cleverly avoided the citizens of Portsmouth having to use the dreaded word 'Southampton', by renaming the company the London & South Western Railway.

■ *Adams A12 class 0-4-2 No 644 heads a goods train outside Gosport locomotive shed. No 644, built in March 1893, was withdrawn in January 1939, but due to a wartime shortage of locomotives, was reinstated in September 1939 and only finally withdrawn in March 1946. Between the solitary wagon and the engines is a bin of pebbles, the contents of which were used to stop clinker forming on the firebars. (Author's collection)* ■

The trusted Thomas Brassey was contracted to build the line and all appeared to be ready for opening on 26 July 1841 when, on 15 July, part of Fareham Tunnel slipped, despite having walls 3 feet thick. It was deemed more economic to open out the affected part rather than to make a repair. The line opened on 29 November 1841 but, on 3 December, fresh slips appeared and passenger services were withdrawn until 7 February 1842.

Portsmouth Direct
The LSWR route to Portsmouth was devious as after travelling nearly 90 miles from London, the journey had to involve the ferry from Gosport. A direct route was sought.

The line from Cosham to Portsmouth was jointly run between the LSWR and the LBSCR. London to Portsmouth receipts were pooled five-eighths to the LSWR and three-eighths to the LBSCR.

Thomas Brassey saw an opening for building a direct route from Godalming to Havant and hoped that on completion he could lease it to either the LSWR or the LBSCR. However, neither company was interested as by shortening the route to Portsmouth by 20 miles, fares would be reduced and thus also their profit. Then the LSWR, perhaps fearing that the South Eastern Railway might lease the line, decided to take up the option.

Although the Direct Portsmouth had running powers from Havant to Portsmouth Junction, the LBSCR decided that the LSWR had not, so blocked working. The LSWR informed the LBSCR that it would send a goods train through on

28 December 1858 but, as Sam Fay recounts, when it steamed into Havant:

> … it was manned by upwards of a hundred platelayers and other rough and ready employees of the Company, under the orders of Mr Scott [Archibald Scott, traffic manager]. The South Western train was not expected until about 10 o' clock, but Mr Scott took time by the forelock and reached the junction at 7.0 a.m. He found the Brighton people had prepared for a surprise by removing the points, and placing an engine on the crossing during the night. No time was lost in relaying the points and the Brighton engine was forcibly seized. By this time the rival army had mustered in force and before Mr Scott could get clear they had lifted a rail on their main line. The South Western goods was then on the crossing, blocking both lines, and in that position Mr Scott and his force remained for two hours. At one time a serious fight appeared imminent, but at length Mr Scott retreated on Guildford leaving the question to be fought out before the Queen's Bench.

When LSWR passenger traffic began on 1 January 1859, as rail throughout was impossible, bus connections were made at Havant. An injunction was sought restraining the LBSCR and through LSWR running commenced on 24 January. Having lost the battle in court, the LBSCR began the battle of fares by charging only 5s 0d return and then a further reduction to 3s 6d. The LBSCR even attacked the LSWR's Southampton

■ *A busy scene at Havant: K10 class mixed traffic 4-4-0 No 386, built in June 1902 and withdrawn September 1949, works a Waterloo to Portsmouth express, while G6 class 0-6-0T shunts. The wheel to work the level crossing gates can be seen on the signalman's right. To ease sighting, the tall signals have repeater arms set at a lower level. A train from Hayling Island stands in the bay platform, left.* (Author's collection) ■

■ *Havant, view Up, circa 1910. 'LV' on the Hayling Island set of coaches, left, stands for 'Last Vehicle' and indicates to a signalman that the train is complete.* (Author's collection) ■

traffic by running a steamer service between Portsmouth and Southampton and offering a very low inclusive fare to London. After some months of competition, the companies realised that they were both losers and reverted to the former pooled arrangements, the LSWR taking two-thirds as operators of the shortest route and the LBSCR one-third.

Eastleigh (Bishopstoke) to Salisbury

The LSWR, with expansion to the west of England in mind, cast its eyes towards Salisbury, so a line from Eastleigh, then called Bishopstoke, to Milford, on the outskirts of Salisbury, was authorised in 1844. Initially things did not appear auspicious. Landowners proved obstructive and prices offered for their properties had to go to arbitration. Then, instead of employing the reliable Thomas Brassey, the contract of the delightfully-named Hoof & Hill was accepted since it was £18,000 below that of its competitors. However, it proved an excellent example of cheap proving dear.

Due to the delay in obtaining land in turn delaying the contractors, Joseph Locke, the LSWR engineer, offered Hoof & Hill an extra £1,000 if the line could be opened on 10 August 1846. This they were unable to do as farmers gathering in the harvest were able to offer higher wages than the contractors.

■ *An early view of Romsey. Notice the low-height platform, the shunting horse and the ballast covering the sleepers – this makes the footing more comfortable for the horse.* (Author's collection) ■

Opening was postponed until October and then, due to unfavourable weather, November, then December. Finally it was opened to Salisbury for coal and goods on 27 January 1847, the first train arriving behind 0-6-0 No 52 *Rhinoceros* in

■ A 2-2-2, Elk, *as reconstructed in February 1856, with feed water heating equipment, seen here at Romsey on a Portsmouth to Salisbury working. Built in September 1838 it was withdrawn in July 1871. At that period when metallurgy was not so advanced, side safety chains were used in addition to the centre coupling. Here the two safety chains are coupled to each other. (Author's collection)* ■

the charge of Driver Naylor who usually drove the Royal Train. Sixteen tons of coal were earmarked for 'distressed persons'. One of the chief benefits the railway brought was cheaper coal, advantageous both to households and industry and thus helping to raise living standards.

The branch opened to passenger traffic on 1 March 1847 and thus enabled Salisbury citizens to reach London by one of the four daily trains after making a change at Bishopstoke. As this was a roundabout route, in due course a direct line was built from Salisbury, joining the main Southampton line west of Basingstoke.

LINKS BETWEEN THE MIDLANDS AND HAMPSHIRE

Hampshire was served by four lines from the Midlands:

1 The Midland & South Western Junction Railway (MSWJR), providing a link between the Midland Railway at Cheltenham and the LSWR at Andover from where a line through Horsebridge brought trains to Southampton.
2 The Didcot, Newbury & Southampton Railway (DNSR), which brought trains from Oxford and the North to Winchester where they could be taken to various destinations on the LSWR.
3 The Reading and Basingstoke line which served as a link between the Midlands and Hampshire, and indeed is the one currently surviving, running parallel with the DNSR.
4 The Somerset & Dorset Joint Railway, which brought trains from the North and Midlands to Bournemouth via Bath.

The MSWJR and the Sprat & Winkle Line

During the railway mania of 1845 several schemes were proposed for linking Southampton and Manchester, but were defeated either by lack of finance or by the GWR strongly objecting to a rival railway cutting across its territory.

The grand idea was whittled down to the Swindon, Marlborough & Andover Railway, which eventually was extended northwards to reach the MR at Cheltenham. This meant that from 1 May 1892 through trains could run from Southampton to Cheltenham, hauled throughout by MSWJR locomotives and onwards by those of the MR. The LSWR made no charge for the MSWJR using Southampton Terminus station, while regarding its running powers from Andover to Southampton, the MSWJR received an allowance as working expenses of 25% on passenger traffic and 33% on goods. From 1 June 1892 Burton beer for export and consumption at Portsmouth travelled via the MSWJR.

The MSWJR entered Hampshire a mile south of Ludgershall. From there a branch ran to a large military camp at Tidworth. Although this branch was in Wiltshire, a curiosity was that when purchasing a ticket, the passenger stood in Hampshire facing the booking clerk in Wiltshire! A further curiosity was that the branch had only one Sunday train and this comprised the first half of an Andover to Swindon service, the rest of the train being left at Ludgershall, while the first half travelled the 2¼ miles to Tidworth and back. Apart from passengers for Swindon suffering a delay of 30 minutes, they could get very cold as the removal of the engine meant the removal of the supply for the steam heating.

■ *A Midland & South Western Junction Railway 0-6-0T and rake of coaches at Tidworth. One advertisement board proclaims 'White Star Line' and another, the 'Japan British Exhibition'.* (Author's collection) ■

The MSWJR provided a highly useful direct link between Southampton, the Midlands and the North, meaning that passengers to and from vessels could travel direct in through coaches, rather than go via London and have to cross the city before catching another train to their destination. The MSWJR went all out to seek traffic for the North and to this end employed an agent at Southampton to visit hotels in the town and try and persuade passengers to use the MSWJR's route.

On summer weekends two South expresses were run to Southampton, one from Manchester and the other from Birmingham, in addition to six other through trains between Cheltenham and Southampton. Pre-1914 a through train was run from Whitehaven carrying migrants from the depressed area, while each Friday morning a train ran from Liverpool, where emigrants from Bulgaria, Italy, Romania and the Ukraine had gathered before being sent to Southampton. These passengers were often a pitiful sight. At Southampton the MSWJR's canvassing agent checked these passengers. All wore identity-discs around their necks and his task was often rendered more difficult by the fact that quite a few children had chewed theirs to illegibility. These trains reeked of garlic and had to be fumigated before further use. From July to September 1913, it is recorded that 2,891½ emigrants were carried (the half being a child).

Another important traffic carried by the MSWJR was milk for London. Every evening between 9 pm and 10 pm an MSWJR train arrived at Andover with seventeen loaded milk vans holding the product of Wiltshire cows. From Andover an LSWR engine and guard took them on to Clapham Junction and Waterloo.

South of Andover, the MSWJR reached Southampton via

the Sprat & Winkle line, or the Andover & Redbridge Railway, as it was officially known. It ran from Andover to Kimbridge Junction. On 20 September 1859 Lord Palmerston turned the first sod near his home at Broadlands, Romsey. The contractor Richard Hattersley was rather cunning. The line was to be built principally on the site of the Andover Canal, which meant that when following contours, it encountered many curves. Instead of immediately draining the canal so that the mud would harden, Hattersley delayed this action until he was almost ready to commence work and then could charge for the cost of removing the sticky mud. His work proved to be very poorly executed, so he was dismissed in May 1861.

Financial difficulties caused further delays and the line was not opened until 6 March 1865. The first train was hardly a roaring success as it arrived at Andover with only five passengers and having twice slipped to a standstill. The opening of the Swindon, Marlborough & Andover Railway on 1 May 1882 placed it on a through route and boosted the line's traffic to such an extent that during the three subsequent years the line was actually doubled between Andover and Kimbridge Junction to cope with it.

A curiosity was that in 1886 at Leckford, which had no station, every weekday a small black dog collected for its master a wrapped newspaper thrown by the guard of the passing 12.56 pm from Andover.

The combined route of the MSWJR and Sprat & Winkle proved invaluable in the First World War carrying troops and supplies to the Channel ports and wounded soldiers northwards in hospital trains. Throughout the war, in addition to normal traffic, an average of four troop trains and one ambulance train ran daily. In fact, drivers were so busy that they sometimes had to work 24 hours without a rest and occasionally were unable to see their families for a fortnight.

The Second World War saw the line again proving a vital artery, but with the rise in road transport in the 1950s, the MSWJR became uneconomic and most of it closed on 11 September 1961. Similarly, the Sprat & Winkle closed on 7 September 1964, despite its local passenger trains having been dieselised seven years previously. It is interesting to record that one of the first internal-combustion engined railcars in the country appeared on the Sprat & Winkle line in 1928. Built by Drewry, it had a 50 hp engine and seated 26 passengers.

The Didcot, Newbury & Southampton Railway
The DNSR ran parallel with the MSWJR and had similar aims. The portion in Hampshire ran from Woodhay to Winchester, Southampton being reached over the LSWR's main line.

The Hampshire section of the DNSR was to have been opened on 24 March 1885, but due to the working company, the GWR, being unable to find sufficiently skilled staff, the inauguration was not held until 4 May 1885. Laid as a single line, earthworks and bridges were sufficiently wide to allow for doubling the track. Most DNSR stations were in a cottage-style, having a small gable over each first floor window. Winchester station used a GWR design. Initially designated Winchester Cheesehill, in 1949 BR took note of the local pronunciation and renamed it Chesil.

Like the MSWJR, the DNSR was an important link in both World Wars. Between 6 and 22 August 1914 all public

■ *Highclere, view Down, circa 1918.* (Lens of Sutton) ■

passenger trains on the line were suspended to allow troop trains to run continuously day and night to Southampton Docks. Then, in the Second World War, the Hampshire section of the DNSR was not doubled like the rest of the line, but instead all crossing loops were extended to a length of 700 yards to enable the longest trains to be crossed. As this made the distance between a signal box and some points too far apart for mechanical operation due to the lack of a signalman's physical strength, a hand-generator provided current for electrically-worked points. It is claimed that 16,000 military trains used the DNSR to reach Southampton during the twelve months prior to D-Day in June 1944, so without the DNSR, the Normandy landings could have been impossible.

During the Second World War, naval officers accompanied the late evening train from Winchester to the camp at Worthy Down in order to quell boisterous ratings. They made sure that any vomit was cleared up and if there was insufficient time at Worthy Down, the sailors completed the task as the train returned empty to Winchester, thus leaving them a walk of four miles back to camp.

The Reading and Basingstoke Line

The Berks & Hants Railway linked the GWR at Reading with the LSWR at Basingstoke, Bramley being the first station on the line in Hampshire. Engineered by I.K. Brunel, it was a broad gauge line and due to this factor, goods and passengers had to be transhipped between the two gauges at Basingstoke. Through trains were unable to run between the two systems until mixed gauge was ready on 22 December 1856. Mixing the gauge was the relatively simple matter of laying a third rail at the standard gauge distance within the broad gauge rails, one rail being common to both. Initially just a branch line, it has now become a vital route for expresses from the south to the Midlands, north of England and Scotland. Another important feature of the line is that it avoids London.

■ *Bramley, view Up. The GWR track is on longitudinal, rather than on the cross sleepers favoured by other railways. There is no room for a flowerbed on the Down platform, so the keen staff have used pots.* (Author's collection) ■

The Somerset & Dorset Joint Railway

The Somerset & Dorset Joint Railway was similar to that of the MSWJR as both linked the MR with the LSWR. All its route was in the counties of Somerset and Dorset, joining the LSWR at Wimborne and Broadstone and using running powers to reach Bournemouth West, which was its only station in Hampshire.

Useful in both World Wars, in the summers of the 1950s, it was particularly busy with holiday trains. A procession of expresses brought holidaymakers from the north and the Midlands to Bournemouth, arriving early on Saturday morning. The coaches were then cleaned, the locomotives turned and serviced ready to take other holidaymakers home. One very interesting feature of the SDJR was that it brought LMS locomotives to Bournemouth, which could hardly be classified as either London, Midland or Scottish. Like the MSWJR and the DNSR, the SDJR succumbed to road competition and most of the line closed on 7 March 1966.

■ Ex-LMS Class 4F 0-6-0s No 44100 and No 43875 head a Bath to Bournemouth West stopping train at Parkstone, 5 August 1950.
The Somerset & Dorset Joint Railway was usually short of locomotives in the height of the summer, and
No 44100 is from Burton-on-Trent shed. (S.W. Baker) ■

■ *BR Standard Class 9 2-10-0 No 92220* Evening Star *(now preserved) heads a Bath train at Bournemouth West,* *30 September 1963.* (Revd Alan Newman) ■

CASTLEMAN'S CORKSCREW

In 1844 Charles Castleman, a Wimborne solicitor, proposed building a railway between Southampton and Dorchester. His route was circuitous and therefore nicknamed 'Castleman's Corkscrew' or 'The Water Snake'.

Southampton inhabitants had found that the arrival of the LSWR in their town was to a certain extent detrimental. Instead of travellers staying in the town for a while, as they had in coaching days, following the advent of the railway they were immediately whisked off from train to ship, or vice versa. This lack of customers had an unpleasant economic effect on both hotels and shops. In an attempt to counteract this trend, Southampton managed to place a clause in the Southampton to Weymouth Act, requiring a station to be built at Blechynden Terrace near the town centre and make most trains call there (this station became the present Southampton Central).

Unfortunately, this station led to legal problems – the case of Fotheringham versus the Southampton & Dorchester Railway. The plaintiff claimed that the site where the station was being built infringed his agreement with that company as the station was within sight of his home, King's Bridge House. Consequently, construction of the station ceased and when the town council discovered that the railway was to be opened, but not the station, thus contravening the clause they had put into the bill, they tried to secure an injunction.

On the grapevine, two railway directors heard of this move, so on 30 May 1847, only two days before the line was to be opened, the LSWR managed to rent Ivy House for two years and use it as a temporary station. A permanent station was eventually opened in 1850 when Ivy House reverted to a private residence.

The 'Corkscrew' opened on 1 June 1847, the first train leaving from Blechynden rather than Southampton Terminus. This was because on 30 May the tunnel between the two Southampton stations had collapsed. The problem was caused by the disused Andover & Southampton Canal tunnel, which crossed below the railway tunnel with only about a foot clearance. Peto, the contractor, had appeased owners of the property above by filling the canal tunnel with rubble, but unfortunately this damming prevented drainage from the canal tunnel. This resulted in water so saturating the clay on which the railway tunnel stood that it collapsed.

Until the train service could begin, horse buses linked the two stations. The tunnel collapse caused confusion on the opening day, as that morning the notice on the doors of Ringwood station announcing postponement of the opening had to be hastily removed when the first train arrived at 10 am and definitely proved it a lie. Following remedial work, the tunnel eventually opened on 6 August 1847. The Southampton & Dorchester Railway amalgamated with the LSWR on 11 October 1848.

This was not the only trouble caused by Southampton Tunnel. In 1964 the floor moved up towards the roof and for six months single line working had to be adopted while repairs were carried out. The trouble re-occurred in 1984.

The development of Bournemouth called for a direct line from London, rather than the circuitous 'Corkscrew' which

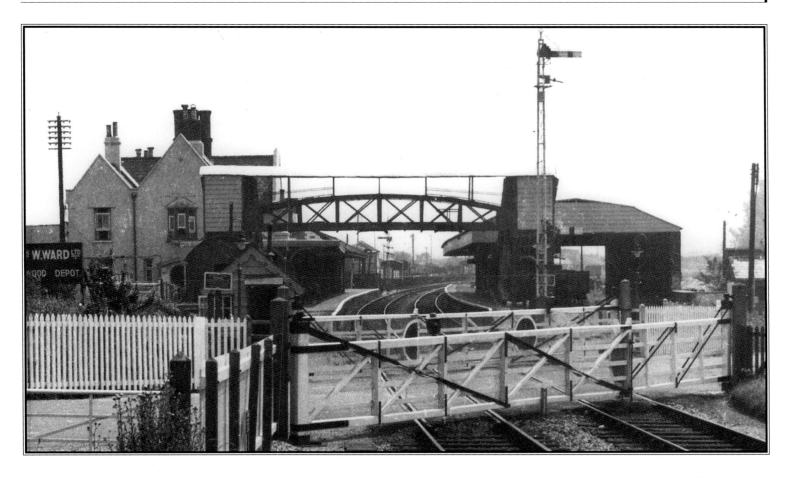

■ *Ringwood, view Up, circa 1950. The former Christchurch branch bay platform was on the right below the train shed. The tall signal, which can be seen from a distance, has a lower repeater arm. Pity the poor lamp man struggling up the ladder in a gale with a lamp in one hand and holding on for dear life with the other.* (Author's collection) ■

approached the town from the west. On 5 March 1888 a direct line was opened from Brockenhurst so Bournemouth was able to enjoy express trains to and from London and this enabled the watering place to develop rapidly.

THE DEVELOPING SYSTEM

The LSWR coped well with increasing traffic. Quadruple tracks reached Basingstoke in 1905 and were extended to Battledown Junction three years later. At the latter location a flyover – the first in the country – was arranged so that Up trains from Southampton crossed over the Salisbury line and thus avoided a conflicting movement. The junctions were laid to allow for speeds up to 55 mph.

Sam Fay, as the LSWR's go-ahead Superintendent in the early 1900s, visited the USA and returned with several innovations, one being electro-pneumatic signalling whereby a stationary steam engine at Fleet supplied compressed air to a pipe to work signals actuated by air pressure. A back-up auxiliary compressor was sited at Basingstoke. Some intermediate signals were even arranged to change aspect automatically as a train passed, this being carried out by track circuiting being applied, probably for the first time in the United Kingdom. This compressed air system gave excellent service and was faster than mechanical signalling. Installed around 1906, it was eventually replaced by coloured lights in 1966.

R.A. Riddles (1892–1983) Chief Mechanical Engineer to BR in the 1950s believed that, ideally, steam would be withdrawn as lines were electrified, with little need for intermediate diesel propulsion. The Southern Region came nearest to fulfilling this ideal, especially the Waterloo to Bournemouth line, which went straight from steam to electric.

The 1960s was an important decade for railways in Hampshire. Many branch lines were closed; the electric current was switched on to Southampton in December 1966 and to Bournemouth the following April, while a colour light signalling centre opened at Eastleigh in November 1966 to control all trains from St Denys to Worting Junction.

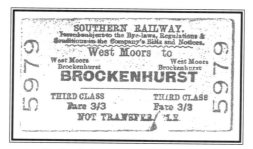

■ *An SR third class single ticket for a journey from West Moors to Brockenhurst; fare 3s 3d.* ■

THE BUILDINGS

RAILWAY ARCHITECTURE TENDS TO GET overlooked by the travelling public. Passengers who do not travel frequently are often worried about whether they are standing on the correct platform, whether the train will be on time, or whether they will have a seat, so fail to look around and enjoy any architectural features. Passengers who use the station regularly often fail to appreciate the architecture because they see it every day and therefore find it ordinary – a case of familiarity breeding contempt.

Many of the LSWR stations in Hampshire were designed by Sir William Tite, whose father was a Russian merchant. Born in 1798, Tite won fame for rebuilding the Royal Exchange in 1841. His designs were usually severe, solid-looking and practical – in keeping with his instructions that they should have 'utility and desirability at the smallest possible cost'.

Micheldever, Grade II listed, is one such structure. Initially called Andover Road, it was a very unfortunate name for passengers who believed they were getting off near Andover when in reality they were faced with a ten-mile walk. Micheldever's two-storey building is of local flint, faced with yellow brick dressings. The roof has a low hip, while a flat canopy is carried round all four sides on slender iron columns.

Eastleigh, called Bishopstoke until 1889, is a small twin-storey block of classical design rendered in stucco. The chimney stacks have fine detail. The building now stands on an island platform accessed from a new entrance building via a footbridge. An interesting and unusual feature, also found at Brockenhurst, was that luggage could be carried across the line on a swivel bridge.

Swaythling station, built in 1883, is another Grade II building. In domestic style it has a prominent Dutch gable. The main building in dark brick is connected to the platform by a curious short covered way.

St Denys, built between 1866 and 1868, was originally Portswood, but renamed in 1876. It is a two-storey red brick structure with stone dressings and is also designated Grade II. Woolston, also Grade II, is of the same design as St Denys, but in stucco. St Denys was carefully and sympathetically restored in 1987. Initially Portswood had been opened on an experimental basis to see if it would prove an economic proposition.

The former Southampton Terminus station, now closed, is Grade II listed. Designed by Tite in classical style, a five-bay arcade forms the entrance. A low, hipped roof is concealed behind a cornice. Nearby is South Western House, also Grade II listed, designed by John Norton as a four-storey hotel in red brick, with stone and terracotta decorations in French Renaissance style. The upper attic dormer windows have unusual circular panes.

Gosport station was another of Tite's designs. As the military authorities demanded that the station building had to be kept low in order not to interfere with the nearby fortifications, its chimneys were no higher than the train shed roof. The station has a very long, fourteen-bay Tuscan colonnade. The building's roof was badly damaged in a bombing raid in 1941 but was repaired. Pevsner describes the south façade as 'one of the finest pieces of external station architecture surviving from the beginning of the railway age'. It cost almost £11,000 to build in comparison with that at Fareham which only cost about £1,400. Gosport station was near St George's Barracks and when troops arrived home from duty abroad, they were cheered as they marched out of the station. In the late 1920s and early '30s, crowds arrived at the station to view the Schneider Trophy seaplane races.

Tite also designed Liphook station on the Portsmouth Direct line. Built in brick it is a Palladian, domestic-style villa. In contrast, Petersfield is in his Tudor style, with a three-storey house on one side, a central entrance, booking window and

■ *An early view of the Up side of Southampton Terminus.* (Author's collection) ■

gabled waiting room on the other side.

The height of early LSWR platforms averaged 21 inches and although this low level made it difficult for passengers to board or alight from trains, it allowed people to step down to cross the line easily in the days before footbridges or subways. In order to reduce the number of passengers killed or injured crossing the line and to make access to trains easier, the platform height was standardised at 30 inches around 1878.

■ *The colonnaded exterior of Gosport station.* (Lens of Sutton) ■

Coin-in-the-slot machines on stations were introduced in 1869, the first being a weighing chair, while others sold items such as chocolate and fortune-telling cards. These brought in useful rent, as did bookstalls. Some stations had boxes for collecting used newspapers and magazines for distribution to hospitals.

Other Grade II listed railway structures in Hampshire are Portchester Road and Quay Street viaducts, Fareham. Designed by Joseph Locke, both are of red brick relieved with white brick string courses and stone copings.

Hockley Viaduct, now owned by Winchester City Council, is the largest brick-built structure in Hampshire. Its friends hope it will be listed soon and form part of a cycle route from the centre of Winchester towards Southampton.

■ *A 700 class 0-6-0 No 350 at Gosport awaits departure to Netley, circa 1935. Built in August 1897 No 350 was fitted with a Maunsell superheater in July 1929 and withdrawn in March 1962. (Author's collection)* ■

RUNNING THE RAILWAYS

■

RAILWAY COMPANIES, LIKE MANY OTHER organisations, were arranged in departments. Generally, a railwayman started as a lad in one of the departments and, if capable, rose up the ladder through the various grades. Promotion from one step to the next was usually determined by length of service, but when a railwayman left his base grade he was also expected to acquire a good deal of specialised knowledge.

Staff at an average locomotive shed would include a superintendent or foreman, clerks, including stores' issuer, boiler washers, coalmen, chargemen, cleaners, boiler smith and mate, fitters, apprentices and enginemen.

A driver started as a cleaner, which meant that he became intimate with the various parts of a locomotive. In addition to cleaning he might be assigned to other tasks such as assisting a boiler smith, or a firebox brick-arch repairer.

A cleaner was tested and, if successful, became a Passed Cleaner, that is, he could be called upon for firing duty. After 313 firing days (a year minus 52 rest days) he was paid a fireman's rate whether he was firing or cleaning. The progress of an aspiring footplate man was usually:

Cleaner
Passed Cleaner (i.e. passed for firing duty)
Fireman
Registered Fireman (i.e. covered a minimum of 313 firing turns)
Passed Fireman (i.e. passed for driving duty)
Driver
Registered Driver (i.e. covered a minimum of 313 driving turns).

The next grades on the ladder were supervisory and their occupants known as Inspectors. Promotion to a supervisory position was determined by suitability.

The work of a steam locomotive depot fell into two main divisions: that of maintaining engines in good repair and that of arranging for suitable engines and footplate staff to be available and out at the times required by the operating department.

The staff compiling the locomotive workings needed to have an exact knowledge of the type of engine suitable for each train and the number of locomotives of each type allocated to their shed. Duties of enginemen were organised in the form of a roster, which was subdivided into 'links', arranged on a seniority basis. They started with engine preparation and disposal within the depot yard, then progress was made to shunting and with local freight, long-distance freight, local passenger and, finally, express passenger. In each link the men worked round weekly, thus sharing equally the early and late turns.

Under Southern Railway management (SR absorbed the

LSWR in the Grouping of 1923) there were three types of locomotive depots:

1 A premier depot, the one for the Hampshire area being Eastleigh, under a locomotive running shed superintendent.
2 Moderately important depots under a locomotive foreman.
3 A small shed with just a few engines, often serving a branch line. Repairs were carried out at a larger depot.

Servicing facilities at sheds were often poor, particularly in small sheds. Coal was moved into tenders manually, often transferred from wagons into wheeled tubs before being manually tipped into a tender or bunker. Ash was required to be manually shovelled from engines. Sheds were often draughty and lighting poor. Curiously, the Factories Act of 1937, which made staff amenities mandatory, inserted a clause excluding engine sheds from its provisions.

Water tanks were installed at sheds in order to give a good head of water. It was usually pumped to the tank by a pump housed below and it was fed to the locomotives from columns with a leather hose, colloquially a 'bag'. Water was sometimes softened to prevent hard water causing scaling in the boilers.

Details of the Larger Engine Sheds
At Basingstoke, the LSWR three-road shed, opened in 1905, as well as catering for regular trains, always had a stand-by locomotive in steam ready to take over any engine that failed on the main line. It had an allocation of 24 locomotives in January 1947. When the GWR shed at Basingstoke closed in 1950, it serviced ex-GWR engines. It remained open as a signing-on point until July 1967, which was the end of steam traction on the SR.

Bournemouth Central was rebuilt as a four-road shed in the mid-1930s when nearly 50 engines were allocated there. In January 1947 its allocation was 60. It closed in July 1967.

The sixteen-road Eastleigh shed opened in 1903 with an allocation of 100 to 126 locomotives. A 20,000-gallon water softener was installed in 1930. The shed closed in July 1967. Locomotive water was drawn from the River Itchen and when the tank was drained for cleaning, a good supply of fish was found. The large water storage tank was over a building of which the first and second floors had been locomen's dormitories, but at the outbreak of the Second World War it was decided to abolish lodging turns so the former accommodation became offices and mess rooms.

Fratton shed was shared by the LSWR and the LBSCR, each company having its own coal stage, offices, cleaners' and drivers' lobbies, only the turntable being shared. A spirit of rivalry developed between the two companies, the LBSCR stock being considered marginally cleaner in the beautiful yellow livery.

The shed was of the roundhouse pattern, set around a turntable that gave access to stalls. An advantage of this pattern was that it was easier to get an individual engine out, but if the turntable failed, all locomotives were blocked in!

Originally each company had 30 to 40 engines allocated to Fratton, but due to electrification the number approximately

■ *Bournemouth Central locomotive depot – Battle of Britain class 4-6-2 No 34063* 229 Squadron *and BR Standard class 4MT 4-6-0 No 75066 with a double chimney.* (Revd Alan Newman) ■

halved. Forty-three locomotives were shedded there in January 1947. The shed closed in November 1959, after which it housed SR locomotives scheduled for preservation.

A two-road shed opened at Gosport in 1842. It was used by engines shunting the station and Clarence Yard and also those working the Meon Valley line to Alton. As no turntable was provided, engines were reversed by running round the triangle formed by the Stokes Bay Pier branch. Considered by the SR as a sub-shed of Fratton, it was partly demolished in 1953 and out of use by 1962.

Southampton had three facilities for maintaining locomotives: an independent three-road shed at Old Dock where eighteen locomotives were allocated in 1947. Although closed in January 1966, it continued to be used. Another shed offered facilities at the Terminus station while the third depot was in the New Docks. The turntable from New Docks shed was sold to the Great Western Society and can be seen today at Didcot Steam Centre. The principal Southampton shed, a fifteen-road depot, was at Northam, but this closed when the Eastleigh depot opened in 1903.

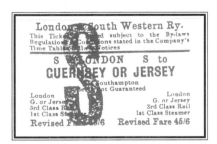

■ *An LSWR single ticket London to Guernsey or Jersey, third class rail, but available in the first class saloon aboard the steam from Southampton. Fare: £2. 5s 6d.* ■

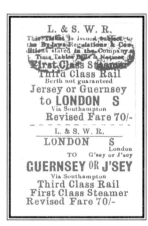

■ *An LSWR return ticket Jersey/Guernsey to London available in the first class saloon aboard the steamer to Southampton, but third class onwards by rail. Fare: £3.10s.* ■

SOUTHAMPTON DOCKS

SOUTHAMPTON IS IN A SPLENDID SITUATION for a port, being sheltered by the Isle of Wight, and favoured with four, instead of the normal two, high tides daily. It is surprising then that it was as late as 1836 before the Southampton Dock Company was formed. The facilities opened on 29 August 1842 and the new steam ships helped its development as sailing vessels had sometimes found the six miles of sheltered Southampton Water a problem.

On 14 August 1848 Parliament authorised the LSWR to operate steam packets from, among other places, Southampton, Portsmouth, Gosport and Lymington, so in 1849 the LSWR leased fourteen paddle steamers. At Southampton these steamers used the Royal Pier – vessels from there serving Le Havre, Guernsey and Jersey. Other ships sailed from Portsmouth to Le Havre.

Seasonal potato traffic from the Channel Islands was important. Over 23 days in 1883 the LSWR carried potatoes in 139 special trains from Southampton to London.

In December 1891 the LSWR wisely purchased Southampton Docks and immediately set about their enlargement. It created the Prince of Wales Graving Dock, at

An advertisement from the Illustrated London News *of 11 July 1903.*

that time the largest in the world. On 4 March 1893 the liner *New York* called at Southampton and this marked the start of the transatlantic traffic, which developed at the expense of Liverpool, Southampton having the great advantage of being so much closer to London.

In 1898 the largest cold store in Europe was opened on the Test Quay. It could hold 4,800 quarters of beef, 155,000 carcases of sheep and still have 1,300,000 cubic feet for miscellaneous goods such as butter, fish, game, poultry, eggs and fruit. In nearby lairage and slaughter houses, 600 head of cattle could be killed and dealt with daily.

The LSWR was very efficient. The imported meat was

packed into horse-drawn carts, which were placed on flat wagons where, on arrival in London, they could be drawn immediately to their destination. Bullion from South Africa was sent to Waterloo in a specially-strengthened bogie parcels van, with an asphalt floor. One interesting import was South African crayfish, curiously transported from Southampton to Folkestone and then exported to France.

Apart from international shipping lines serving the port, the LSWR ran its own services to Cherbourg, the Channel Islands, Granville, Le Havre and St Malo. Many discerning passengers preferred the Southampton to Le Havre route when travelling from London to Paris rather than taking one of the shorter sea crossings. Utilising the Southampton route, you left Waterloo in the evening, crossed the Channel by night and French railways took you to Paris the next morning – all very civilised.

Southampton handled most of the military traffic for the Boer War, 528,000 men and 28,000 horses, so the new quays and sheds proved invaluable.

When the docks were taken over by the LSWR there were no hydraulic cranes and no electric lighting, while the shed accommodation was insufficient and the railway very inadequate. By 1911 the LSWR had laid 25 miles of track, built grain and timber warehouses, two storage sheds on the quays, the finest cold storage and lairage in Europe and added several thousand feet of new deep water quayage. Between 1892 and 1911, goods traffic increased by about 90% and passenger traffic by 70%.

When the LSWR purchased Southampton Docks it required 0-4-0Ts for shunting on the sharply-curved lines and,

following the practice of the docks company, these were named from places in the Duchy of Normandy and the Province of Britttany. The first were built in 1891 and the class remained intact until 1948 when they were replaced by war surplus ex-US Army 0-6-0Ts, which, in turn, were displaced by diesels in 1962.

Although some of the engines taken over from the dock company were withdrawn at an early date, one lasted into the British Railways' era. R.W. Kidner in *The Waterloo to Southampton Line* records that the dock locomotives were subject to marine law, for when one driver had been found carrying contraband, his locomotive was placed in a siding with its motion officially sealed.

Ever larger vessels required the lengthening of some docks. Just prior to the 1923 amalgamation, the LSWR proposed enclosing the mudland between the Royal Pier and Millbrook Point. The Southern Railway carried out this work in 1929 and built a two-mile-long quay wall from the Royal Pier to Millbrook, reclaiming 407 acres of mud. They then infilled this area with chalk excavated from behind Micheldever station. This work placed Southampton Central station inland, instead of being set beside the water as formerly.

By VE Day 1945 a total of 3,500,000 troops had sailed from Southampton and military stores tonnage shipped in the seventeen weeks after D-Day equalled the total imports/exports from Southampton for the whole of 1938. Train ferries ran between Southampton and Cherbourg, with locomotives, ambulance trains and petrol tank wagons. Many of the engines had been built in the USA and prepared for Continental use at such places as Eastleigh Works.

■ *A line of 0-4-0T dock shunters at Eastleigh in clean condition, 24 June 1954: C14 class No 30589 and B4 class No 30096 (now preserved) and No 30082. (Revd Alan Newman)* ■

■ *USA class 0-6-0T No 30065 (now preserved) at Eastleigh, 5 November 1962, having been ousted from Southampton Docks by a diesel shunter. A US Army Transportation design, it was purchased by the SR in 1946 and fitted with a modified cab and bunker. (Revd Alan Newman)* ■

On 31 July 1950 the Ocean Terminal was opened by the Prime Minister, Clement Attlee. The pre-cast concrete building, nearly a quarter of a mile in length, occupied almost the entire length of the east side of the Ocean Dock where the largest liners berthed. There was a 1,000-ft island platform, sufficiently long to accommodate two full-length boat trains.

■ *BR Standard class 5 MT 4-6-0 No 73080 is being stoked up at Southampton Central, 22 April 1966, while working a Salisbury to Portsmouth train.* (Revd Alan Newman) ■

BOAT AND OTHER SPECIAL TRAINS

∎

IN **1893** THE LSWR BUILT LUXURIOUS saloon coaches for the American Line boat trains known as American Eagles. In 1895 the Railway Engineer carried the following description:

Mr. Wm. Panter, Carriage and Wagon Superintendent of the L&SWR, has designed and built 20 First-class Saloon carriages for the special express service between London and Southampton, in connection with the American Line and other Mail Steamers which sail from Southampton.

The length of these carriages overall is 47 ft 6 ins. They are divided into four compartments or saloons, the largest being 20 ft 1 in long, and with a seating accommodation for 12. In connection with this saloon there is also a small ladies' compartment of 4 seats, and at the other end a smoking compartment with 4 seats. The ladies' lavatory leads out of the ladies' compartment and the gentlemen's lavatory out of the smoking compartment. There is also at one end of the carriage a private compartment with 5 seats and lavatory accommodation. The width of the carriage is 8 ft 0¾ ins, and the height of the carriage from the floor to the top of the side plate 6 ft 5 ins, and to the middle of the roof 7 ft 11 ins.

These carriages are very sumptuously furnished with figured moquette of the finest quality. The seats and back are stuffed with the best curled hair over Peters' patent springs. The interior framing is of American walnut, filled with panels veneered with unrolled Hungarian ash. This ash is largely used for decorating the interior of South Western carriages, and presents a pleasing appearance on account of its light colour and the beautiful figuring obtained by unrolling the wood. The roofs are covered with large panels of Lincrusta-Walton. The ends of the seats are ornamented and fitted with carved panels.

The main framing of the carriage is teak with mahogany panels backed with canvas. The roof sticks are strengthened with iron carlines, 1¾ ins x ½ in.

The bogies are 3 ft 9 ins between the centres, the bogie wheels 8 ft between the centres. The bogies are constructed entirely of Fox's patent pressed frames, and are of a pattern to which we have before drawn attention as being one which gives practically no trouble and requires no attention.

The body is supported throughout its length by Spencer's India-rubber pads; the carriage is efficiently ventilated by Laycock's torpedo ventilators. It is lighted by compressed gas on Pintsch's system, and fitted with the vacuum automatic brake. In connection with this last the difficulty of running the train pipe below the underframe has been ingeniously surmounted by running it under the continuous footboard, where it is held in position by clips secured by the same bolts that fix the board on to the step irons. The weight of the carriage is 23 tons.

The Spithead Review of 28 June 1902, intended to mark the coronation of Edward VII but actually aborted due to his illness, would have been an exceptionally busy time for the LSWR. The signalman at Worthy – a temporary box opened specifically to shorten the section between Winchester Junction and Winchester – between 8 am and 11.30 am was to have dealt with 49 special trains at a rate of one every four to five minutes. One minute after each one passed, he would receive the 'Train out of section' bell from Winchester. Two minutes later he would have received the 'Be ready' bell from Winchester Junction for the next train. During this period of duty he would have made 196 lever operations and exchanged 296 bell signals, excluding those for trains on the Up line. To cope with any locomotive failures, standby engines were provided at Basingstoke, Mitcheldever and Eastleigh, while the Northam breakdown train and a crane outstabled in Southampton Docks were ready for immediate use. In the event, a reduced Spithead Review was held on 16 August 1902 and only seventeen special trains were run between Waterloo and Southampton.

When a boat train approached Canute Road level crossing near Southampton Terminus station, the gates were opened and a gateman bearing a flag and hand-bell walked into the centre of the road and stopped traffic, while the crossing keeper guarded the other side. This delightful ceremony ceased in 1981 when flashing lights were installed. In the 1950s over 1,000 boat trains ran each way annually while, in the 1930s, a Bank Holiday weekend could see over twenty ships arriving or departing, served by up to 40 boat trains.

'Imperial Airways' was the named train for flying-boat passengers. In 1937 it consisted merely of two Pullman cars and a van added to an ordinary express from Waterloo, but from June 1939 these special trains were run from Victoria, adjacent to the London Air Terminal. As take-off was at dawn, Imperial Airways asked for sleeping cars, but normal Pullman cars were provided. As trains consisted of no more than four cars, they could be economically worked by T9 class 4-4-0s. This service lasted until the 1950s when flying boats were phased out.

The SR gave the title 'Ocean Liner Express' to the Waterloo to Southampton Docks trains. Traffic ceased during the Second World War, but by the 1950s had resumed its pre-war level and each summer saw about 150 boat trains monthly, this total being halved during the winter. As they did not run at regular intervals, they were given 'Q', or conditional paths, in the working timetable. Between 89 and 112 minutes were allotted for the 79-mile run to Southampton Dock Gates, or two or three minutes more for using the Millbrook Dock entrance. The line to Old Docks crossed Canute Road, as well as several internal road crossings, all of which were ungated and so needed protection by flagmen.

The two-platformed Ocean Terminal opened in 1950 and was used by the *Queen Mary* and the *Queen Elizabeth*. The two

■ *A boat train, with servicemen leaning out, enters Southampton Docks during the First World War.* (Author's collection) ■

Queens could only arrive and depart on certain tidal conditions, so the weekly Cunard service to New York was not always at the same time. Smaller vessels were less dependent on tides, so the Union Castle Line mailboat for the Cape always left on Thursdays at 4 pm.

The boat trains for the French ports were named the 'Normandy Express' and 'Brittany Express', in 1952 and 1954 respectively.

The early 1950s saw a spate of train naming since a named train carries a certain amount of extra glamour. From 2 July 1952 the principal first class train for the *Queens* was named the 'Cunarder' and often was an all-Pullman. Later that month the train serving the *United States* was named 'Statesman'. In 1953 came the 'Union Castle Express', while Royal Mail Line trains were named 'Holland American' and 'South American'. Other Ocean Liner trains were named 'Arosa Line', 'Springbok' and 'Sitmar Line'.

In the 1950s and early '60s, the arrival or departure of the *Queen Mary*, *Queen Elizabeth* and the *United States*, with up to 1,500 passengers requiring rail transport, usually needed three to four boat trains, including a complete Pullman car train. Eastleigh depot was responsible for supplying locomotives for Southampton to Waterloo trains while Nine Elms provided those for Down trains. Eastleigh had 24 crews just for working boat trains. Despite their names, Merchant Navy class locomotives were not normally used as these powerful engines could be better employed elsewhere. At this time, rolling stock was usually one of five eight-coach sets numbered 350 to 354. A Pullman coach was added to serve light refreshments, plus one or two vans to cope with passengers' baggage.

Occasionally ten- or eleven-coach Channel Islands sets were used for Ocean Liner trains. Troopship trains were usually formed of normal boat train stock.

Locomotives and rolling stock for these Ocean Liner specials spent quite a time idle, so enhanced fares were charged to make up for this. For instance, in 1960, a Waterloo to Southampton single ticket cost 22s 6d first class and 15s second, whereas boat train fares were 37s 6d and 22s 6d respectively. The Pullman supplement was 14s 6d, whereas travelling on the 'Bournemouth Belle' from Waterloo to Southampton Central, the supplement was only 4s 6d.

When cruising recommenced in the 1950s, many started on a Saturday and great difficulty was experienced finding a path for these special trains in the summer, so in later years some cruise sailings moved to Sundays.

In 1963 the number of boat trains run was 1,727 and 4,997 freight trains served Southampton Docks but, by 1966, slightly more cargo was leaving by road than by rail and the seamen's strike of that year caused a serious decline in traffic. By 1992 Associated British Ports, then owner of the docks, raised charges, so Intercity ceased operating boat trains.

Canon Roger Lloyd in *The Fascination of Railways*, published in 1951, experienced travelling on the Channel Islands Boat Train:

We slow down steadily until Southampton Terminus station comes into sight, where a tank engine is shunting rolling stock ready for the morning trains, and it seems almost as if we were going to enter it, but at the last moment we lurch to the left, and slowly glide round the outside of it. By now we are crawling at no more than walking pace, and we go across what is in daytime a very busy road, our passage being guarded by a man with a bell and a red lamp. Then the train passes through the dock gates, and grinds round a left-hand curve so sharp that one wonders so large an engine can negotiate it. In less than a minute more we pass out of the darkness and into the glaring, metallic light of the dock shed, where at last we come to rest.

Introduced around 1900, a pioneer of Britain's cross-country services was the 7.05 am Great Central Railway's Newcastle to Bournemouth Buffet Car Express which ran every day except Sundays. In summer it ran throughout as a complete train, but for the rest of the year it terminated at Southampton, just one coach being taken on to Bournemouth. On 1 July 1903 an introduction was the 7.15 am from Southampton Docks. A Great Central corridor train with breakfast car, it ran to York and on 11 July was extended to Scarborough. Similarly a luncheon car train ran south.

Likewise the GWR ran a through train between Birkenhead and Bournemouth via Oxford and Basingstoke. At peak times this service was so well used that it was required to run in two portions. GWR engines worked the train throughout, an LSWR pilotman boarding the footplate at Basingstoke to conduct the GWR crew to Bournemouth.

■ *Handbill giving information about cheap Sunday fares from London on the Bournemouth Belle Pullman train from August 1931.* ■

ONTO THE PIER

SOUTHAMPTON'S ROYAL PIER WAS OPENED in 1833 by the Duchess of Kent and her daughter Princess Victoria and, in the latter's honour, it was named 'Victoria Pier'. When the London & Southampton Railway arrived in 1840, passengers were conveyed between the station and pier by horse bus until a horse tramway opened in 1847. This tramway could also be used by railway goods wagons as it was connected to the main line via a turntable, but the tramway was only suitable for tramcars and not passenger coaches. In 1851 the LSWR took over the lease of the tramway and in 1871 a direct connection was made with the main line. In 1876 steam trains were permitted to use the line, so horse traction ended. Due to a severe weight limitation, normal engines could not be used so three small condensing locomotives were purchased to work the line. A service of about six trains ran daily at a maximum speed of 5 mph.

By the 1890s, having an open platform at the pier station was considered rather uncivilised, so the station was rebuilt and given two platforms with canopies. This opened on 2 June 1892. The improved pier was given the name 'Royal Pier'.

In 1906 the C14 class 0-4-0Ts took over the working and three years later they were replaced by steam railmotors. The service was withdrawn on 6 August 1914 to facilitate troop trains to the docks and this service was never restored, the station being officially closed in 1921.

Portsmouth Harbour station opened on 2 October 1876. Initially it was constructed above the water on wooden piles, but later these were replaced with iron. The station was, and is,

■ Southampton Pier, with the railway running along on the left.
(Lens of Sutton) ■

■ *Southampton Pier station.* (Author's collection) ■

kept busy with connections to the Isle of Wight and Gosport. When the line to Portsmouth Harbour station was built, a branch was made from just short of the terminus, across a swing bridge to a railway station with a waiting room. This branch is now closed.

The Stokes Bay Railway & Pier Company was created to form a short route to the Isle of Wight. At Stokes Bay passengers could step from the train, which ran along the pier, straight into the ferry. The railway's engineer was Hamilton Henry Fulton whose greatest achievement was the Manchester Ship Canal.

The line experienced several initial problems. Lack of finance delayed construction work for four years and then when it was completed, Capt H.W. Tyler arrived to make the necessary Board of Trade inspection, but could not run a test engine over the line as the contractor, Messrs Brassey, had lifted a rail due to a financial dispute with the directors. When the ferry made a test run on 28 February 1863, it was unable to land passengers at Stokes Bay as Brassey's men barred the way with clubs. The line was eventually opened on 6 April 1863. In 1869 complaints were received from passengers using the pier because touts pestered them to use certain Isle of Wight hotels.

The LSWR purchased the line on 1 January 1872 and, because of the ease of transfer at the pier, advertised it as 'The Family Route'. It also made much of the fact that the fifteen-minutes crossing was shorter than that from Portsmouth and avoided that 'unsavoury town'. It was not, in fact, ideally

■ *Gosport Road station on the Stokes Bay line, view north. The Up track has been lifted.* (Author's collection) ■

situated as ferry boats experienced difficulty in mooring beside the pier when a south-westerly gale was blowing. Care for passengers was important and the railway was required to have a boat standing by for life-saving. Queen Victoria herself never used the route, but her luggage did.

From 1874 through coaches were run from Waterloo. The opening of Portsmouth Harbour station in 1876 partly nullified Stokes Bay's advantage. Through tickets could be used for return by either route. In 1911 the GWR ran a through coach from Reading to Stokes Bay. As railway staff at Stokes Bay were unable to find housing, in May 1899 the LSWR constructed a row of five cottages for £1,235.

1677. Lymington Pier

■ *A three-coach push-pull set leaves Lymington Pier, circa 1914, propelled by the engine. The paddle steamer to Yarmouth is moored at the pier.* (Author's collection) ■

■ *A 0-4-4T heads a Down train at Lymington Pier, circa 1935.* (Author's collection) ■

■ *An M7 0-4-4T stands at Lymington Pier station, 12 July 1950. In the foreground is the car ferry* Farringford. *(F.F. Moss)* ■

and made the branch a long siding. The track, except that on the pier, was lifted by 1936. Today, much of the branch is a public footpath.

The branch line from Brockenhurst to Lymington opened ceremonially on 8 May 1858, but the public opening was delayed as the sleepers were frugally laid at 3 ft 9 in intervals instead of 3 ft. The LSWR, which was to work the line, insisted that they be placed closer. This work was carried out and the public opening took place on 12 July 1858. The Solent Steam Packet Company's paddle steamers made four connecting return sailings daily. The railway was taken over by the LSWR on 23 March 1878.

Due to the difficulty in reaching steamers at low water, an extension to a new pier opened on 1 May 1884 and two months later the LSWR purchased the ferry. The ferries continued running through both world wars.

When the Spithead Review was held on 16 August 1902, coronation year, Stokes Bay was one of the best viewpoints. The LSWR charged five shillings for admission to the pier and one shilling for the evening illuminations and fireworks. That day 32 trains ran over the branch.

From 1 November 1915 Stokes Bay station was closed and in 1918 the Admiralty used the pier as an experimental site for torpedo research, running torpedo trolleys along the pier's standard gauge track. In 1922 the Admiralty took over the line

Boat trains of up to ten coaches in length ran from Waterloo to Lymington Pier. This had the dubious honour of being the last BR branch line to be worked by steam, which ceased to be used on 2 April 1967. Diesel-electric multiple units took over temporarily until the line was electrified on 2 June 1967. A new terminal on reclaimed lands opened in January 1976.

THE ROYAL TRAIN COMES TO HAMPSHIRE

O N **28 AUGUST 1843 QUEEN VICTORIA** made her very first journey on the LSWR when she travelled from Farnborough to Southampton accompanied by the Duke of Wellington. The latter was strongly prejudiced against all railways and prior to this trip, when travelling between London and his Stratfield Saye residence had always used his own horse-drawn coach, even though the LSWR directors informed him that a special train was always at his command.

'Standard Working Instructions' were issued regarding Royal Train travel. The locomotive superintendent was required to 'select the Engines and take every precaution to secure the most perfect class to avoid any possible failure or delay; he will also select the Enginemen for the Royal Train and for the Pilot Engine, from the most steady and experienced drivers who know the road well.' The pilot engine was despatched approximately ten minutes ahead of the Royal Train.

Further instructions were that all signal boxes on the route had to be open – even those normally closed – for at least an hour before the passage of the pilot engine. Goods trains were prohibited from leaving any station unless they could be shunted at least thirty minutes before the Royal Train was due. Likewise, all shunting operations adjacent to the line used by the Royal Train were to cease thirty minutes before it was due. Stationmasters and guards were responsible for checking that loads on the wagons that were halted did not cause any obstruction by fouling the gauge.

Everything was required to be as quiet and clean as possible for Her Majesty. Drivers of waiting engines had to prevent their engines emitting smoke, blowing off steam, or whistling when the Royal Train passed. Stationmasters had to arrange for permanent way inspectors to position men at facing points thirty minutes before the Royal Train was due and the points had to be carefully examined before the passing of the pilot engine and again before the Royal Train; during the whole of this period the points were to remain unaltered. Speed over facing points was restricted to a maximum of 20 mph and steam had to be shut off until the entire train had passed over them. Platelayers equipped with flags and detonators were required to be at all unstaffed level crossings. 'The Servants of the Company are to perform the necessary work on the platforms without noise; and no cheering or other demonstration must be offered, the object being that the Royal Party shall be quite undisturbed during the journey.' The Queen disliked high speeds and stipulated a maximum speed of 40 mph during the day and 30 mph at night.

At the station where the royal journey was to terminate, a chalk mark was made at the exact spot at which the footplate of the engine should be when the Royal Train stopped and a man with a red hand-signal was stationed at this mark. This ensured that the train would stop in the correct position for the Queen to step onto the red carpet. On arriving at a station, the Queen would be greeted by the stationmaster and the company's chief officers, while the locomotive superintendent usually travelled on the locomotive footplate.

On the LSWR, Her Majesty travelled in a special saloon designed by Joseph Hamilton Beattie who was responsible for the company's carriage and wagon department. The coach was a four-wheeler, 17 ft 4½ in long and 7 ft 3 in wide, designed in the style of a contemporary three-compartment first class vehicle, but with two compartments made into one. This formed a handsome and comfortable saloon for Her Majesty, while the end compartment, with an internal communicating door, served the Queen's equerries.

The saloon contained a long cross seat at one end and four fixed armchairs, upholstered in silk damask laced in crimson and white. The ceiling was quilted in white watered silk, embroidered with roses, thistles and shamrocks in velvet and silver thread. The curtains were peach-coloured silk with silver tassels. Externally the body was very grandiose, with moulded cartouches bearing the royal arms and the insignia of the highest orders of chivalry. Surprisingly, this splendid vehicle was still in use a century later on the Shropshire & Montgomeryshire Railway where, as an inspection car, it had outlived that line's passenger service.

When Netley Hospital opened in 1856, Queen Victoria made frequent visits, generally starting from Windsor. She made her last visit on 16 May 1900, only about eight months before her death.

After Osborne House was completed in 1846, the Royal family made bi-annual visits to the Isle of Wight, using the special station built in 1845 in Clarence Yard, Gosport, which was found to be more convenient for boarding the royal yacht than the splendid town station. The Clarence Yard platform was quite narrow and only three people could walk abreast, but from the platform a short covered way led to a pontoon and a draped portable gangway to the Royal Yacht. The platform was also quite short, so portable steps were required for access to vehicles at the front of the train. Certainly, in later years, the pupils of St Matthew's school lined the route to Clarence Yard station waving flags and singing patriotic songs. One lady, Mabel Brooks, recalled standing on the station with her fellow pupils when the Royal Train steamed in. Queen Victoria leaned out of her coach and spoke to the awe-struck children saying that she hoped they all helped their mothers at home. One girl replied that she was fed up with housework and when the Queen asked why, replied that she was one of a large family and that it was her task to wash the babies' nappies. Her Majesty was impressed with the children and sent the teacher money to buy them sweets.

When travelling to the Isle of Wight, the Queen enjoyed the beautiful scenery on the Whitchurch to Fullerton line. When returning, the Queen's luggage was sent to Stokes Bay earlier and joined the Royal Train at Basingstoke.

The Queen died at Osborne House on 22 January 1901 and on 1 February the Royal Yacht carried her body to Clarence Yard. The following day, the funeral train headed by Jubilee class 0-4-2 No 555 worked the funeral train from Gosport to Fareham. This engine was selected because it was one of the class that was fitted with the Westinghouse brake, as well as the vacuum type. LBSCR B4 class 4-4-0 No 54 *Empress* (the LBSCR used the Westinghouse brake) hauled the funeral train from Fareham to Victoria station. No 54 was decorated with a gilt crown resting on a crimson cushion attached to the front of the chimney base, while its handrails were draped in white and purple cloth.

Unlike the splendid arrangements made for the Queen's travel when she was alive, her funeral train arrangements were appalling. A plan of the train had been prepared for guiding the guests, but this had been made out for when it arrived at Victoria. Someone had overlooked the fact that the train would need to reverse at Fareham and at Clarence Yard everything was found back-to-front. The eight-coach train was too long for the short platform so the imperial and royal mourners had to scuttle from one end of the train to the other.

All this fuss and bother caused much delay and the LSWR and LBSCR officers were not slow at blaming each other for the deficiency. Departure from Gosport was eight minutes late, while two more minutes were lost at Fareham. As King Edward abhorred unpunctuality, the LBSCR obliged by making a very fast run to Victoria, conveying the Queen's corpse at approximately twice the speed she had ever travelled in her lifetime.

King Edward VII did not share his mother's fondness for Osborne House and the twice-yearly pilgrimages ceased.

Railways continued to take the greatest care of the Royal Family, though, as is seen by a special notice issued when King George VI and his family were to travel from Waterloo to Portsmouth & Southsea (High Level).

The train travelled via the Portsmouth Direct line, running to timing similar to the standard 90-minute expresses. Double block working was in force, to keep twice the normal space clear ahead of the train. 'Care must be taken that any Horses, with or without vehicles, which may be within Station Limits are under strict control during the approach and passing of the Royal Train.' Level crossings were guarded and 'at all level crossings which are in the charge of Gatewomen, a competent man must be employed 30 minutes before the Royal Train is due to pass and remain until 10 minutes after.' The three tunnels were to be inspected 'immediately prior to the running of the Royal Train' to check their condition while a competent man was to be posted 'at each end an hour ahead so as to prevent any unauthorised person being upon the Railway in or near the tunnel.' Another competent man was to be stationed at each ventilation shaft on top. Stationmasters were required to watch the passage of the train and passing times from certain specified stations were telephoned to Waterloo. The distance from the centre of the footplate to the centre of the leading door of the Pullman car *Marjorie*, from which the Royal party would alight, was 159 ft 4 in.

LIGHT RAILWAYS

∎

LIGHT RAILWAYS ALWAYS FASCINATE as they often used types of locomotives not seen elsewhere and sometimes had strange working practices. They were constructed under the provisions of the Light Railways Act of 1896. This allowed a simpler railway to be run in an area where a normal line would have been uneconomic. Gradients could be steeper, curves sharper and have level crossings without gates, thus saving the costs of a gatekeeper. Gateless level crossings were protected by cattle grids. In the interests of safety, speed on light railways was severely restricted. Hampshire had several of these lines.

∎ H12 class steam railmotor No 2 at Cliddesden on a Basingstoke to Alton working. Part of the station name in white can be seen to the left of the left-hand buffer. (Author's collection) ∎

The Basingstoke & Alton Light Railway

Opened on 1 June 1901, this 14¼-mile-long line was owned and worked by the LSWR. Because of the curvature adopted by the route, in order to minimise the earthworks required, Cliddesden, Herriard and Bentworth and Lasham stations were distant from the communities they purported to serve. Each station had a well and water tank, Herriard using a pump powered by an oil engine, while the others used wind pumps. Speed over the branch was limited to a maximum of 25 mph,

with a lower limit of 10 mph approaching level crossings. The axle load was limited to 14 tons. The only place where trains in opposite directions could cross was Herriard.

Locomotives were used initially but, in the spring of 1904, a railcar was tried. However, the steep gradients and sharp curves caused failures and that August it was replaced by a conventional locomotive.

A siding served Thornycroft's works, Basingstoke, while another carried coal to a 500-bed hospital near Alton, which had been established during the Boer War. In 1918 a platform called Alton Park was provided for the hospital, but the name never appeared in public timetables.

The Basingstoke & Alton Light Railway closed on 1 January 1917 so that the rails could be lifted and sent to France where there was a grave shortage of track for military lines. From this date, a motor lorry carried goods, milk and parcels traffic.

The Southern Railway, which had taken over the LSWR, had hoped not to have to reopen the line as, with increasing road traffic, it would have been uneconomic. Local pressure, however, forced the SR to re-lay and open the railway on 18 August 1924, but no passing loop was provided at Herriard or elsewhere. As anticipated, it ran at a loss and passenger trains were withdrawn on 12 September 1932, but Basingstoke to Bentworth and Lasham remained open for freight traffic until 1 June 1936.

The line was used for making two films. The first was *The Wrecker*, shot in August 1928, which involved a collision between a train and a Foden lorry at Salter's Ash level crossing. In order for the event to be really spectacular, the lorry was packed with dynamite. The second film was the Will Hay comedy *Oh, Mr Porter!*, shot in June 1937. As the scenes were set in Ireland, Cliddesden station was renamed 'Buggleskelly'. Elderly SR locomotives were used and also Kent & East Sussex Light Railway 2-4-0T No 2 *Northiam*, which was provided with an extra tall chimney to give it an even older appearance.

The filming gave rise to an amusing incident. One morning the film crew arrived and found an old woman sitting on the station seat waiting for a train. When informed that she was five years too late and that the station was now part of a film set, she strongly remonstrated with them and the more they insisted it was not a working station, the more she insisted that she would write to *The Times* about the matter.

The Bentley & Bordon Light Railway

When the War Office planned Longmoor Camp in Woolmer Forest, it invited the LSWR to provide a rail link. This was the Bentley & Bordon Light Railway, 4½ miles in length. Instead of a contractor being employed as was normal practice, the LSWR's own Engineering Department staff carried out the work. When the work was in full swing, 155 men were employed plus three locomotives hired from the LSWR's Mechanical Department, three horses and 40 tip wagons. The line was constructed in eighteen months at a cost of £30,000.

As with most light railways, level crossings were gateless and were provided with cattle grids to prevent livestock from wandering along the track. An overall speed limit of 25 mph was imposed, with a lower restriction of 10 mph or 5 mph near crossings. Only a single line was laid, but sufficient land was purchased to allow for doubling should this have ever become necessary.

Most of the station buildings at Bordon were constructed of corrugated iron, but the platform was capable of handling up to four ten-coach trains. The station was lit from the product of a small coal-gas producing plant. As there was no existing housing available for railway staff, the LSWR constructed ten terraced homes and a detached stationmaster's residence. The partition walls between the houses were of brick, but for economy, those within a house were of tongue and grooved timber. As was contemporary custom, an earth privy was situated outside.

■ A scene at Bentley in the 1930s: A12 class 0-4-2 No 632 heads a main line train, while push-pull fitted M7 class 0-4-4T No 28 is in charge of a train to Bordon. No 632 was withdrawn in August 1937. (Lens of Sutton) ■

An interesting feature of the line was that in the early 1920s, an Adams 415 class 4-4-2T, with pulley and cable apparatus, was used for push and pull operation. This meant that the engine stayed at one end, pulling in one direction and then pushing on the return journey. This avoided the trouble of uncoupling the engine, running round the train and recoupling. When the engine propelled the train, the driver stood in a control compartment of what had been the rear of the train. Adjacent to the station, a branch line engine driver kept an allotment and profitably spent much of his waiting time between trains gardening.

Until 1941, the largest engines permitted to run over the branch were 4-4-0s, but that year a 2-6-0 was tried. Its weight damaged an underline bridge and rail services had to be suspended until it was repaired and strengthened by the Royal Engineers. Subsequently, engines of this wheel arrangement were allowed to use the line.

The line opened on 11 December 1905 worked by locomotives, but four months later a steam railcar operated the passenger services. It was a railmotor of the H13 class, which differed from the H12 class tried on the Basingstoke & Alton Light Railway, as the former had its engine completely enclosed in coach bodywork. On the Bordon branch a railmotor burnt 13.2 lb of coal per mile, compared with 26.8 lb of an O2 class 0-4-4T.

The branch had a most curious passenger timetable in the early 1930s. Such were its idiosyncrasies that if you travelled from Bordon on a Monday, you could not return by rail until the following Sunday while if on a train from Bordon you got off at Kingsley Halt, you were unable to return as the Sunday train back to Bordon did not call there!

The passenger service was withdrawn on 16 September

1957 and the line closed completely on 4 April 1966, by which time traffic to and from Longmoor Camp had seriously declined. Interestingly, the Association of Train Operating Companies' report *Connecting Communities*, published in June 2009, recommended restoring the branch as a single track electric line. Such a development would ease pressure on Liphook and Farnham stations, at both of which car parking is fully utilised.

The Lee-on-the-Solent Railway
The 3-mile-long Lee-on-the-Solent Railway was unusual in that it was not built under an Act of Parliament, but was one of the very few constructed under an order of the Railway Construction Facilities Act of 1864. Powers were granted in 1894 to build a line from Gosport to the hamlet of Lee Britten as Dr John Newton Robinson, who was the light railway's main shareholder, had the intention of turning the place into a resort. Construction proceeded very sluggishly until 1893 when Messrs Pauling & Elliott took over the contract. The permanent way consisted of flat-bottomed rail spiked directly to the sleepers American-style, rather than being held in the usual British chairs. When Major Yorke from the Board of Trade made an inspection on 15 July 1893 he found that the platforms were only 4 inches high and were without any shelter or booking offices, so he was forced to declare the line incomplete. Matters improved, he carried out a re-inspection and sanctioned opening for 12 May 1894 in readiness for the Whit Monday traffic two days later.

At the two intermediate halts, a lad with a red flag signalled to the driver if there were passengers to be picked up, while any needing to alight were required to inform the guard before leaving a terminus. Between Fort Brockhurst and Fort Gomer, the railway ran tramway-like unfenced beside the road. Fort Gomer was originally called 'Privett' but was renamed in October 1909 to avoid confusion with the station of the same name on the Meon Valley line. Unlike a tramway, through bookings could be made to main line stations.

Locomotives hired from the LSWR were 2-4-0T No 21 *Scott* and 0-6-0ST No 392 *Lady Portsmouth*, the latter having worked on the construction of the Bentley & Bordon Light Railway. Coaches had longitudinal seating of tramway pattern and end balconies. Due to the light nature of the permanent way, speed was restricted to 10 mph.

In June 1908 the LSWR declared that both locomotives were life-expired and that it had no others available with such a light axle loading of 8 tons. As the light railway had failed to make a profit due to the fact that the new resort did not develop to the hoped for extent, there was no rush to lend suitable engines. On 26 July 1909 the LSWR took over working, almost immediately introducing its H13 class steam railmotors, which were ideal for the task. These continued until October 1915 when push-pull trains took over. Facilities for the engine stabled overnight at Lee-on-the-Solent were quite primitive – merely a water tank and coal stage. No shed was provided and having no protection from the weather, it was uncomfortable for the man responsible for cleaning and coaling.

Elmore Halt opened on 11 April 1910 and like the other intermediate halts closed on 1 May 1930. Due to road

Lee-on-the-Solent, 1 January 1931, the final day of passenger working. (Author's collection)

Scouts at Lee-on-the-Solent, circa 1933. (Author's collection)

competition, the line closed to passengers on 1 January 1931 and to goods traffic on 30 September 1935.

Totton, Hythe & Fawley Light Railway

The 9-mile-long Totton, Hythe & Fawley Light Railway was a nominally independent line constructed to serve Fawley oil refinery. Although granted a Light Railway Order in 1921, no active steps were taken until after the 1923 railway amalgamation when the SR got things moving. The single line, with no passing loops, opened on 20 July 1925, with intermediate stations at Marchwood and Hythe. Although five trains were run daily, many potential passengers preferred using the Hythe–Southampton ferry. No turntable was provided at Fawley so the use of tank engines would be expected but, surprisingly, tender engines hauled most trains.

Originally the branch was worked as one section from Totton to Fawley, but with the extension of the Royal Engineers' dock at Marchwood in 1943, that station became an intermediate block post with a crossing loop. The signal box was created from a station office. It is now one of the very few Network Rail mechanical boxes in the south of England.

Much of the traffic was from the AGWI (Atlantic Gulf West Indies Corporation) refinery at Fawley and in 1951 its new owners, Esso, operated Europe's largest refinery. Construction workers were drawn up the hill to a special platform by a diesel-electric locomotive built in the USA. When the extension was completed, products were taken down the gradient of approximately 1 in 40 and returning empty wagons always had an ex-LMS brake van at the rear to guard against runaways. The line actually in the refinery for safety has

■ *The inaugural passenger train from Fawley arrives at Hythe,*
20 July 1925. (Author's collection) ■

always used internal-combustion engines and today there are two Hunslet 0-6-0 diesel-electric locomotives *Bluebird* and *Redwing* bearing brass nameplates also carrying a reproduction of the bird, while the whole engine is painted in the appropriate colour. They are maintained in a single-road shed just long enough to hold one locomotive.

Breakdown crews thoroughly enjoyed going to Fawley because if they were working inside the refinery, free refreshments were offered in the canteen.

In the 1950s a power station was built at Marchwood, while a synthetic rubber factory at Hythe brought more traffic to the line. New factories opened at Hardley, where a new platform opened on 3 March 1958, but it had a brief life and was closed on 5 April 1964. In 1963 the ungated level crossing at Frost Lane, south of Hythe, received one of the first lifting barriers in the country, this enabling the speed restriction of 10 mph to be removed. Passenger traffic was withdrawn from the branch on 14 February 1966, not surprisingly as latterly only about twenty-five passengers were carried daily. However, oil traffic still flourishes though it is only a fraction of the 60 trains weekly that used the line in the late 1960s.

In June 2009 the Association of Train Operating Companies' report *Connecting Communities* recommended

■ *Sharp, Stewart 2-4-0T* Hayling Island *at Hayling Island. This engine worked the branch from 1874 to 1889. (Author's collection)* ■

that the line from Totton to Hythe be reopened to passenger traffic and believed this would do something to ease road congestion in the Hythe and Totton areas.

The Hayling Island Railway

Although not officially a 'light railway', the delightful Hayling Island line had several of its characteristics. It opened in 1867 and although the Receiver was called in two years later, by 1872 its finances were in the black. Initially passenger trains

■ *A Terrier 0-6-0T and seven coaches at Hayling Island. (Author's collection)*■

were operated by a contractor's locomotive and four-wheeled coaches, but from 1871 the line was run by the LBSCR, prior to being absorbed by the SR in 1923.

Hayling Island station was a most attractive structure, half-timbered with herringbone-pattern brickwork and roof tiles of two designs.

The most significant engineering feature was the Langston Bridge (the final 'e' was never used by the railway). This consisted of a timber trestle 370 yards in length, comprising 49 spans of which the highest was 25 ft above high water. Regulations stated that ships must not sail through when the 30 ft swing span was opened, but were required to moor at posts and be hauled through. Swinging the bridge required two railwaymen: a signalman to work the box, disconnect and reconnect signal wires, while a lengthman had to remove and replace the locking fishplates and push the span open. Masters and pilots were ordered:

> On a vessel approaching the railway bridge, the Bridgeman will hoist on the flagstaff at the centre of the bridge, a white flag by day and a white light by night to denote that the vessel is seen. If the bridge can be safely opened, a black ball will be hoisted by day and a green light at night. When the bridge is actually open a red flag will be hoisted by day and a red light by night and shown when the bridge is about to be closed again for the passage of trains.

Severe weight restrictions over the bridge limited the choice of engines that could be used, so for the last 73 years of its life it was worked by Terrier class 0-6-0Ts. Latterly, spark-arresters were fitted to their chimneys to protect lineside crops. No separate freight trains were run, one train each way being designated 'mixed' and carrying both passengers and freight. Around 1900, a siding was installed just south of North Hayling Halt so that oysters could be transferred directly from boats to railway wagons. Latterly the normal weekday service of fourteen trains each way required only one engine in steam, but the 24 trains on summer weekends required three. On one summer Sunday in 1961, no fewer than around 7,000 passengers were carried.

In 1963 Langston Bridge required repairs that would cost £400,000. As this would have proved uneconomic, the line was closed on 4 November 1963. The final train was six coaches in length and as it was heavier than one engine could handle, a locomotive was coupled at each end in order to spread the weight on the aged viaduct, rather than couple two engines together in the normal way.

EASTLEIGH WORKS

IN **1891** WHEN THE **LSWR** DECIDED to build its carriage and wagon works at Bishopstoke, the novelist Charlotte M. Yonge, who lived at nearby Horsley, was asked to propose a name and suggested Eastleigh, after the manor, rather than New Bishopstoke.

No new town was planned and the work of the local builders was so poor that a public inquiry was held. Professor Jack Simmons in *The Railway in Town & Country, 1830–1914* wrote: 'Bad material, bad construction and bad arrangement were everywhere and evident – the only redeeming feature a good supply of water.' The scandal led to a public inquiry and a Local Board of Health was set up in 1892. The population of Eastleigh grew from about 700 in 1888 to 7,500 in 1898.

The works consisted initially of six buildings 330 ft by 200 ft, while a wagon shop erected later measured 375 ft by 300 ft. There was a sawmill for turning logs into planks and these were seasoned before being cut into shapes for carriage building. Nothing was wasted; all sawdust and chippings were fed into boiler furnaces. The electrician's shop dealt with carriage lighting and in the body shop coach assembly was in stages: underframe; sides, ends, corridor and compartment partitions erected; doors hung and polished; roof covered in canvas; rain strips fitted. The vehicle then proceeded to the paint shop.

The LSWR's locomotive construction and repair works were originally at Nine Elms but, as the company's territory expanded, the works had become sorely inadequate and needed to be moved to a larger site. It therefore made sense to develop the Eastleigh site and erect the country's most advanced locomotive works there to enable the company to construct all its own locomotives, instead of having them erected by tendering firms. Additionally, Eastleigh offered a much better environment for the works' staff than South London.

In 1898 the LSWR acquired 200 acres of the Chickenhall Farm estate near Eastleigh, between the London to Southampton and the Portsmouth line, for the new factory, whereas the carriage works were situated to the east of the Southampton to London line. The estimated cost of the new locomotive works and a replacement locomotive shed for engines transferred from Northam, Southampton, was £277,000. Work on constructing the depot began in November 1900 and the transfer from Northam was in January 1903. Eastleigh became the second largest shed on the LSWR. When the footplate crews and locomotive depot staff arrived at Eastleigh, they added 250 more men and families to the crowded area. In view of the grave shortage of homes, in January 1903 the LSWR agreed to build 54 cottages in Campbell Road – named after the company chairman, the Honourable H.W. Campbell. Costing £255 each, they were all completed by December 1904.

■ *Work on L12 class 4-4-0 No 419 being carried out at Eastleigh.* (Author's collection) ■

roof, while the separate buildings required for the forge, foundry and stores were given space around them for expansion. The works were designed with wide bays to allow easy movement. Stone for the concrete was nearly all obtained on site.

Interestingly, as the boiler shop at Nine Elms had only been built in 1892–3, part was transferred to Eastleigh, as were many of its machine tools. The yard floor was composed of chalk and ash, which was brought from various parts of the LSWR's system. Robert Urie, appointed Works Manager at Nine Elms in 1897, transferred to the new works at Eastleigh in 1909. In 1912 he succeeded Drummond as Chief Mechanical Engineer and held this post until the LSWR became part of the SR in 1923.

In 1908 the LSWR announced that it would not erect houses for its locomotive works staff as their needs would be provided for by private enterprise. The reason behind this statement was that the LSWR was experiencing a temporary cash shortage, due to a greater expenditure than usual on capital projects.

By the summer of 1909 some locomotive repair work began and by the end of that year 350 men were employed there. As might be expected, land prices rose and no speculative

Although the decision to start constructing the locomotive shops was taken in December 1902, progress was slow as authority had to be sought for each stage. The works were planned and supervised by Dugald Drummond, the Chief Mechanical Engineer, who made frequent visits in his special saloon 'The Bug' (see page 78). He designed the works so that as many tasks as possible could be carried out under one building was carried out, so those transferred from Nine Elms tried fruitlessly to find accommodation. Many had to take lodgings in Romsey, Chandler's Ford, Swaything, Southampton and nearby villages, thus facing a daily commute to the works, the company providing cheap tickets. The kindly LSWR at least provided a special train to Waterloo at midday on Saturday, with a return on Sunday evening, to enable the workers to travel home at weekends in order to see their families and friends. This situation was quite intolerable, so in January 1910 a hundred more cottages were erected on land in Campbell Road. Built at a cost of £30,758, they were let at a weekly rent of 5s 6d. The main transfer from Nine Elms involved 1,500 men.

At the LSWR's half-yearly meeting in February 1910, the company chairman, Sir Charles Scotter, said that Drummond had reported: 'The locomotive works at Nine Elms are now closed and the men and machinery are removed to Eastleigh. The works are designed to reduce to the minimum the handling of material, and the process of manufacture and the machinery are the finest that can be procured for our requirements. This transfer has been accomplished without an employee of the department being one hour out of work or the output of the works interfered with. I have no hesitation in saying that the company possesses the most complete and up-to-date works owned by any railway company.'

■ *Campbell Road, Eastleigh, sited between the locomotive running shed and the works. Notice the railway track, to aid the transportation of construction materials, and the kerbs made from rail. (Author's collection)* ■

Eastleigh turned out its first new locomotive on 12 September 1910, the 0-4-0 motor tank No 101. Between 1910 and 1961 the number of steam locomotives built or rebuilt at Eastleigh was 425. The last steam engine to be constructed was West Country class No 34104 *Bere Alston* and by a strange coincidence this was the last to be rebuilt in May 1961. The last steam engine to be repaired was Battle of Britain class No 34089 *602 Squadron* on 3 October 1966.

■ *The erecting shop, Eastleigh, circa 1910. (Author's collection)* ■

The workshops, 882 ft by 407 ft, were constructed of steel framing covered by non-load-bearing brick walls. They were erected by LSWR staff under the chief resident engineer, J.W. Jacomb-Hood, rather than by outside contractors. Due to Rendle's patent glazing in the roof, the shops did not require artificial light during the daytime. During the hours of darkness 'Davy' arc lamps were used. Unusual for the time, no gas lighting was installed, gas only being utilised for heating furnaces, cooking food and burning off paint.

The Pattern Shop supplied all patterns for use in the iron and brass foundries. The iron foundry consisted of two bays. In one was set a continuous casting plant. Moulds were placed on a moving belt and filled with molten metal as they passed the three cupolas. The moulds were then broken open and the casting placed on a conveyor, which took it to the fettling shop for trimming.

The Wheel Shop had a wheel press and also lathes capable of turning locomotive wheels up to 7 ft 6 ins in diameter. Eastleigh manufactured fire bricks for firebox arches and for lining furnaces. The kilns attached to the Brick Shop held 10,000 bricks and two kiln-loads were produced monthly. Other departments included a metallurgical laboratory, stores and an ambulance room.

The boiler and machine shops were also well equipped and the tube shop repaired damaged boiler tubes by welding. The erecting shop had four bays, two used for dealing with large and small locomotives respectively. Engines for repair entered at one end and were stripped. The parts were cleaned by being passed through a bath of boiling caustic soda. The stripped locomotive frames were then moved up the shop and the reassembly of the engine began. A third bay was used for building new locomotives while a fourth bay repaired tenders.

The three-road paint shop measured 45 ft by 360 ft and was steam-heated for drying the paint and gas was provided for burning it off.

On entering the workshop yard there was the Time Office where employees took metal discs. All the office rooms were steam-heated. Recycling was practised – engine drivers' and cleaners' oily cloths were placed in a perforated drum, spun at high speed and the oil collected for further use, while the clean cloths were reissued.

The LSWR cared for its employees. As early as 1891, at a cost of over £3,000, it set up an institute with a large reading room, a well-patronised library, a billiard room with three tables and a 500-seat concert hall. In the classrooms, courses were offered in mathematics, shorthand, drawing and first aid.

The Railwaymen's Institute, Eastleigh, circa 1910.
(Author's collection) ■

By 1898 its membership totalled almost a thousand. There were sports fields and a banked cycle track that was one of the best in the country. The company also contributed £500 towards the enlargement of the parish church so that it could cater for the increased population. Each of the nonconformist chapels was given £50. The works had a canteen for 600 men and a dining room for clerical staff where a hot meal could be obtained for sixpence, though initially workmen provided their own meals, which were heated free of charge, the only cost being a penny a week for condiments.

Throughout the summer months hours of labour were so arranged that every Saturday was a holiday. Special travelling facilities were provided so that Eastleigh residents could visit the sea, as well as attractions inland, and at fares that seldom exceeded one shilling return.

By 1898 near the dining hall were 26 cosy little cottages built by the LSWR for its emergency men – each being a well-trained fire-fighter. All these cottages were linked by telephone to the works so that in the case of fire, the men could be summoned quickly. These fire-fighters were supplied with a uniform and were paid for every attendance at fire drill. Normally the fire appliance was in the hands of two permanent brigade firemen who patrolled day and night. Water for the works was obtained by pumping.

The miners' strike of 1912 led to staff at the works being placed on short time. In October and November 1917 workers at Eastleigh struck because their pay had not kept pace with that paid to workers in munitions factories at Southampton and elsewhere. Arbitration awarded a 12% increase.

In 1923, with the formation of the SR from the amalgamation of the LSWR, LBSCR and other companies, the Eastleigh Works were reorganised and became the SR's main centre for locomotive and carriage construction. This step was taken because they were equipped with modern machine tools, which speeded work, thus returning locomotives to service sooner and reducing the number required to run the trains. In 1936 over 1,000 engines for repair passed through the works in addition to the construction of new ones.

During both World Wars, Eastleigh manufactured armaments, while various marine fittings were supplied to

Harland & Wolff and Thornycroft & Co for vessels constructed at Southampton.

In the 1930s the locomotive erecting shop changed from the traditional method of one gang carrying out a complete overhaul, to using specialist gangs, the engine being progressively moved down the shop. This method was considerably faster. Previously, a King Arthur class 4-6-0 took three months to overhaul, including about a month in the paint shop, but the new method reduced the overhaul to nineteen days, painting being carried out while the fitters were still at work.

■ *Two King Arthur class 4-6-0s at Eastleigh, 25 October 1960: No 30768* Sir Balin *and No 30802* Sir Durnore. *(Revd Alan Newman)* ■

■ *Merchant Navy class 4-6-2 No 35016* Elders Fyffes *at Eastleigh, 5 October 1962.* (Revd Alan Newman) ■

■ *Q1 class 0-6-0 No 33015 at Eastleigh, 5 October 1962, having just undergone an overhaul at the works.* (Revd Alan Newman) ■

Recollections of Eastleigh

Peter Martin, a lifelong Hampshire railway enthusiast, gives a fascinating first-hand account of the area:

My memories of Eastleigh stretch from after the Second World War until the present time. Eastleigh station was situated between the staggered road junctions of Leigh Road, Southampton Road, Station Hill and Bishopstoke Road. Immediately outside the station and situated in Southampton Road, was for many years the local office of the Hants & Dorset Omnibus Company, with stops in Leigh Road, Southampton Road and the surrounding streets.

Access to the carriage works was via Bishopstoke Road and that to the locomotive works via Southampton Road and Campbell Road, the latter known locally as 'Spike Island', presumably because of the many iron railings fencing off the locomotive works and running sheds from the public highway. In Campbell Road were a number of houses erected specifically for the workers and their families.

The whole area was definitely a place to be avoided, if you possibly could, in the early morning, lunchtime and teatime. The mass of workers coming and going from their homes, or exiting the station and walking to either the carriage, or locomotive works was certainly a sight to behold. Added to this, of course, were workers joining or alighting from buses, as well as those cycling.

Control of the junction of Station Hill, Southampton Road and Leigh Road, was in the hands of a lone policeman on point duty here. Although he always appeared to be in control, I am sure he must have experienced many hairy moments at these busy times.

One of the comical sights to be enjoyed was the workers on Bishopstoke and Campbell road bridges. If you were on the station, or outside of it, their bodies concealed, all you could see were the peak caps, or heads of the workers bobbing along as they made their way across both bridges to or from the two works.

A further complication occurred in Bishopstoke Road at lunchtimes. Here workers would leave the carriage works for their canteen situated just across the road, so it you were travelling to or from Bishopstoke at this time, you took your life in your hands dodging the hungry workers crossing the road. Further complications were caused by the existence of two factories situated in Leigh Road a short distance from the station. These were the Pirelli General Cable factory and Causton's printing works, both set almost opposite each other. Workers from both these establishments added further to the hordes of people milling around at busy times.

For many years, the railway workers entered floats into the annual Eastleigh Carnival held in August and won many prizes for their ingenuity and comical endeavours. They were great fundraisers during this event and it was sad to see them go when Health and Safety issues reared their head in later years, coupled of course, with closure of much of the works. In my opinion, after this, Eastleigh's carnival was never the same.

In the 1970s and '80s many Open Days were held at the works, mainly the locomotive side, and these were always a great success, bringing many people in, while helping to raise funds for the Southern Railway's children's home at Woking, in Surrey. Railway work was dangerous, so quite a few children became fatherless. To help with this problem, the South Western Railway Servants' Orphanage was established at Clapham in 1885, moving to Woking in 1909. It still stands today, but is now a retirement home for railway workers.

Another fascinating aspect of the railway was the boat traffic to and from Southampton Docks generated by the many international shipping companies using it as their port of arrival or departure to faraway places across the world. Many of these great liners, as they were arriving or departing, let out loud blasts from their fog horns, which could be heard several miles inland, so you were always aware then these giants of the seas were about their business.

As a child at that time, it was exciting for me to watch the boat trains passing through Eastleigh at full speed, their individual name boards at carriage roof level indicating which shipping company's passengers they were carrying. My curiosity always left me wondering which celebrities had just embarked, or disembarked, from the two giant 'Queen' liners on the North Atlantic Route to New York. However, one could always rely on the local evening paper the following day to reveal who exactly had arrived or departed by this means of transport, including Hollywood film stars and others deemed equally famous in their various fields.

Around Eastleigh station were situated a number of drinking establishments, which one would imagine were deliberately built to slake the thirst of all the workers. Immediately outside the station were the Junction Hotel, the Home Tavern, while around the corner in Upper Market Street was the Crown. On the corner of Upper Market Street and Leigh Road was the Railway Institute, later rebuilt in Romsey Road on the site of the rectory of the Church of the Resurrection. On Station Hill, almost opposite Bishopstoke Road, was the Locomotive & Firemen's Club. Both these were built by the railway company for their employees' recreation.

Today, in the 21st century, unfortunately only one of these works is still in existence, and that is as a maintenance depot, a far cry from the many departments established there at the start of the 20th century. However, Eastleigh can be very proud of its railway traditions over the past hundred years and its involvement in providing and maintaining the various forms of rolling stock and locomotives required for working on the LSWR and its successors, the Southern Railway and the Southern Region of British Railways. Many local people were employed either in the works, or as station staff, and many others were required as drivers, firemen, guards, signalmen or track maintenance workers, all of whom were vital to keep the trains running.

LOCOMOTIVES AND LOCOMOTIVE WORKING

■ *A 2-2-2T at Gosport 1859. (Author's collection)* ■

ONE INTERESTING **LSWR** TRAIN in 1874 was the 2.10 pm from Waterloo. Nicknamed the 'Beeswing', probably after a racehorse, it was the fastest Down train on the system. It left Waterloo behind two engines, the train engine from the LSWR's London shed at Nine Elms, with the leading locomotive having come from Southampton. It was really two trains in one, for at Basingstoke it divided: the leading engine was detached to allow the second engine to take the main portion of the train on to Exeter. Following its departure, the Southampton engine set back to the remaining coaches.

Having sped the 47¾ miles to Basingstoke in just over an hour, progress through Hampshire was more leisurely, taking about 55 minutes for the 31½ miles to Southampton, making just one stop at Winchester. Progress from Southampton along the twisting Castleman's Corkscrew was snail-like, Weymouth not being reached until 6.25 pm, thus having taken about two hours to cover the 64 miles from Southampton. By July 1880 the 2.10 pm Down had become just a train to Southampton and Weymouth and quite independent of one to Exeter. It

covered the 79 miles to Southampton in two hours one minute and arrived at Weymouth at 6.04 pm.

E.L. Ahrons in *Locomotive & Train Working in the Latter Part of the Nineteenth Century* wrote that in the 1890s the average speed from London to Portsmouth was well under 40 mph:

> *To the South Western official mind, Portsmouth seems to have been an obscure and unimportant village somewhere on the south coast, and for the life of them they could not see why anybody should want to get there quickly. And so they decided that nobody should. At one time Southampton was in a like case, but being on the main line to Bournemouth it did*

afterwards manage to pick up a few crumbs that fell from the table of the latter town, by virtue of the stopping there of one or two of the through expresses.

A class of engine that worked Southampton trains for many years was the 2-4-0 designed by Joseph Beattie. This was the first standard gauge coupled engine ever to be built with driving wheels as large as 7 ft diameter. The 95, or Centaur class, was constructed in 1859 and withdrawn between 1894 and 1899 after each had covered about a million miles.

Joseph Beattie was anxious to reduce the LSWR's coal bill as the company, unlike most other large railways, did not serve a colliery and thus had to pay to have its coal hauled for some distance over other companies' lines. Beattie's solution was to invent a patent firebox with a combustion chamber. These fireboxes succeeded in saving on coal, but at the expense of leaks and cost a good deal to keep in repair, so the financial saving was minimal.

His patent firebox consisted of a front and back chamber separated by a transverse partition. There were two fireholes of which the lower formed the opening into the back chamber nearest the footplate. The upper firehole was placed so that coal could be thrown over the transverse partition into the front chamber. The fire in this front chamber was kept in a white-hot incandescent condition, while most of the new coal was fired into the rear chamber. This meant that smoke and unburnt gases from the rear chamber passed over into the front chamber and were combusted and gave heat, instead of going to waste up the chimney. This invention could reduce coal consumption by up to 42%. Most other railway companies used the cheaper and less complex brick arch and deflection plate, which served the same purpose.

Beattie had what he considered another bright coal-saving idea. Instead of cold water being fed into the boiler to replace what had been used as steam, he believed it advantageous to warm it by the exhaust steam from the cylinders that was just going to waste. This warmed water would need less coal to turn it into steam. Thus, Beattie's engines fitted with this device appeared to have two chimneys: a smaller one being placed in front of the other, but in reality, the smaller 'chimney' was a condenser. Exhaust steam from the cylinders passed through a tubular heater into this condenser where it met a jet of cold water from the tender. The resultant hot water was then either delivered into the boiler or, if not required there, could be taken back to the tender to warm the cold water.

Although brilliant in theory, it proved not to be so excellent in practice. One problem was that the exhaust steam was polluted with cylinder oil and when this oil entered the boiler, it proved detrimental to the plates and also caused priming, which is when water, instead of steam, entered the cylinders and when ejected from the chimney soiled everything it touched. Determined not to be beaten, Beattie devised a modification – a double pipe. Exhaust steam was in the outer pipe and the fresh water heated in the inner pipe.

In 1877 Beattie designed a 4-4-0 and had twenty built. With hindsight it would have been a better decision had only one been built and then given extensive trials and any problems solved before launching out with a large order. The

Locomotive Committee should have been suspicious because one reputable manufacturer, the Vulcan Foundry, declined to tender to erect these engines, while Robert Stephenson & Co and Neilson & Co both suggested design modifications. The locomotives did indeed prove to be a disaster. They suffered defects such as bolts and buffers falling off, cylinders and piston heads becoming loose, fractured driving wheel spokes and jammed regulators, while all members of the class suffered from leaking boiler tubes.

The LBSCR locomotive engineer, William Stroudley, named his engines after stations and villages along the line. Although a pleasant idea, it led to confusion with people inexperienced in railway ways and dear old ladies, seeing the name of their destination on an engine, assuming that that was where the engine was going.

Stroudley also had an unusual livery for his passenger locomotives. 'Improved Engine Green' was actually ochre yellow; it is believed that he was colour-blind. His engines were kept beautifully clean and looked splendid, their coupling rods claret-coloured and the number plates of polished brass.

Stroudley's first express engine with single 6 ft 9 in diameter driving wheels was No 151 *Grosvenor*, built in 1874. In August of the following year, it was the first engine to make the through 86¾-mile-run from Victoria to Portsmouth. It covered the distance in 110 minutes at an average speed of 47.3 mph. A similar type of engine but with 6 ft 6 in driving wheels, the G class, appeared in 1877 and was built for the Portsmouth traffic. They remained on this duty until 1895

when they were displaced by the 4-4-0s of Robert Billinton who had succeeded Stroudley in 1890.

Stroudley was keen on standardisation and interchange ability, and arranged for the tender wheels to be outside, instead of inside, the frames – to make them interchangeable with the carrying wheels of tank and express engines. This meant that when the tyres at the leading end of an engine had worn below a certain thickness, instead of being discarded, they could be safely used on a tender. The disadvantage was that it placed the tender springs in a less accessible position so that broken spring plates could not so readily be observed.

'One driver, one engine' was the LBSCR practice and Stroudley favoured the pleasant idea of painting the driver's name inside the cab. It meant that a driver always looked after his engine more carefully. When the hours of a working day were reduced, however, double-manning was introduced and although more mileage was obtained from a locomotive, it was not looked after so carefully.

The LSWR and LBSCR jointly owned the 1¼-mile-long branch between Fratton and East Southsea. Traffic was light as the service was irregular, running in connection with Brighton, Fareham and London services rather than aimed at serving purely local needs; in fact, unless a train was imminent, it was quicker to walk. Down main line trains were often late and as these East Southsea branch trains connected, they too were late. One good thing was that the waiting room at Fratton was well supplied with current newspapers and magazines, available free to passengers.

To save time when running late, on at least one occasion when a very tardy Down train stopped at Albert Road Halt, the guard told the passengers waiting for the Up service, 'Jump in mates, she's at Fratton and then we shan't have to stop coming back.' They jumped in, travelled to East Southsea and back to Fratton in three minutes fifteen seconds.

The job of being a guard on this service was no sinecure. In addition to his normal guard's duties, he was required to issue tickets, keep a sharp look ahead and be prepared to apply the hand-brake should it be necessary to do so. He was also expected to apply it when approaching Fratton, East Southsea and the intermediate halts. An electric bell communication between the guard and driver allowed the guard to request the driver to stop in an emergency and it also gave the driver the signal to proceed. In the event of the railcar becoming disabled on the East Southsea branch, as there was no fireman to carry out the duty, the guard was required to obtain assistance from Fratton.

The First World War brought passenger services on this branch to a halt for on 8 August 1914 a notice was chalked at Fratton: 'NO MOOR TRAINES TO EAST SOUTHSEA – FISCHAL'.

E.L. Ahrons revealed the foolishness of the LBSCR's Traffic Department:

> *Near Fratton there existed a junction with the London & South Western Railway … It would, perhaps, naturally be concluded that there would have been some arrangement as to suitably connecting trains. One train from Southampton was due to reach Fratton two minutes before the departure of the Brighton train, but the latter never waited for it in case it was two or three minutes late. Fratton was the one station on the line where the Brighton Traffic Department appeared to make every endeavour to get the trains away to time. On the other hand, the South-Western train for Southampton left Fratton six minutes before the Brighton train was due. I believe the London and South-Western authorities did their level best to get London Bridge [the Brighton company's headquarters] to agree to suitable times for connecting trains, but were met with a stolid non possumus. The Brighton traffic people conducted their extensive non possumus proceedings with other companies, and with the general public with great politeness and courtesy – everybody admitted that – and it is but a duty to record that whatever their administrative sins, which were many, they were most affable sinners to deal with so long as the long-suffering public did not expect to get any tangible results out of them. Which nobody ever did!*

As you will have gathered, the LBSCR was not noted for the excellence of its timekeeping and one passenger referred to it as the 'Long time Blighted and Slow Coach Railway'.

In 1898 Mr Rous-Marten, a noted railway recorder,

reported in his annual report to the International Railway Congress:

> *With reference to the work of the London, Brighton and South Coast Railway I have again little of interest to relate. The booked speed is poor, and in my experience much time is lost by signal checks or otherwise. Travelling by the train known as the Isle of Wight special express from London Bridge, the time lost to Portsmouth Harbour (86¾ miles) was no less than 64 minutes! The engine was not blameable for the loss, which was due to defective traffic arrangements along the line. It is curious to note that the time of the London, Brighton and South Coast's fastest run, viz.: - London to Brighton (50½ miles) in 65 minutes is exactly the same as it was in 1857, forty years ago!*

Ahrons revealed one reason for the poor timekeeping was that the company:

> *… scrupulously weighed every particle of luggage with the same scientific exactitude as the modern provision shops weigh tea and margarine, inclusive of the paper. The fine-art avoirdupois proclivities of London Bridge and Victoria would have done credit to the troy methods of a dispensing chemist in the poison business. Consequently there was naturally insufficient time for the process. The company seemed*

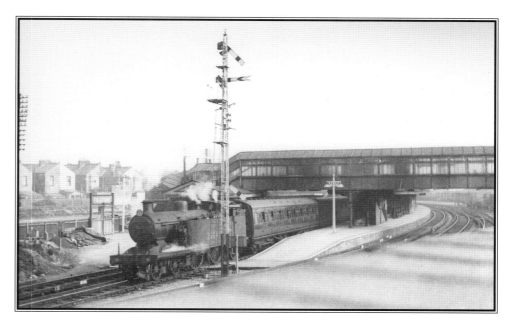

■ *I3 class 4-4-2T No 2084 designed by D.E. Marsh of the LBSCR, seen here at Fratton. Marsh began his career in the GWR's Swindon Works and was an early advocate of superheating, whereby apparatus in the smoke box raised the temperature and volume of the steam leaving the boiler, thus creating better fuel efficiency. He abandoned the Stroudley yellow livery for passenger engines and replaced it with a dark umber brown. (Lens of Sutton)* ■

to expect the long-suffering public to attend the place of execution hours beforehand so that due time should be provided for their satellites to extract excess shekels for a few extra pennyweights of luggage.

In the early days of railways, the only braking on trains, whether passenger or goods, was provided by guards in brake vans and the fireman applying the brake on the tender, for often the locomotives themselves were brakeless. The ability not to be able to stop quickly led to accidents and in due course the Board of Trade which regulated railways, demanded that passenger trains should be fitted with continuous brakes so that a driver could control brakes on all the vehicles. There were two main systems: the automatic vacuum and the Westinghouse. For some time, 2-2-2WT No 1 *Sussex* was fitted with the automatic vacuum and No 2 *Tartar* with the Westinghouse and both ran London to Portsmouth. The LSWR settled for the automatic vacuum, whereas the LBSCR chose the Westinghouse.

This was the one good thing about the LBSCR, it was one of the first to adopt an efficient continuous brake and, thus, pay due regard to the safety of its passengers. By June 1879 the company had largely fitted its locomotives and coaches with the Westinghouse system.

Passenger communication with the guard was another feature in which the Brighton was miles ahead of the large northern railways. The latter clung to the obsolete cord communication in which a passenger had first of all to read a lengthy notice fixed in the compartment, then having digested that, had to lean out of the window and haul in a few yards of

slack cord and finally, as often as not, he drew a blank. Yet the Brighton Company arranged an electric bell in each compartment and this communicated with the guard's van. According to *Punch*, one of the super-first-class patrons of the line, on the earliest appearance of the then new apparatus, rang the bell for a whisky and soda. What he actually got *Punch* did not state; possibly it was forty shillings or a month's imprisonment for improper use of the equipment!

Special Engines

The LSWR's Dugald Drummond had something no other British locomotive engineer had – his own inspection saloon. He had one constructed so that he could run over the system and check that all was in order. A 4-2-4T, it had a short saloon mounted behind the bunker. Officially known as 'Mr Drummond's Car' but colloquially referred to as 'The Bug', it could reach a speed in excess of 80 mph. On the four-track main line London to Basingstoke, he could, on another track, overtake a train and check that all was well on the footplate.

Following Drummond's death in 1912, aged 72 and still in harness, it saw little use. In 1932 it was refurbished with a six-wheel coach and was employed carrying officials and visitors around the construction works in Southampton New Docks. Its firebox failed in 1937 and during the Second World War the frame, minus driving wheels, carried heavy loads around Eastleigh Works. Until 1974 the saloon provided office accommodation for the timber inspector.

The LSWR and LBSCR Joint Committee decided it wished to work the branch between Fratton and East Southsea as cheaply as possible. To this end, Drummond and William

Panter, the LSWR Carriage & Wagon Superintendent, planned a steam railmotor – really a coach constructed with an integral locomotive. The engine part or Railcar No 1 was painted in LSWR green, while the coach portion was painted in LBSCR chocolate and cream livery. Railcar No 2 had its coach portion painted in the LSWR salmon and dark brown colours. Both railcars were lettered with the initials of both companies. Their boilers proved too small even for this short run, so the

■ *'The Bug', Dugald Drummond's personal transport, seen here at Nine Elms, 23 March 1905. (J.B. Ashford)* ■

■ *LSWR/LBSCR Joint steam railcar No 1 in its original condition. Notice the solid wheels.* (Author's collection) ■

The Basingstoke & Alton Light Railway opened in 1901 to prevent the GWR from having direct access to Portsmouth. Right from the start, the line was not economic and was always run at a loss. The LSWR sought to reduce working expenses, so Drummond proposed using a steam railcar.

Learning from experience with those on the East Southsea branch, he built railcars of a more powerful pattern. After construction they were run-in on the Basingstoke & Alton Light Railway and between Whitchurch and Fullerton. The car working the latter service proved so popular that one trip daily was extended to Basingstoke, the Up journey being via Fullerton, Longparish and Whitchurch, while the return was routed over the main line to Andover Junction. At night the spare car was used to carry signalmen, permanent way gangs, staff coal and drinking water in churns to remote signal boxes and level crossing keepers' lodges. The Board of Trade strongly objected to the hand braking and oil lights of the first two railcars so, within six months, vacuum brakes and electric lighting were fitted. Following this improvement, one railcar took over the Bishop's Waltham branch working. In May 1906 this railcar made trial runs from Aldershot to Alton with fifty fully-equipped troops to evaluate the use of railcars in the event of mobilisation.

heavily-patronised morning and evening services required them to be piloted by a conventional tank engine. Drummond improved them to some extent by fitting a larger boiler. The small boilers were not wasted – one was used on a steam crane at Fratton coal stage while the other was used at Redbridge permanent way depot.

The wheel bearings tended to run hot and when this occurred, the railmotor was jacked up in Fratton locomotive yard for the necessary treatment to be carried out. One day the jacks descended too quickly and the body tipped over on its side.

■ *LSWR/LBSCR Joint steam railcar No 1 with the initial vertical boiler replaced by one laid horizontally.*
(Author's collection) ■

■ *H13 class steam railmotor No 13 at Eastleigh.* (Author's collection) ■

■ *An H13 class steam railmotor approaches Andover Town.* (Author's collection) ■

■ *C14 class 2-2-0T No 742 at Whitchurch, October 1909.* (Author's collection) ■

Although dealing with the sparse traffic on the Basingstoke & Alton Light Railway proved no problem, steep gradients and tight curves near Cliddesden frequently defeated a railcar and locomotive assistance had to be sought from Basingstoke. Consequently, the railcars only worked over the line for six weeks before being transferred elsewhere. At the end of 1912, railcar No 1 worked on the Southampton Town to Royal Pier tramway.

One problem experienced with railcars was that their maintenance in smoky engine sheds was unkind to the upholstery, windows and door handles. Another disadvantage was that they could not cope with additional traffic. If, say, on market day a longer train was required, then a conventional engine and coaches had to be used and it was uneconomic to keep these at hand just for stand-by duties. The one advantage of railcars was the economies of using them; their coal consumption was less than half that of a conventional tank engine.

Occasionally a railcar came to a stop with the piston at the top of its stroke and thus unable to move off again under its own power. The solution was for the driver to step down and ease his 24½ ton car forward a few inches from dead centre using a long pinch bar.

All the railcars were withdrawn by 1919, with their coach portions turned into pull and push trailers and the boilers sold to market gardeners.

In 1906 Drummond and Panter had produced push and pull trains whereby an engine drew the coaches in one direction and then pushed them on the return journey, the engine remaining at what had become the rear, and the driver in charge of the train from a special control compartment in what became the leading coach. For working these trains, Drummond designed a 2-2-0T – really a compromise between the power portion of a steam railcar and a conventional tank engine. Costing £910 each, their moving parts were based on those of the larger railcars, but the boiler was considerably bigger. Almost square in appearance, they were nicknamed 'Humpty-Dumpties'. They hauled one or two trailers, which were designed to be pulled or pushed. Whistles were sited on the cab roof in order that they could be heard when the engine was pulling or pushing. In Hampshire these engines worked on the Whitchurch–Fullerton branch and between Cosham and Havant. They were not a success, so some Adams tank engines were adapted for push and pull working and proved very effective. Just prior to his death in 1912, Drummond acknowledged that push and pull services were better operated by conventional locomotives suitably equipped and so rebuilt these 2-2-0Ts to the 0-4-0T wheel arrangement. In the First World War, the War Department's desperate need for locomotives meant that the LSWR could sell these feeble engines and at the same time feel patriotic. Three of these machines lasted into SR and BR days, two shunting at Southampton Town quay and the third employed at Redbridge Permanent Way Depot.

HOSPITAL RAILWAYS

■

Of the Hampshire hospitals served by rail, the Royal Victoria Military Hospital, Netley, was the most important. Queen Victoria always had a great compassion for her troops, especially those wounded, and it was she who laid the foundation stone on 19 May 1856. The completed building was to accommodate wounded soldiers, initially those from the Crimean War. The vast building, a quarter of a mile in length, was designed by the War Department architect R.O. Mennie. Florence Nightingale had wished to help in its planning, but construction had already commenced by the time she returned from the Crimea.

The building contractors used 2-2-0 locomotives, not to haul wagons, but to power mortar mixers. A landing stage was adjacent to the hospital, but the pier was too short to reach deep water and so could not be used by hospital ships. The railway station was also inconvenient as it was about ¾ mile distant from the hospital. Although a special hospital siding and platform were provided, this was unsatisfactory as it was unroofed and lacked a waiting room.

To obviate this unsatisfactory state of affairs, at the suggestion of Queen Victoria, the War Department spent £4,090 on constructing a branch line to the hospital. The first two trains arrived on St George's Day 1900, with casualties from the Siege of Ladysmith. The line was difficult to work as it fell on a gradient of 1 in 70 towards the hospital and in autumn, when the line was covered with leaves from overhanging trees, both ascending and descending could lead to problems.

The 196-ft-long hospital platform had a small ticket office, which could be manned when required. Five ambulance coaches were stabled in a corrugated-iron carriage shed, the hospital's steam supply being connected to warm them before use.

The first casualties of the First World War arrived on 24 August 1914. During that war approximately 1,200 hospital trains arrived and each Tuesday and Friday a train left with discharged patients. In the inter-war years, trains averaged about five per annum.

The United States' Military (Army and Navy) took over Netley during the Second World War and it is said that they believed the ¼-mile-long corridor too lengthy to travel on foot, so drove their jeeps along the ground floor. As a form of escapism from their injuries, some patients used the same corridor for wheelchair races. Following D-Day, casualties arrived by road, but after treatment and when fit to travel, were moved by ambulance train to other hospitals. In June and July 1944 as many as five 14- to 16-coach trains left daily. Even with an engine at each end, wet rails could cause a train to take as long as 45 minutes to cover the distance of less than a mile. The final train on the branch ran on 30 August 1955 when the last ward cars were removed. The hospital itself

■ *The platform at Netley Hospital; some passengers are in uniform and some in 'civvies'. Three permanent way men stand on the track.* (Author's collection) ■

closed in 1958 and much of it was demolished in 1966. Only two buildings remain today: the Royal Chapel, now a museum, and the officers' mess building, converted into luxury apartments. The grounds were purchased in 1979 by Hampshire County Council and opened to the public the following year as the Royal Victoria Country Park.

The most curious train to use the line arrived in 1942. It consisted of about 20 horse boxes. It transpired that their occupants had been bombed out and had been brought to enjoy the grass at the hospital.

Just north of Butts Junction, Alton, on the Basingstoke & Alton Light Railway, a siding was laid to a hospital and convalescent camp with accommodation for 500 soldiers wounded in the South African War. It was built by the charmingly-titled 'Absent Minded Beggar Fund'. This curious name came from the fact that at concerts that raised funds for its construction, Rudyard Kipling's poem *The Absent Minded Beggar* was recited.

In due course the siding was removed, but a similar one was laid on 5 April 1910 for the Lord Mayor of London, Sir William Treloar's Cripples' Home which, in 1908, had taken over the convalescent camp huts. Some 1,500 tons of coal arrived annually at the siding. Additionally, to serve the

hospital in 1918 a 200-ft-long platform called Alton Park was provided on the Basingstoke & Alton Light Railway. On Founder's Day a special train would be run with an engine at each end in order to make the return journey safe as there were no run-round facilities at Alton Park. The platform survived until 1939.

West of Basingstoke a siding off the main line took coal to Park Prewett Hospital.

North of Fareham was Knowle Farm. In 1849 this was the selected site for the Hampshire County Asylum. The LSWR declined requests for a station and coal siding as being unremunerative but by September 1849 had relented sufficiently to allow two trains each way to call daily. Further, it stated that should the Asylum authorities build a station and lay a siding, it would arrange for three trains to call. The matter seems to have died, but in November 1906 a halt was built there at a cost of £53 and served only by the Meon Valley trains. The company minutes reveal that there existed 'a long standing custom of stopping trains at Knowle Junction on certain days for the convenience of persons visiting the Hampshire County Asylum'.

MILITARY RAILWAYS

•

Longmoor Military Railway

HAMPSHIRE HAD QUITE A NUMBER of military railways, the most impressive of which was at Longmoor. It really started in May 1903 when the 53rd Railway Company of the Royal Engineers arrived for the task of relocating huts for Longmoor Camp to that at Bordon, a distance of five miles.

Rather than face the tedious task of dismantling, transportation and re-erection, they had the ingenious notion of laying down two parallel narrow gauge tracks between Longmoor and Bordon and moving the huts whole. Placed on bogies, they were moved by the expedient of attaching a cable to a nearby tree and then winding it in with a steam winch. The fastest hut reached Bordon in a day.

In 1908 the Woolmer Instructional Military Railway was established at Longmoor to train military railwaymen, as Army needs and equipment could vary from that required for civilian use. As well as training regular soldiers, it was also used for training reservists recruited from British railway companies. Over forty skills were taught, including surveying, draughtsmanship and plate-laying, as well as training for footplate crews, traffic control staff, workshop staff and railway clerical work. The organisation was divided into three departments: railway construction, operating and workshop. The quality of training was summed up in the remark, 'You can tell a Longmoor-trained Sapper anywhere, but you can't tell him much.'

The First World War required the centre's expansion and the line was taken over by the Railway Operating Department. Then, in the post-war period, the centre was enlarged still further and reserve units of men from the Big Four (GWR, LMS, LNER and SR) arrived to carry out their fortnight's annual training.

In addition to providing railway training, the line carried supplies to and from the camp. Men could experience both double and single line working and a variety of token instruments. Then, in order to give the staff experience of long runs rather than just a few miles, in 1932 the 4-mile-long Hollywater Loop was surveyed and laid, but then lifted. Ten years later it was re-laid so that if required, a train could keep going round and round Hornby-style for any distance desired.

In its early days, connection with the main line was at Bentley, but in 1924 work on the 3½-mile line to Liss was begun and eventually opened in 1933. That year, stock at Longmoor comprised six locomotives and over 100 coaches and wagons. The railway was run by 22 officers and 385 other ranks.

Details survive of the skills the Supplementary Reserve Transportation Units, Royal Engineers practised during their annual training between May and September 1935. Each

■ *LMR 0-6-2T* Kitchener, *built by Bagnall in 1938, with a train of ex-GWR stock, 1940.* (E.J.M. Hayward) ■

company passed a fortnight in the camp, spending approximately one week on technical training such as the construction and operation of military railways, while the remainder of the time was used for military training. Each of the two operating companies took over working the Woolmer

Instructional Military Railway for two days, during which an operating exercise was staged, reproducing as far as possible the difficulties that might be encountered under active service conditions. The Docks & Stores Companies each carried out a practical exercise in addition to a theoretical exercise on paper.

The three constructional companies continued their previous work on the Hollywater Loop and pushed the line further into Woolmer Forest. They also started work on the construction of a landing wharf in Cranmere Pond. Directors and officers of the Big Four visited Longmoor during the annual camps.

When the Second World War broke out, there were 4,000 trained transportation officers and men, both regular and reservists, available for duty and, by September 1942, the 500-man strength of Longmoor had grown to 7,000. During the war a total of 6,960 officers and 51,350 men had been trained at Longmoor, while, additionally, over 80,000 had passed through to form drafts or on postings.

Traffic was extremely busy during both World Wars and during the 1939–45 war over 800 wagons at times were exchanged daily with the SR. From 1948 the number of trains

■ *LMR 0-6-0ST No 195 at Longmoor Downs, with a train to Liss, 3 June 1967. Both locomotive and coaches are lettered 'LMR'.*
The signal box is in modern style. (Author) ■

■ *LMR 2-10-0 No 600* Gordon *(now preserved) at Longmoor Open Day on 28 September 1968.*
The track is flat-bottomed. (Revd Alan Newman) ■

operated declined. In the post-war era, volunteer recruits were joined by national servicemen who served for four years in the reserve after their period of service with the active army. The Bordon Light Railway closed on 4 April 1966 and the Longmoor Military Railway itself closed 31 October 1969 and, subsequently, parts of the line were used for filming *The Young Winston*. It was not Longmoor's first use as a location because it had been previously used for filming *The Great St Trinian's Train Robbery*.

The Marchwood Military Railways
In the Second World War, the portable Mulberry harbour was designed in order to cater for shipping in the Normandy landings at Arromanches, where no suitable harbour existed. A location was needed for fabricating part of this harbour and an area of ground was selected at Marchwood, opposite Southampton and conveniently adjacent to the Fawley branch.

In June 1943 the Royal Engineers built there a jetty, stage sheds, workshop and living accommodation. This base was served by the Marchwood Military Railways, opened on 28

■ *War Department No 106* Spyck *at Marchwood Military Railways, 17 May 1958. Both locomotive and coach are lettered 'MMR'.* (Hugh Davies) ■

November 1943, and consisting of 22 miles of flat-bottomed track. The standard War Department locomotives were supplied by the Longmoor Military Railway. From about 1948 Marchwood became the No 1 Port & Inland Water Transport & Repair Depot and since 1977 the line has been run by civilians. Today, still open though not using steam traction, it is used for shipping army equipment. It receives approximately one train daily from the main line.

When the Central Electricity Authority's Marchwood power station was built in 1955, it was served by a branch from the Marchwood Military Railways, the line being worked by a 0-4-0ST. Following completion of the works, it was little used and the track was lifted in 1963.

Ludgershall to Tidworth

The Midland & South Western Junction Railway sought traffic eagerly. When its general manager, James Purkess, heard of a new military camp being set up at Tidworth, he arranged for a railway to connect it with the existing line at Ludgershall. As the proposed line was to be laid entirely on War Department land, no Act of Parliament was required. At first it was for War Department use only; later, public goods and civilian passenger traffic were carried.

Vital in the First World War, even in 1922 the garrison accommodated approximately 8,000 troops while up to 100,000 were quartered in the nearby summer camps. The

■ *Tidworth station, circa 1910; view towards the buffers. The extra wide platform permits room for entraining and detraining troops. The water tank stands on the left.* (Author's collection) ■

seven sidings at Tidworth could hold ten twelve-coach trains, or 290 wagons. Receipts at Tidworth, the only MSWJR station electrically-lit, were the highest on the system, so the station, although at the end of a branch, was put in the charge of the company's highest-ranking stationmaster.

Until the system closed in 1953, Tidworth Camp was served by a variety of standard gauge steam engines.

WHERE THE CALSHOT EXPRESS CROSSES THE ROAD.

■ *The 'Calshot Express' crosses the road. Notice the check rail on the inside rail to reduce the force on the outside rail. On the left is a Horstmann car.* (Author's collection) ■

The Calshot Light Railway

In 1913 the Air Ministry opened a base at Calshot Spit to service seaplanes. Around 1916, a 2-ft gauge railway system was constructed by Henry Boot & Son to transport material for the jetties at Calshot to Eaglehurst Camp, a distance of about 1¾ miles. In addition to stores, it carried passengers. Due to the deterioration of rolling stock, it closed on 16 August 1945. One of the railway's 0-4-0 well tanks built in 1918, now named *Douglas*, works on the Talyllyn Railway in Wales.

Ministry of Munitions Bramley Depot

North of Basingstoke and south of Bramley station, in 1916 an extensive Command Ammunition Depot was set up on each side of the GWR line. The mixed stud of locomotives used by W. Alban Richards Ltd on the building contract was later used by the Ministry of Munitions for operating lines within the depot, the eastern side becoming operational in 1917 and the western side in 1918. From 1922 English Electric battery-electric locomotives appeared on the line, being deemed safer for use in the proximity of explosives than steam engines. A workmen's service operated on the extensive system.

Portsmouth Dockyard

The dockyard had a horse-worked plateway before 1800, then when the LSWR and LBSCR Joint line to Portsmouth Town opened in 1847, a standard gauge line was laid into the yard. This line was later altered to connect with the High Level lines when the Portsmouth Town to Harbour extension was opened on 2 October 1876. Steam-worked until the late 1950s, traffic declined from 8,500 wagons per annum in 1957 to 700 in 1977, when the line closed.

Royal Naval Armament Depot, Bedenham, Bridgemary

The line consisted of four sections: Bedenham, Frater, Elson and Priddy's Hard, Gosport. The last was detached from the other three, but connected by a line passing through the intervening residential area. The main locomotive shed for maintaining the steam stock was at Bedenham, with a repair shed at Frater, while that at Priddy's Hard was for stabling the locomotive out-stationed there.

Stokes Bay Depot, Gosport

For some years the Royal Engineers' Electric Light School was served by a 600 mm line worked from 1919 by two Hunslet 4-6-0Ts. The school's presence brought trains to the branch that were much longer than normal. For instance, on 21 June 1914, fourteen Great Northern Railway coaches conveyed 254 officers and men of the Tyne Division Electrical Engineers from Tynemouth to Stokes Bay.

HOLIDAYS AND DAYS OUT

HAMPSHIRE HAS BEEN A HOLIDAY DESTINATION from the early days of railways. On 21 July 1850 so many passengers wished to avail themselves of an excursion from Waterloo to Southampton that a train of no fewer than 33 coaches was needed, to be supplemented by a duplicate train of another 18; this at a time when regular trains usually only consisted of about 7 coaches.

The Great Exhibition of 1851 spurred excursion traffic and many people used the opportunity to travel by train for the very first time. To provide for these extra passengers, the LSWR constructed 84 new coaches and it was estimated that the LSWR carried about 450,000 to the Exhibition. This increased traffic that year by 29.9%. The passengers were not all English, though, because the LSWR also conveyed some from the continent, as about 1,000 each week travelled from Le Havre to Southampton.

Pre-First World War excursion tickets cost about a third of a penny per mile, which contrasted very favourably with the normal third class fare of a penny a mile. For example, a return excursion ticket from Waterloo to Bournemouth cost 6s 0d compared with the ordinary third class return fare

of 16s 0d. Between these two fare structures were 'Cheap Tickets'. These were advertised in connection with special events and could be used on ordinary services. The cost of a Cheap Ticket for a return journey was usually the cost of a single journey plus a third. Using Waterloo to Bournemouth as an example, an ordinary third class single ticket cost 9s 0d and a cheap return ticket cost 12s 0d, compared with the ordinary return of 16s 0d.

On 27 June 1914 no fewer than nine excursion trains arrived at Portsmouth, eight hauled by GWR engines and one by a MSWJR locomotive. On that same day four GWR engines worked through to Bournemouth. From Salisbury they reached their destination via Fordingbridge. These 'foreign' engines were serviced at Fratton and Bournemouth respectively.

The GWR ran excursions from Birmingham to Portsmouth and back via the MSWJR. An LSWR driver accompanied the MSWJR engine from Andover Junction as its driver would have been unfamiliar with the route from Romsey to Portsmouth via Chandler's Ford.

Special trains could be hired and the LSWR summer timetable for 1914 offered details:

Special trains may be hired at the principal Stations at a few hours' notice at a charge of not less than Seven Shillings per mile for a single journey and Ten Shillings and Sixpence per mile on the single journey distances for a double journey (minimum Five Pounds), in addition to the full ordinary first, second

■ *A group of children from All Saints' School, Weston, Bath board the 4.44 pm to Cardiff on 4 July 1961 at Southampton Central, after visiting Southampton on an educational outing. The train engine is BR Standard class 4MT 2-6-0 No 76054. (Author)* ■

or third class fares as the case may be of the passengers conveyed.

By way of an example, this meant that a first class passenger could hire a special train from Waterloo to Bournemouth for his sole use at a cost of £38 14s 0d.

As many people worked on Saturdays, or at least on Saturday mornings, in the 1930s, excursions tended to be run on Sundays.

Schools made educational visits to Southampton. Sometimes a special was run, usually carrying several schools or, on other occasions, a coach, or coaches, would be added to ordinary service trains.

Hampshire is blessed with an attractive coastline and the major resorts of Bournemouth and Southsea, as well as many other smaller places. Summer Saturdays saw many extra trains serving them, some running through from the north of England, the Midlands and South Wales. So intensive was the traffic that some expresses used subsidiary lines in order to ease pressure on the main lines. For instance, some Weymouth trains travelled via Ringwood instead of through Bournemouth; South Wales to Bournemouth trains travelled via Fordingbridge and some trains for Southampton travelled over the Mid-Hants through Alresford.

A few principal trains were named. The *Bournemouth Limited* was an ordinary train that ran non-stop to or from London in just under two hours. Designed for long-distance commuters, it ran up in the morning and returned in the late afternoon. The title was dropped in 1939. In 1951, the year of the Festival of Britain, quite a few trains were named and what had been the *Bournemouth Limited*, though unnamed, was called the *Royal Wessex*. The *Bournemouth Belle* was an all-Pullman train introduced on 5 July 1931. That summer it served Southampton and Bournemouth, while on weekdays it additionally served Poole, Wareham, Dorchester and Weymouth. When serving Weymouth, half of the ten cars went forward, the others remaining at Bournemouth West until the other five returned on the Up working. For the winter of 1931–2 the train ran on Sundays to Bournemouth and for the resumption of the summer service in 1932, this remained the terminus. This was because the 2¼-hour stay at Weymouth was insufficiently long to entice tourists for the day. From 1 January 1936 the train ran daily all the year round until the Second World War ended it.

VANLOADS OF STRAWBERRIES

---■---

FOR WELL OVER A CENTURY, the land on the east side of Southampton Water has been used for strawberry-growing. In 1882 a total of 595 wagonloads of bark (to act like straw) were unloaded at Fareham. That year, between mid-June and late-July, 816 tons 6 cwt of strawberries were despatched from Fareham and Botley stations. Until a few years previously, the crop had never been grown commercially.

Before the season opened, the LSWR assembled between 600 and 700 luggage, milk and other vacuum fitted vans and, at least from 1898, installed special fruit vans with tiers of shelves. Some old four-wheeled passenger coaches had their seats removed and 'Fruit' painted on their frames. If the supply of vans ran out, old excursion passenger coaches were used, the baskets loaded on seats, luggage racks and placed on the floor. Using coaches was an expensive alternative to vans as they could not convey as much fruit. Sometimes a train of 21 old coaches filled with strawberries was run from Hampshire to the north of England.

The chief stations dealing with strawberries were Botley, Bursledon, Eastleigh, Fareham, Netley, Sholing, Swanwick, Wickham and Woolston. Some strawberries were grown on large fruit farms, while others came from smallholdings of between a half and four acres worked by the owner and his family. Hampshire growers favoured the Royal Sovereign and Sir Joseph Paxton varieties, these having an exquisite flavour and travelling better by rail than other types. Some pickers arrived from outside the area, often by rail, and camped out in the fields. They were paid about a penny for each basket they brought to the despatching shed where the chip baskets were labelled. The Swanwick & District Fruit Growers' Association had more than 600 growers on its register and in a good year Swanwick station would handle over three million baskets of fruit.

In the early morning, a train of empty vans left Bevois Park Sidings near Southampton and fruit was loaded at the intermediate stations: Bitterne, Woolston, Sholing, Netley and Bursledon and then after it had left Swanwick, more loading took place at Fareham and Botley. As the train had to reverse at Fareham, since no turntable was situated there, engines had to work tender-first from Bevois Park sidings to Fareham, with the consequent disadvantages of coal dust blowing into the footplate crew's eyes and facing rain and the cold wind. Non-stop runs were made from Eastleigh to London at an average speed of about 40 mph. Signalled as passenger trains, the heaviest could be up to 30 vehicles in length. Many trains were exchanged with other railway companies at Willesden Junction. One train conveyed strawberries for Belfast and Dublin. Pressure on rolling stock was so great that sometimes as little as two hours elapsed between the arrival of a loaded train at its destination employed to load the fruit as they were able to crawl in between the shelves and pack the chip baskets into the furthest corners. As the influx of workers created a scarcity of lodgings, the LSWR provided a cookhouse and dining tent for its employees, with meals and drinks provided at low cost – just sufficient to cover the company's expenses.

Three loading sidings were provided at Swanwick. Each van was in charge of a checker to tally the consignment notes with the baskets, which were then packed by two boys. A foreman was in charge of each group of vans and he arranged the vans' loading and marshalling. Often the farm carts, drawn by donkeys, mules and horses, were lined up for almost a mile waiting to be unloaded. Traffic within the yard was regulated by an LSWR policeman.

■ *LSWR Metropolitan class 4-4-0T No 322 shunts strawberry traffic at Botley. Built in February 1875 it was withdrawn in January 1908, having run 791,694 miles.* (Author's collection) ■

and the departure of those empty vans back to Bevois Park Sidings.

To deal with this important traffic, which lasted about six weeks, the LSWR required extra manpower: two inspectors, ten clerks, fifty porters and thirty boys. The latter were

Each consignment note showed the consignee's name, the destination and the route by which the consignment was to travel. After it had been checked on the van, it was passed to the office where clerks were at work booking the fruit. For charge purposes, 26 baskets of fruit were reckoned to weigh one hundredweight.

■ *Transferring baskets of strawberries at Bursledon from carts to railway vans.*
(Author's collection) ■

In the office each clerk was assigned to dealing with a particular town, or group of stations. All entries were attributed to the Passenger Account except the fruit for jam-making, which was forwarded at the end of the season in tubs and charged at goods train rates. Each of the railway companies was allotted a group of stations or district which they served best and the fruit booked accordingly by agreed routes. Dual-braked vans were required to be used for destinations where the railway companies used the Westinghouse brake, while those running on the underground Metropolitan Extension Line had to be within the Metropolitan Railway's restricted loading gauge. As long as all the vehicles were equipped with an automatic brake, be it vacuum or Westinghouse, a train could be signalled as a passenger train, thus giving it the high level of priority required for the transport of fruit with a relatively short shelf life.

In addition to special trains, vans containing strawberries were attached to scheduled passenger trains and a large number of small consignments to private persons were booked on the Parcels Account and carried in guards' vans.

On 29 June 1923, 64 vans were needed at Botley to load strawberries and brought to the SR an income of £571.19s 0d for carriage. On an average day Botley dealt with about 50,000 baskets and employed about 50 additional staff for the season, including one foreman, six clerks, thirty porters and thirteen loading boys. Bursledon dealt with about 30,000 baskets daily and its extra staff comprised three clerks, six porters and six boys. Extra staff at Wickham was three porters, while Sholing employed two extra porters and a boy.

■ *Vans for two strawberry specials at Swanwick, circa 1914. The nearest belongs to the London & North Western Railway. (Author's collection)* ■

FALLING ASLEEP ON THE FOOTPLATE AND OTHER ACCIDENTS

■

MERCIFULLY, **H**AMPSHIRE has been free of serious railway accidents. In the early days of the London & Southampton, there was plenty of scope for things to go wrong. Until 1840 the only signals provided were flags by day and common horn lanterns by night. Standard signals were then erected, but distant signals giving advance warning of the position of a home signal did not come into use until eight or ten years later.

At first, when starting one train after another on the same line or rails, the only precaution deemed necessary to ensure safety was that of delaying a following train until its predecessor was 'well out of sight'. Such a haphazard system was likely to produce accidents and sure enough it did. On 15 August 1840 a goods train left Southampton for London. After going six miles the load was found too heavy for the engine, so a portion was left behind in charge of the guard. He sent a boy back to warn the following train, but the 11.00 am mail consisting of 30 first class coaches drawn by two engines failed to stop and ran into the goods, injuring many passengers.

This and similar accidents elsewhere led James E. McCabe to insert a long and costly advertisement in *The Times* stating: 'It is incumbent upon every man, however humble his ideas may be, to give any suggestion he may consider likely to prevent accidents.' He went on to describe his suggested method, which was to have the engine a mile, or a mile and a half in advance of the train, connected with it by a sufficiently strong rope. 'In the event of an accident,' he observed, 'the engineer only would be imperilled.'

Notwithstanding the undoubted ingenuity and eminently philanthropic character of Mr McCabe's device, no railway adopted his scheme.

On 21 July 1850 Bison class 0-6-0 *Rhinoceros*, working the 33-coach Waterloo to Southampton excursion, was steaming poorly and 2 miles east of Basingstoke had to stop to raise steam. The engine of the train behind gave rear banking assistance. Despite repeated warnings, one passenger refused to sit, so when the train started, the violent jerk flung him across the compartment and killed him. Around the same year, *Lioness* of the same class stalled with a goods train near Andover Road (Micheldever) and was run into from behind by an engine. The guard was seriously injured.

A curious and unusual accident occurred near Eastleigh, or Bishopstoke as it was then known, on the night of 4 August 1851. Driver William Priswell, on a locomotive heading a goods train, fell asleep on the footplate as did his fireman, so the train proceeded on its way without anyone in control except the guard, who, quite unaware of the condition of his colleagues, made no attempt to stir them into life. Near Bishopstoke, Driver Priswell tumbled from his engine receiving serious injuries, which included breaking both legs. Fortunately the guard was alert and witnessed this and had the good sense to apply his brakes. Despite the fact that he could only control the brakes on his van and not those of the engine or the rest of the train, he succeeded in bringing it to a standstill because steam pressure was low, the firebox not having been fed with fuel for some time. The guard walked alongside the train and when he reached the tender he found the fireman so fast asleep that he was obliged to take him by the shoulders and shake him violently in order to wake him. The injured driver was lifted up and taken to receive surgical attention. The fireman revived the fire and was able to draw the train forward to its destination.

The reason for the footplate crew sleeping? Both men were perfectly sober when they started working the train but were greatly fatigued, having been on duty for two days and two nights.

On 30 June 1856 at Andover 2-2-2 *Gem*'s firebox burst, seriously injuring its driver, blowing the roof off the station and killing chickens in a line-side coop. On 20 October 1856 *Ruby* of the same class was waiting at Northam until its goods train could be accepted at Southampton. The driver and fireman filled its boiler, made up the fire and decided to patronise the local inn. Unattended, the train started moving towards Southampton. A ganger fortunately was able to speed along the track, leap onto the footplate, sound the whistle and apply the tender handbrake, reducing speed to walking pace

and alerting the station staff. No one was injured, but an express engine was struck and derailed.

The regular duties of 7ft-diameter driving wheel 2-4-0 No 96 *Castor* and its crew was to work the 6.30 am Southampton to Weymouth, the 2.20 pm passenger to Eastleigh, and the 6.05 goods to Salisbury – an unusual duty for a locomotive with such large driving wheels. It then shunted at Salisbury before returning light engine to Northam. The crew worked a 16½-hour-day so were far from being lazy. Approaching Eastleigh on the evening of 12 July 1870, they ran through danger signals and crashed into the rear of a goods train. The accident was caused through the tiredness of the crew.

On the evening of 26 November 1947, the 3.05 pm Bournemouth to Waterloo, headed by Lord Nelson class 4-6-0 No 860 *Lord Hawke*, was waiting at a failed signal near Farnborough and the driver was unfortunately unable to communicate with the Farnborough signalman. The Fleet signalman allowed the 12.15 pm Ilfracombe to Waterloo, headed by N15 class 4-6-0 No 453 *King Arthur*, to enter the section. It struck the rear of the first train, killing a passenger and the guard, and then turned over on its side. Its crew survived but were severely injured. The last three coaches of the train from Bournemouth were wrecked.

The 36-ton Eastleigh breakdown crane rushed to the scene. Officially it was restricted to 25 mph, but this was somewhat exceeded as it could have been required to release trapped passengers. However, by the time the crane arrived, soldiers from a nearby camp had freed most of the injured, including the crew of *King Arthur*. All four tracks were blocked, but the

■ *Lord Nelson class 4-6-0 No 857* Lord Howe, *sister engine to* Lord Hawke, *seen here shunting at New Milton, circa 1932. (E.J.M. Hayward)* ■

soldiers assisted in clearing the lines and helping with the cutting equipment, while their catering facilities provided meat pies, sandwiches and tea, the latter being particularly welcome as there was a hard frost. Cranes from Salisbury, Nine Elms and Guildford also assisted. When re-railed *King Arthur* was towed to the goods yard at Fleet where a new front bogie was fitted before the engine was taken to Eastleigh for repair.

A curious mishap occurred in the summer of 1950. Porter Sell at Christchurch station had already dealt with the last Up Friday night/Saturday morning train and there only remained the 10.30 pm from Waterloo for him to deal with when it called at a few minutes after 2 am. The country was experiencing a heat wave, so the presence of a good quantity of moisture on the Up track, just after the Hamworthy to Eastleigh goods had passed at 12.25 am, puzzled Porter Sell. As he detected the smell of what he believed to be creosote, he advised the signalman who, in turn arranged for the train to be stopped and examined when it arrived at Brockenhurst.

There in the darkness, nothing untoward was found, but on arrival at Bevois Park, Southampton, it was noticed that the end of a wagon was heavily splashed with tar. Closer examination revealed that the wagon in front, a tank car, had its outlet missing as well as its contents. Meanwhile the 3.25 am Up freight from Bournemouth had passed through Christchurch without incident. When dawn came it was found that the outlet valve had come off just after the Hamworthy to Eastleigh goods had crossed the bridge over the River Stour, west of Christchurch and, because the internal valve was not properly shut, approximately 3,000 gallons of compound had

discharged itself on the climb up through Hinton Admiral. By the time it reached Sway, the wagon was empty.

The normal passage of that 3.25 am Up freight gave false assurance. The sun rose and quickly its heat caused the compound to act as a lubricant so that the driving wheels could not grip the rails.

The first victim was the 5.38 am Poole to Southampton passenger train and seven more trains suffered before a light engine was sent through to apply sand. Bulleid's Pacifics were at the best of times light-footed and with this added lubricant the wheels spun round on the rising gradient, which was in places as steep as 1 in 107. The locomotives' sandboxes were quickly depleted and firemen cast ballast and dirt under the driving wheels in an attempt to obtain a grip.

The worst-affected train was the 7.20 am from Bournemouth West to Waterloo, which had to borrow the engine off the 4.20 am Down freight from Eastleigh to assist it to Brockenhurst. The loss of 41 minutes by this train contributed to a total loss of 155 minutes by the eight trains, this figure ignoring the disruption to connecting services.

Level crossings could be the scene of accidents. One such occurred at Cosham. A train had passed over the crossing so the signalman opened the gates for road traffic. Not realising this, and also because the train was on a curve, the driver stopped and then set back over the crossing, striking a car driven by the local general practitioner. It was dragged for a hundred yards and the good doctor was lucky to escape with only a foot injury.

The Eastleigh steam crane, or any other rail-mounted crane, required a skilled driver. As the cranes ran on a relatively narrow track, they could easily become unstable so it was essential to extend girders housed in the frames to form a wider base. It was not always possible to extend these girders because sometimes the ground beside the track was soft, or alongside a platform. Overhead telephone wires could form an obstruction to the jib, but it was surprising how far the wires could be pushed before they broke with a 'ping'. Also the unexpected could happen, perhaps a gust of wind would cause a load to be blown out beyond the safe radius for operating a crane.

On the Castleman's Corkscrew line, the many crossing keepers' lodges had gardens. One night a crane was working and its jib was slewed above a garden and when it was about to be returned to its normal position, the operator spotted that it had an apple tree attached. The jib was quickly slewed back, the tree replaced in the ground and the loose earth stamped down. There were no repercussions.

On 20 July 1952 an accident that could have been very serious occurred. Lord Nelson class 4-6-0 No 30854 *Howard of Effingham*, hauling an Up train to Waterloo normally running on the fast line, was placed on the local line near Shawford to allow a boat train to overtake. The driver of No 30854, seeing the Up fast line signal off, forgot that he was not on that line and failed to close the regulator. At the end of the slow line, the engine ran into the sand drag and fell down the embankment. Fortunately no one was injured.

THE RAILWAYS AT WAR

The First World War

ROYAL ENGINEERS FROM LONGMOOR laid a railway from the main line at Farnborough to the Royal Aircraft Factory and another at Hamble to serve the naval airfield. To construct the airfield, 300 workmen were conveyed daily from Southampton to Netley to cope with the many military and naval establishments in the Portsmouth area, and extensive sidings were laid at Fratton. The SR purchased these in 1923.

The Ministry of Munitions required a halt at Crow Park near Bursledon, its two platforms coming into use on 20 and 27 July 1918. Interestingly, they were built of planks on empty ammunition boxes filled with clay. It never appeared in a working timetable. War Department sidings were laid at Micheldever. Redundant in 1922, they were purchased by the SR to relieve pressure on sidings at Eastleigh. The United States' Army engineers built a platform and siding just north of Winchester to serve their large camp on Winnall Down.

Pre-1914, the War Department had a few ambulance coaches at Netley Hospital, but many more were required, so the main line railways were asked to provide these. The LSWR responded with a nine-coach train in November 1914, and a ten-coach rake the following year. On 7 July 1916 after the first Battle of the Somme, 6,174 wounded men left Southampton in 29 trains, sitting cases being conveyed in ordinary corridor coaches. German prisoners were also carried in corridor trains so that armed guards could patrol the corridors and also to avoid having to make lavatory stops.

In December 1917, for use in France, the LSWR supplied Overseas Ambulance train No 35, comprising thirteen vehicles. Train No 62 consisted of fourteen corridor coaches and two vans to carry 418 stretcher cases, or 680 walking wounded. Sold to the War Office in 1917 for £22,233, it was sent to France by train ferry from Southampton and re-purchased by the LSWR in 1919 for £12,800.

Seven million troops passed through Southampton Docks in the First World War, averaging about 4,500 daily. Southampton could be reached from South Wales, the North and Midlands by five separate routes without travelling through London. This was done by travelling via the Somerset & Dorset Railway, Salisbury, Andover, Newbury or Basingstoke. On 22 August 1914 the British Expeditionary Force in 73 trains, the majority of these originating from the London area, passed through Southampton Town station into the docks. They were drawn to the required berth by the engine that had brought the train to Southampton.

The LSWR organisation was superb. Between 10 and 31 August 1914, 5,006 officers, 125,171 non-commissioned officers and other ranks, 38,805 horses, 344 guns, 1,574 limbers and wagons, 277 cars and 1,802 motor cycles were taken to Southampton – all this in addition to the normal traffic. A total of 670 trains were booked to enter the docks at 12-minute intervals. This continued into September and one day 100 trains arrived with a total of 31,192 men.

Some lines in Hampshire were closed, the track lifted and sent to France to carry war supplies to the front line; Basingstoke to Alton was one of these (see page 55). Under the 1923 bill the SR sought Parliamentary powers to abandon the line as uneconomic, but landowners and MPs successfully opposed it and so it was re-laid.

A train ferry terminal was built just west of the Royal Pier, Southampton. A service to Dieppe opened in November 1917 and to Cherbourg in November 1918. Each ferry made three crossings weekly.

The Royal Navy depended on coal for its ships' boilers. Some 283,353 tons were sent to Southampton and 213,224 to Gosport. Sixty wagon trains were worked by LSWR 4-6-0s between Salisbury and Eastleigh.

Railway enthusiasts saw interesting sights. One observer at Swaything in April 1915 noted two Great Eastern

■ *Soldiers and Boy Scouts at Redbridge during the First World War.* (Author's collection) ■

Railway trains within a few minutes: a Great Western Railway 4-4-0 hauling a London & North Western Railway train and a South Eastern & Chatham Railway train.

The Second World War

From October 1939 British Expeditionary Forces' leave trains ran from Southampton. Two SR ambulance trains ran daily from Southampton Docks via Winchester Chesil and the DNSR to army depots on Salisbury Plain and elsewhere.

Initially, German bombers made raids during daylight hours and much time was lost at Eastleigh when workers took shelter. To obviate this, spotters were posted to give warning of the approach of hostile aircraft and only then did workers take shelter. Eastleigh Works were fortunate to remain undamaged throughout the war.

The first bomb on SR property fell on Redbridge sleeper works in June 1940. Portsmouth Harbour station received a direct hit on 12 August 1940 and four trains in the station were damaged. The station received further damage in January 1941.

One raid wrecked a bridge at Woolston on the Southampton to Portsmouth line. The Fratton crane crew were clearing the wreckage when a daylight raid occurred. Three of the crane crew took cover in a shelter at the Supermarine aircraft factory, but it received a direct hit, killing all inside. The crane driver sheltering under his crane escaped. A fund set up to help the families who had lost their breadwinner received over 700 contributions, and not all these were from railwaymen.

For obvious reasons, crane crews dealt very rapidly with derailments at Fawley oil refinery and the Royal Naval armament depot at Bedenham.

Portsmouth received more than its fair share of bombing and the Harbour station received a direct hit on 12 August 1940. Four trains standing in the station were damaged, while fire gutted access to the landing stage. This and further damage in January 1941 was so serious that only one platform was repaired and no rebuilding carried out until the end of the war.

In one of the saturation raids on Portsmouth, bombs were falling almost continuously and houses were blazing and fires could not be put out due to damage to the water mains. In all this chaos, a railwayman, acting as fire watcher on the highest part of the Town station roof, was standing ready to kick or shovel away any incendiary bomb that landed on the roof before it could set the building alight. Whenever there was a lull in the noise, this railwayman, sticking bravely to his post, could be heard giving a dissertation on mountain goats and how fortunate they were to be able to leap from rock to rock.

Two engines were in steam at the station, a T9 class 4-4-0 No 287 and an Adams Jubilee 0-4-2 No 620. Both drivers were loyally remaining with their locomotives, yet both had sent their fireman to shelter. The driver of Jubilee No 620 remarked: 'Someone's got to stay with her, otherwise she might blow up!' As if everything else around was cool and calm.

Gosport received regular bombing raids and its engine shed was destroyed in December 1940 by an unexploded bomb that had been declared 'safe'. The following year Fratton locomotive shed was bombed and twenty engines damaged. Lord Nelson class 4-6-0 No 860 *Lord Hawke* on a Down Bournemouth

■ *The locomotive shed at Fratton following a bomb attack in the Second World War.* (Author's collection) ■

■ At Redbridge permanent way depot, women during the Second World War propel a trolley-load of sleepers into the pickling plant where air is extracted and then preservative introduced under pressure. (Author's collection) ■

express was derailed near Swaything when a German plane dropped three bombs on the line. T9 class 4-4-0 No 115 had a similar experience two weeks later.

In January 1941 a bomb fell through the Swaything booking office roof and floor without exploding. The authorities believed that the bomb had gone off and allowed staff to return to work. The next day, the landlord of the public house opposite insisted that it had not exploded. Digging began and in due course the live bomb was discovered and duly rendered safe.

Later in the war, many of the ammunition dumps for the Normandy invasion were sited on the DNSR. A large transit camp was set up at Eastleigh. During 1944 a train, including two LNER sleeping cars, ran from Waterloo to Southampton for VIP traffic.

CURIOSITIES

∎

SHIRLEY HOLMS ON THE Lymington branch opened 10 October 1860 and may have been the very first British halt, ie an unmanned station. Opened to serve the residents of Sway and Boldre, trains only stopped at Shirley Holms to pick up in the Up direction and set down in the Down. On arrival at Brockenhurst, passengers were required to pay the full fare from Lymington, and likewise those travelling from Brockenhurst were required to pay the fare to Lymington. Trains did not stop at Shirley Holms in the dark and its name never appeared on timetables or on tickets. In 1888, with the opening of Sway station on the main line, its usefulness diminished and the timber-built platform closed that year.

Brockenhurst has an interesting platform that can be swung at right-angles over the track to enable luggage to be taken on the level from an unloading dock for road vehicles across to a passenger platform.

In 1905 the LSWR operated a Clarkson steam bus from Lymington to Milford-on-Sea and New Milton. It sank in the muddy roads, so to counteract this, wider tyres were fitted. It was withdrawn the following year.

During the cutting of Privett Tunnel on the Alton to Fareham line, two men were buried when a vertical shaft collapsed. One died almost instantly, but the other managed to dig himself to the surface with a knife and when he got out ate six loaves.

A platelayer on the Basingstoke to Alton branch related:

∎ *Luggage bridge at Brockenhurst, 19 September 1986. To facilitate transfer of luggage from one platform to another, the bridge is swung at right angles to span the track. (Author)* ∎

'Once I mouched from a parson. The parson went into the house to see what he could do and brought out a basin full of cold 'taties. My mate was very hungry, so he clutched at one of these. "No," said the parson, "you shan't eat meals at this house until you've said Grace. Come on, say your Grace." Joe was unable to recall one, so the parson looked at me, but I'd forgotten all my mother taught me, so I said, "May the Lord pity us poor chaps and give us a bit of meat to eat with these cold 'taties." The parson laughed and went and fetched us half a leg of mutton.'

Sam Fay, who rose to become Superintendent of the LSWR, joined the company as a junior clerk at Itchen Abbas. His first move was to Stockbridge, of which he reminisced:

'Stationmasters as a rule are proper persons. David Worsley was by no means a proper person. He drank hard; his possession of a revolver was a menace to his neighbours. Sometimes he leapt from a fence on the opposite side of the platform, then turned to a fire in the porters' room, which he tried to put out by repeated shots.

At the station was also a red-haired porter nicknamed "Coppertop". He was once sent to ask an engine driver "for the key of the tunnel". The driver's reply was unprintable.'

Fareham was a junction and keeping a connection with other trains was vitally important, as a story by Roger Arnold, regarding Sir Herbert Walker, the SR's General Manager reveals. One evening in the 1920s:

'We approached Fareham and just as our train came to a halt, I espied another M7 0-4-4T heading a two-coach salmon and umber outfit standing in the bay. The guard was fingering his green flag, ready to wave it just as we drew to a halt. But he did not! A

■ *The stark exterior of Itchen Abbas station where Sam Fay began his railway career.* (Author's collection) ■

■ *Stockbridge, view Up, 31 May 1967. The station closed on
7 September 1964. (Author)* ■

As it seemed to Roger Arnold:

'A huge square-shouldered man in a tweed overcoat, with pince-nez gold spectacles, came down and hurtled over the timber crossing from the island to the bay platform with the alacrity of a young athlete, rather than a staid man in his forties. Once more his instinct for the detail paid off. With his furled umbrella like a foil at the ready, he came up to the startled guard. "Your name is George Grant? Mine is Herbert Ashcombe Walker. You were about to start this train before the passengers from

stentorian roar from the footbridge came like a thunderclap to Guard Grant, "George Grant, hold that train!"'

*the 5.50 pm from Southampton could join, although this is the last train up the Meon Valley today!"
By this time the capless stationmaster came*

■ *D15 class 4-4-0 No 30467 leaves Fareham with the 4.48 pm Portsmouth to Eastleigh, 29 May 1949. It is formed of ex-GWR stock. The fireman is reaching out to pick up the single line staff.* (Pursey Short) ■

■ *Wellworthy's Ampress Works Halt, which did not appear in the public timetables, opened 1 October 1956 and closed in May 1977.* (Author's collection) ■

running up to see what had caused the disturbance. Before he could collect his thoughts, Walker was speaking again. "Your name is Mr Peter Cooper; does this heinous thing happen every evening? If it does, let me assure you it will not again without your coming to Waterloo." A faint cheer from the passengers within earshot. By then Walker had boarded the train and from a first class compartment was asking Cooper if he could telephone Alton. "Yes, sir." "Then tell Mr Smith that this train connects with the 8.20 pm to Surbiton and Waterloo and if he does not do so then HE can come to Waterloo and see me in the morning!"'

In the 1930s Gosport had a Station Club, where a bar and billiard table was set up in a parcels office. The club was started because it was rumoured that the stationmaster enjoyed several pints of Bass before lunch.

Around 1966 the Portsmouth Water Company laid a water main to serve houses beside the Fareham to Gosport line, so to facilitate this, rather than them being unloaded at some distant goods yard, 232 railway wagons unloaded the pipes right on the spot where they were required to be laid.

Bramshot Golf Club Halt, for use only by club members, was situated just east of Fleet. It was served by just two trains a week and both were on Sundays. They were thoughtfully timed so that players could stay for lunch. The halt closed on 6 May 1946.

A stopping place not in the timetables was Atlantic Park Hotel Halt, which opened 30 October 1929 between Eastleigh and Swaything as a reception centre for emigrants to the USA. The station re-opened on 1 April 1966 as Southampton Airport.

South of Winchester, the London & Southampton Railway was cut through plague pits, some dating from AD 941.

At Liss in 1900, impure water from the station well caused the stationmaster to develop blood-poisoning. The LSWR gave him £13 15s 0d to cover his doctor's bill.

Railwaymen's cottages at Portcreek Junction could only be reached by walking beside the track, so the Joint Committee (the LSWR and the LBSCR), who operated the line jointly, had to issue track passes to the doctor, district nurse, vicar and school attendance officer to prevent them from being charged with trespass.

In November 1964 ex-London, Midland & Scottish Railway Jubilee class 4-6-0 No 45699 *Galatea* unusually visited the Southern Region and, while there, was condemned at Eastleigh Works, the only member of its class to be condemned in that region. It was towed via Salisbury to Barrow Road shed, Bristol, before being sent onwards to a South Wales scrapyard.

STEAM IN HAMPSHIRE TODAY

■

THE **MID-HANTS RAILWAY** opened on 2 October 1865 and as the extant terminal station was unsuitable for a through line, a new station was built and the original converted to a stationmaster's house. Medstead station, 650 ft above sea level, opened on, or just before, 1 August 1868. On 30 June 1884 the Mid-Hants Railway was taken over by the working company, the LSWR.

The line was very busy during the First World War when hundreds of troop trains used it en route from Aldershot to Southampton. In 1937 push-pull working was introduced between Eastleigh and Alton. M7 class 0-4-4Ts normally propelled a two-coach set to Alton and drew it on the return journey. Regular steam ended on 16 September 1957 when Hampshire diesel-electric multiple-units began work over the line. Due to falling traffic, it closed on 5 February 1973.

Fortunately, this was not the end of the line as the Mid-Hants Railway Limited was formed to preserve the Alton to Alresford section. Alresford to Ropley opened 30 April 1977, Medstead & Four Marks on 28 May 1983 and it finally reached Alton on 25 May 1985. A locomotive shed has been erected in what was Ropley goods yard, the line having a stud of nineteen steam engines.

■ *M7 class 0-4-4T No 30031 at Alton with a Mid-Hants train. Electric unit No 2101 is on the left.* (Lens of Sutton) ■

■ *A 700 class 0-6-0 No 30308 at Medstead & Four Marks with a Down goods train.* (Lens of Sutton) ■

■ *N class 2-6-0 No 31874 and LMR No 196 at Ropley, 23 July 1979.* (Author) ■

■ *Alresford, view Up, circa 1910.* (Author's collection) ■

BIBLIOGRAPHY

———— ■ ————

Ahrons, E.L., *Locomotive & Train Working in the Latter Part of the Nineteenth Century*, Heffer, 1953

Antell, R., *Southern Country Stations: The London & South Western Railway*, Ian Allan, 1984

Bennett, A., *Southern Holiday Lines in Hampshire and Isle of Wight*, Runpast, 1994

Bishop, B., *Off the Rails*, Bracken, 1984

Clinker, C.R., *Register of Closed Passenger Stations and Goods Depots 1830–1977*, Avon Anglia, 1988

Course, E., *The Railways of Southern England: Secondary and Branch Lines*, Batsford, 1974

Course, E., *The Railways of Southern England: Independent and Light Railways*, Batsford 1976

Cox, J.G., *Castleman's Corkscrew: The Southampton & Dorchester Railway 1844–1848*, City of Southampton, 1975

Easdown, M. & Sage, L., *Piers of Hampshire & The Isle of Wight*, Amberley, 2011

Ellis, H., *The South Western Railway*, Allen & Unwin, 1956

Fairman, J.R., *Netley Hospital & Its Railways*, Kingfisher, 1984

Fairman, J.R., *The Fawley Branch*, Oakwood Press, 2002

Faulkner, J.N. & Williams, R.A., *The LSWR in the Twentieth Century*, David & Charles, 1988

Fay, S., *A Royal Road*, E.P. Publishing, 1973

Glenn, D.F., *Roads, Rails & Ferries of the Solent Area*, Ian Allan, 1980

Glenn, D.F., *Rail Routes in Hampshire & East Dorset*, Ian Allan, 1983

Griffith, E., *The Basingstoke & Alton Light Railway*, Kingfisher, 1982

Harding, P.A., *The Longparish Branch Line*, Author, 1992

Hardingham, R., *The Mid Hants Railway*, Runpast, 1995

Kidner, R.W., *Southern Railway Branch Lines in the Thirties*, Oakwood Press, 1976

Kidner, R.W., *The Waterloo to Southampton Line*, Oakwood Press, 1983

Lloyd, R., *The Fascination of Railways*, Allen & Unwin, 1951

MacDermot, E.T., revised Clinker, C.R., *History of the Great Western Railway*, Ian Allan, 1964

Maggs, C.G., *The Midland & South Western Junction Railway*, David & Charles, 1967

Maggs, C.G., *The Branch Lines of Hampshire*, Amberley, 2010

Marshall, C.F.D., revised Kidner, R.W., *A History of the Southern Railway*, Ian Allan, 1963

Paye, P., *The Lymington Branch*, Oakwood Press, 1979

Robertson, K., *Railways of Gosport*, Kingfisher, 1986

Sands, T.B., *The Didcot, Newbury & Southampton Railway*, Oakwood, 1971

Simmonds, R. & Robertson, K., *The Bishop's Waltham Branch*, Wild Swan, 1988

Simmons, J., *The Railway in Town & Country, 1830–1914*, David & Charles, 1987

Stone, R.A., *The Meon Valley Railway*, Kingfisher, 1983

Tavender, L., *Southampton, Ringwood & Dorchester Railway*, A.E. Baker, 1995

Thomas, D. St J. & Whitehouse, P., *SR 150*, David & Charles, 1988

White, H.P., *Regional History of the Railways of Great Britain Vol 2, Southern England*, David & Charles, 1982

Williams, R.A., *The London & South Western Railway Vols 1 & 2*, David & Charles, 1968; 1973

Young, J.A., *The Ringwood Christchurch & Bournemouth Railway*, Bournemouth Local Studies,

ACKNOWLEDGEMENTS

———■———

MANY THANKS ARE DUE TO Peter Martin for checking the manuscript.

Colin Maggs

Index

———— ■ ————